# Levinas for Psychologists

*Levinas for Psychologists* provides a rigorous, yet accessible, examination of Emmanuel Levinas's philosophy and its implications for psychology and the human and social sciences.

Comprehensive in scope, this book traces Levinas's thought across the arc of his oeuvre, from the earliest works to the last interviews and essays. Laubscher provides numerous examples of how Levinas's thought challenges current clinical and psychotherapeutic work, psychological theory, social science research, and social theory but also offers promising alternatives. Such alternative ways to think and practice psychology are richly illuminated by accessible examples from therapy, research, and the social everyday. The volume makes Levinas's dense and demanding philosophical language comprehensible and accessible, without losing the radical, profound, and poetic qualities of the original. Issues of justice, racism, and nature are addressed throughout, and these insights and conclusions are placed within a contemporary context.

This book is essential reading for psychologists, philosophers, and anyone interested in the legacy of Levinas's work.

**Leswin Laubscher** is Associate Professor at the Department of Psychology at Duquesne University, Pittsburgh, USA. He also serves as "Extraordinary Professor" at the University of the Western Cape, South Africa (and in the past at the University of Stellenbosch, South Africa). Dr. Laubscher has authored several scholarly articles and books and, most recently, edited *Fanon, Phenomenology, and Psychology* (2022) with Derek Hook and Miraj U. Desai.

# The Psychology and the Other Book Series

Series editor: David M. Goodman
*Associate editors: Brian W. Becker, Donna M. Orange and Eric R. Severson*

The *Psychology and the Other* book series highlights creative work at the intersections between psychology and the vast array of disciplines relevant to the human psyche. The interdisciplinary focus of this series brings psychology into conversation with continental philosophy, psychoanalysis, religious studies, anthropology, sociology, and social/critical theory. The cross-fertilization of theory and practice, encompassing such a range of perspectives, encourages the exploration of alternative paradigms and newly articulated vocabularies that speak to human identity, freedom, and suffering. Thus, we are encouraged to reimagine our encounters with difference, our notions of the "other," and what constitutes therapeutic modalities.

The study and practices of mental health practitioners, psychoanalysts, and scholars in the humanities will be sharpened, enhanced, and illuminated by these vibrant conversations, representing pluralistic methods of inquiry, including those typically identified as psychoanalytic, humanistic, qualitative, phenomenological, or existential.

Recent titles in the series include:

**misReading Plato**
Continental and Psychoanalytic Glimpses Beyond the Mask
*Edited by Matthew Clemente, Bryan J. Cocchiara, and William J. Hendel*

**Neoliberalism, Ethics and the Social Responsibility of Psychology**
Dialogues at the Edge
*Edited by Heather Macdonald, Sara Carabbio-Thopsey and David M. Goodman*

**Anacarnation and Returning to the Lived Body with Richard Kearney**
*Brian Treanor and James Taylor*

**The Psychology and Philosophy of Eugene Gendlin**
Making Sense of Contemporary Experience
*Edited by Eric R. Severson and Kevin C. Krycka*

For a full list of titles in the series, please visit the Routledge website at: www.routledge.com/Psychology-and-the-Other/book-series/PSYOTH

"This is simply a marvelous book. Leswin Laubscher's understanding of Levinas is deep and comprehensive. He is a psychologist who has been inspired by Levinas's philosophy and has also struggled with its limitations with care and honesty. Accordingly, Laubscher is a trustworthy and seasoned guide for psychologists and others in the social sciences who want to understand the importance of Levinas's ideas. His writing style is so clear and engaging that as a reader I felt like I was drawn into a conversation with him, a conversation that I did not want to end."

**Steen Halling**, *Professor Emeritus, Psychology Department, Seattle University, USA and author of* Intimacy, Transcendence and Psychology

"Leswin Laubscher gives psychologists a roadmap to reading phenomenologist/ prophet Emmanuel Levinas so that we clinicians can find ourselves challenged by the primordial, prior, and exorbitant responsibility. Laubscher further challenges the totalizing tendencies – diagnostics, classifying, reifying – of contemporary psychology, and offers us the opportunity to restore psychology to the human sciences through teaching his way through the major works of Levinas. Those who want to humanize clinical psychology, and those willing to tackle a challenging philosopher in the service of this task, will find themselves grateful for this book."

**Donna M. Orange**, *Postdoctoral Program in Psychoanalysis and Psychotherapy, New York University, USA*

"Readers of Levinas are often compelled by the power of his writing to imagine the way such thinking might inhabit the work of psychotherapy. Laubscher's new book moves chronologically and critically through the escalating challenges to philosophy and psychology offered by Levinas. With Laubscher's help, even the most difficult concepts are given helpful, relevant, and conversational interpretations, a task made difficult by vital but often opaque developments in Levinas's later work. With a constant eye on clinical application, Laubscher offers a deft and memorable introduction to Levinas for psychotherapists."

**Eric R. Severson**, *Associate Teaching Professor of Philosophy, Seattle University, USA*

"Professor Laubscher has written a very welcome and much-needed introduction to the work of one of contemporary philosophy's most difficult and profound figures, and has done so in a most engaging and thought-provoking manner, one that will be of tremendous service to a wide-range of students of psychology. Although Levinas has a well-earned reputation for difficulty because of the often idiosyncratic, analytically nuanced, and genuinely novel approach he takes to examining some of philosophy's most fundamental issues, Laubscher has managed to capture not only the essential features and key arguments of Levinasian phenomenology but has also done so in a way that makes its immediate and practical significance to psychology exceptionally clear and persuasive. While others have done much to pave the way for an increased appreciation of Levinas's ethical phenomenology in psychology, this book represents a significant leap forward in engaging the central themes and ideas of his intellectual project and does so in a way that is accessible to a broad audience of both theorists and practitioners. Whether you are already acquainted with contemporary phenomenological thought or simply interested in learning a bit more about what Levinas might have to offer contemporary psychology, I urge you to read this book."

**Edwin E. Gantt**, *PhD, Professor of Psychology, Brigham Young University, United States*

# Levinas for Psychologists

Leswin Laubscher

Routledge
Taylor & Francis Group

LONDON AND NEW YORK

Designed cover image: "The birth of humankind" © Raimond Spekking/CC BY-SA 4.0 (via Wikimedia Commons). See https://commons.wikimedia.org/wiki/File:Wiederentdeckung_des_Otto-Freundlich-Mosaik_„Die_Geburt_des_Menschen"-8723.jpg.

First published 2024
by Routledge
4 Park Square, Milton Park, Abingdon, Oxon OX14 4RN

and by Routledge
605 Third Avenue, New York, NY 10158

*Routledge is an imprint of the Taylor & Francis Group, an informa business*

*British Library Cataloguing-in-Publication Data*
A catalogue record for this book is available from the British Library

*Library of Congress Cataloging-in-Publication Data*
Names: Laubscher, Leswin, author.
Title: Levinas for psychologists / Leswin Laubscher.
Description: Abingdon, Oxon ; New York, NY : Routledge, 2024. |
    Series: Psychology and the other | Includes bibliographical references
    and index.
Identifiers: LCCN 2023025485 (print) | LCCN 2023025486 (ebook) |
    ISBN 9781032320083 (paperback) | ISBN 9781032325538 (hardback) |
    ISBN 9781003315612 (ebook)
Subjects: LCSH: Lévinas, Emmanuel | Psychology and philosophy. |
    Ethics—Philosophy.
Classification: LCC BF41 .L38 2024 (print) | LCC BF41 (ebook) |
    DDC 150.1—dc23/eng/20230802
LC record available at https://lccn.loc.gov/2023025485
LC ebook record available at https://lccn.loc.gov/2023025486

ISBN: 978-1-032-32553-8 (hbk)
ISBN: 978-1-032-32008-3 (pbk)
ISBN: 978-1-003-31561-2 (ebk)

DOI: 10.4324/9781003315612

Typeset in Times New Roman
by Apex CoVantage, LLC

# Contents

# Acknowledgments

For sixty years now, the Department of Psychology at Duquesne University provided a home and sanctuary for those who dared to think and practice its task as a uniquely human science. This book is dedicated to all those students, faculty, and friends of the department who nurtured and fanned the flames of its mission and dream. Here's hoping it continues to burn bright as beacon and invitation to what psychology could still be. *Respice, Adspice, Prospice.*

# Chapter 1

# Introduction

This book issues an invitation to conversation with Emmanuel Levinas and well from a certain defining positionality which needs to be acknowledged at the outset: I am a psychologist, Emmanuel Levinas was a philosopher. Not unlike the key signature to a musical composition, which organizes and modulates the work in a rather particular way, this statement – of a psychologist reading and presenting a philosopher's work – serves as an analogous structuring scaffold for this book. While there would admittedly be a fair measure of false humility in my claiming that I don't know anything or much about philosophy, it is unequivocally so that my access to the philosophical work of Emmanuel Levinas is from the discipline of psychology. My educational and professional training was as a psychologist, *not* a philosopher, and my professional identity, as clinician, researcher, and university professor, derives powerfully and primarily from its location within psychology. As such, one may ask what business I have reading and teaching Levinas, in a clinical psychology department no less, or writing this book for an imagined audience consisting largely of helping professionals and students of psychology and the human sciences. Already, it is clear that I will have to make two related arguments: why philosophy matters to psychology, in general, and why *this* philosopher, Emmanuel Levinas, needs to be taken seriously in psychology and the social and human sciences, more broadly.

I would venture that most people, including students and scholars within the disciplines of psychology and philosophy, might think of the link between philosophy and psychology, to the extent that there is one, as a predominantly *historical* one. To most contemporary purposes and intentions, there seems little need to think of those disciplines in any relational detail beyond that they have split at some past point, like train tracks, into two separate routes which, by that metaphor, sometimes aim for the same station, but often not, sometimes run close or parallel to each other, but often also use different locomotives or energy sources with which to traverse landscapes and terrain supposedly unique to each's unfolding journey. In some admittedly exaggerated way, like those famed words of Rudyard Kipling's poem, where "east is east, and west is west, and never the twain shall meet," philosophy is philosophy and psychology is psychology, with little need for each other, save perhaps for the knowledge of each other's presence. The assertion

DOI: 10.4324/9781003315612-1

that psychology used to be "part of" philosophy at some point seems to have as little relevance to the living present as saying that South America was once "part of" Africa. Moreover, and more often than not, psychology erases its own history or excises it as something distinct and removed from the present: there is what one *does* in contemporary psychology and then there is the *history* of psychology. That twain, too, it is thought unnecessary to bridge. A philosopher may readily refer to Plato or Aristotle, but the contemporary psychologist has little use for Gustav Fechner, William James, or in some quarters, even Sigmund Freud.

A recent example embroiders on this neighborly tension: I teach in a graduate clinical psychology program which allows and encourages students to take classes in the graduate philosophy program (and vice versa, with philosophy students able to take courses in psychology). In one such class, students were poring over a particularly dense paragraph of Martin Heidegger's, on the difference between the ontological and the ontic, I seem to recall. The philosophy students in the class relished the challenge in a particularly intellectualized way and had the resources of a philosophical grammar and history, from Socrates to Derrida, to reference and offer critical commentary from. The psychology students had a tougher conceptual time of it, almost all of them lacking that broad theoretical background available to their peers from philosophy. But beyond such difficulties (which in large measure were overcome as the psychology students committed themselves to broader philosophical reading and as they opened themselves to asking questions and being taught, as it were, by their philosophy colleagues), the psychology students registered another, thornier issue. At first glance, it seemed a tension of disciplinary application, crystallized in one psychology student's observation that immediately after class, she had to see a patient working through childhood sexual abuse by her stepfather. This student wanted to know how all of this talk about being and "the ontological difference" enhances or otherwise prepares her to be in that room with another person's pain in a manner that's helpful and facilitative of healing. "Right there, in the therapy room, I don't have the luxury of counting philosophers on a pinhead," she said in a testy disciplinary challenge to philosophy and the philosophy students in the class. In many ways, this book is also a kind of response to that student's challenge; it will take her objection very seriously, but it will also provide a response that the philosophy students in that class did not, maybe even could not, offer. In truth, perhaps the response, if not answer, *has* to come from psychology itself. As a psychologist and a philosopher, as a philosophical psychologist (all psychologists really are, but as with this student in my example, without them necessarily recognizing it), it will be my task precisely to demonstrate how/that the work of Emmanuel Levinas, a philosopher, may be brought to bear on the psychologist's craft, art, and/or science – and well in a way that includes, but is also broader than, the therapy room. What, for example, can we learn from Levinas such that our research, our theories, our critique, our specialized community, personality, social, or developmental psychologies are broadened, challenged, and informed to a richer and more invigorating scholarly direction, position, or end?

In one of the precious few existing books explicitly devoted to psychology and Levinas, David Goodman (Goodman & Freeman, 2015) relates a remarkably similar motivational story to the one earlier: he notes that he derived great stimulation from his theology and philosophy classes, where issues of subjectivity and metaphysics provided a picture of the self that was rich and complex, as opposed to the often "flat" and "facile categorizations" of psychology. Yet at the same time, he felt a real discomfort with how those philosophical ideas "engaged the world and where they actually responded to human need in daily life and in the midst of tremendous social ills" (Goodman & Freeman, 2015, p. xii). I cannot help conjuring up a stereotypical image of the philosopher pensively reflecting upon life, under some olive tree, with a good bread and a bottle of wine, to be contrasted with the psychologist running some survey or laboratory experiment, or earnestly talking the suicidal or anorexic patient off death's ledge. These are, of course, ridiculous caricatures, but they do betray a larger tension of thinking versus doing, of the philosopher who ponders life deeply, but abstractly, against the psychologist or social worker in the acting, doing muck of the everyday. Philosophy has wrestled with human suffering more so than any other scholarly discipline, for example (even surpassing theology and religious studies, I daresay, whose insights were often philosophical ones modulated some by the incantation of the specific religion in question), but when last have we heard a philosopher interviewed on television about the suffering aftermath of a traumatic event? Not unlike Goodman and Freeman's aim for their own book (2015), I wish to steer into this tension of the philosophical and the psychological and where the desire is not so much for the twain to meet in some synthesis, integration, or resolution as much as it is for the creative conversation by which both disciplines, ultimately, may be enriched, even changed.

To "bring Levinas to psychology" (and psychology to Levinas), I cannot assume that the reader – especially the reader from psychology and other health, helping, and human sciences – is familiar with Levinas's thought, or with the particular philosophical register and language with which he writes. It is also true, though, as we will learn in due course, that much of Levinas's terms and uses of language are not familiar or usual to philosophy scholars either, which may bode well to their finding use, as well, in this book's attempt to present key aspects of his philosophy in as accessible and intelligible a manner as I can muster. We won't be able to escape the provocative, serpentine, hyperbolic, and excessive language and style that is Levinas's (and we should not try to avoid it, in truth, as much of its poetic and suggestive beauty, much of its writing style, is closely related to its philosophical message, as a performative enactment of the argument), but I will try to lodge my words alongside Levinas's, as vernacular and "more accessible" commentary, or shamelessly as lesser translation.[1]

By appropriating and/or articulating "key aspects" of Levinas's thought, there is an authorial selectivity at work, which begs the question as to how one decides which is key and which is peephole or door stopper, all, of course, important to entry (as to prohibition). I will be guided by whom the book invites to its table – everyone who is generally interested in gaining a fuller understanding of Levinas, to be sure, but also and rather particularly, those who come to Levinas from psychology and the helping and human sciences. As such, I provide a general overview of Levinas's philosophy but also pay particular attention to those aspects of his thought (such as subjectivity, embodiment, the interpersonal, the ethical, the other, justice, for example) which are of clear and present interest to the psycho-social health and human sciences. Other aspects (such as a detailed examination of time, or Levinas's philosophical-conceptual relationship to philosophers such as Rosenzweig, Bergson, Descartes, Kant, Spinoza, Plato, Aristotle, for example) will feature less prominently, if at all.

While there are not very many of them, this book is not the first invitation to Levinas from psychology, or a psychologist. In the next chapter, I examine some of these past and existing invitations and introductions. As was the case with those authors, the invitation necessitates a dual task: firstly, explaining and presenting "key aspects" of Levinas's philosophy to a psychological audience and then wrestling with how such insights challenge psychology to imagine a different way or path. What is different for this book, however, is the broad scope of its Levinasian telling. The story it wishes to bring to psychology is an encompassing one, from the earliest works (which are routinely overlooked and ignored in much Levinas scholarship in general and in psychology even more so) to the essays and interviews of the last few years.[2] Moreover, and as appropriate, we will also make reference to select writings on Judaism, Levinas's so-called "confessional texts," which he was adamant to distinguish, even keep "separate," from the philosophical work. Encompassing, broad, and comprehensive, however, does not translate to all-inclusive, exhaustive, or all-embracing – an impossibility even in the wildest of ambitions or narcissisms. There will be omissions and erasures from the oeuvre, to be sure, but I find confident comfort in the view that such exclusions need not incriminate a claim to comprehensiveness given a clearly circumscribed aim and plot: to tell a big, broad story to psychologists about the work of a philosopher and the implications of that work to their discipline and practice. An analysis of Albert Einstein's mathematics and physics may claim to be comprehensive to the extent that one about his politics and peace initiatives might as well, different as each will be.

A related caveat pertains to the psychological appropriation and aim. This book is not to provide a systematic "Levinasian psychology," even assuming such a thing was possible or desirable. It is not to prescribe a new psychology as it is to ask some of the questions by which one can begin to imagine such a psychology. Questions by which the invitation to Levinas then spins off into a new invitation to other psychologists and scholars to converse (which is to "take turns" speaking; from the Latin *vertere*, "to turn"), to dialogue (which is to "speak through" something; from the Greek *legein* and *dia*), and to creatively wrestle with just what a Levinasian-inspired psychology might look like. As such, this book is both a beginning and a response – it is a turn-taking dialogue with those existing authors and texts of Levinas and/in psychology but in the process also to initiate, to turn questions and issues to a different light, to begin again.

Throughout the book, I allow myself the freedom not only to present Levinas's thought but also to venture from it to context, to the times, and/or to the people contemporaneous to Levinas. This, too, is a distinguishing feature of the book. In this vein, the reader would be well advised not to skip the endnotes, as so many of us in psychology are wont to do, and the American Psychological Association (APA) style guidelines actually dissuade authors from (this is another difference from philosophy, where much – sometimes more – of the action is in the footnotes; philosophers are primed not to neglect those).

In the chapter to follow (Chapter 2), we examine the relation between philosophy and psychology, particularly for the rupture, the faultline, of their difference. It is by psychology's claim as a science that a divorce was wrought from philosophy. It transpires, however, that one can conceive of science in different ways and that there is, in fact, two broad approaches to thinking and practicing a scientific psychology. The chapter explores the assumptions and historical trajectories of psychology as a natural science as opposed to psychology as a human science. Additionally, some attention is paid to phenomenology, which is central to both psychology as a human science and Levinas's philosophical project. It transpires that a welcoming receptivity to Levinas issues most readily from psychology conceived as a human science, and the chapter continues to review existing attempts to "bring Levinas to psychology." It characterizes and organizes such attempts thematically and also highlights and prefigures some of the difficulties of the philosophical translation to psychology, some of which is voiced by Levinas himself.

Chapter 3 introduces Levinas, but it does so in a manner that is performative of the imperatives attendant on his philosophy. Hence, it does not provide a (mere) listing of biographical dates or facts, or a focused, linear narrative of the intellectual and scholarly trajectory, but asks first what it means to introduce or present someone to another. The chapter poses pertinent questions about the relationship of the person to the work, about the social, cultural, and historical pressures on the person and their work, and about our responsibilities towards those we introduce or present to others in their absence. As such, the chapter attempts to demonstrate some of the philosophical issues Levinas grapples with in his work without necessarily giving conceptual or philosophical terms and names to those issues. The intent is to tell a story of Levinas's life and surround, his work and his times, his loves and his disappointments, in a way that involves the reader affectively and by sensibility to the extent that it also does the cognitive and reasoned intellectual.

Chapter 4 examines Levinas's early work, specifically *Existence and Existents* and *Time and the Other*. A feature of this chapter, as with the book as a whole, is that it also provides some social and historical background to the texts, as well as pointers about how to read and approach the texts. Some of the most important yields from the early work are explained, inclusive of the Il y a, or "there is," hypostasis, embodiment, solitude, and transcendence. Additionally, the chapter organizes and clearly presents attempts to flee from existence: these include death, nourishment, reason, work, Eros, and fecundity. Throughout the chapter, reference is made to psychological implications of the work, but the chapter also provides a dedicated section to such questions and challenges. Existential and humanistic psychology, especially, are brought into the conversation, as the chapter explores the possibility of a psychological anthropology/ontology to be gathered from the early work.

Chapter 5 proceeds to an examination of *Totality and Infinity*. Again, the chapter provides important background information to the text's genesis, its reception, as well as a description of the difficulties attendant upon a reading of the text. The architecture of the text is provided, inclusive of its writing style and presentation. We explore how such features of the text are related to the message of the text, its philosophical project. Hereafter, important and defining aims and concepts are described. These include transcendence, need and desire, totality and infinity, same and other, and ethics. References to psychology are woven throughout the chapter, for example, how psychology has traditionally taken up issues of transcendence, ethics, reason and the ego, and need and desire.

Chapter 6 continues the examination and presentation of *Totality and Infinity*. It does so by following the broad itinerary of the text itself, first focusing on the egoic "I" or the "same," whereafter the "other" and the "face" introduces the central Levinasian concern of ethics as first philosophy. The chapter makes the point that inasmuch as psychology is most attracted to this text, *Totality and Infinity*, it has nonetheless given shorter shrift to the exposition of the egoic I in the world. It consequently spends some time examining precisely those aspects of enjoyment, the elemental, the dwelling, labor and possession, and the feminine before it turns to the other and infinity. Here, Levinas's propositions of the face, freedom and responsibility, ethical resistance, language and discourse, as well as justice are presented and explained. Questions of or from psychology are interspersed throughout the chapter, as are practical or "real-world" examples with which to illustrate and/or "clarify" the philosophical.

Chapter 7 turns to *Otherwise than Being*. Again, it provides some background to the text, including for its relationship to Jacques Derrida's influential commentary on *Totality and Infinity*. The chapter provides an organized summary of the differences between *Otherwise than Being* and *Totality and Infinity*, in so doing providing a clear and concise illustration of the movement and development of Levinas's project. Key ideas from the text are explored. These include transcendence, the saying and the said, substitution, subjectivity, proximity, justice, and the neighbor.

Chapter 8 examines several critical responses to Levinas's work, notably with respect to nature, sex/gender, and race/culture. With respect to nature and non human animals and against the present of a looming ecological calamity, there have been those who have looked to Levinas as a source and guidance for an ecological ethics. We examine several of the ways such authors proceed to do so. However, this chapter also highlights the difficulties and pitfalls attendant on such an undertaking, indeed the fundamental claim that Levinas's philosophy is andropocentric and allergic to an ecological ethics. Similarly, the section on women, sex, and gender wrestle with Levinas's references to woman and the feminine in his work. The chapter charts a variety of critical responses, from charges of sexism to complex attempts to see a nuanced nonsexist quality to his use of such terms. The section on race and culture also surveys the critical literature, both as it pertains to the philosophy and certain concepts as well as Levinas's person. Charges of anti-Black prejudice and Eurocentrism are examined closely and both prosecuted and defended by reference to the texts and Levinas's own words.

Chapter 9 offers concluding thoughts and remarks. It does so in a practical manner and by several examples and vignettes with which to bring the whole of the book together, so to speak. The challenges of a Levinasian-inspired psychology is restated and elaborated on, as are the promises and possibilities.

## Notes

1  Fred Alford (2002), in another excellent attempt to put Levinas and psychology in conversation with each other, registers a related sentiment. He notes that "many who write about Levinas adopt his language, as though to understand Levinas means being able to write in the style of Levinas" (Alford, 2002, p. 2). This is a mistake, not because Levinas's language must be avoided but because "sounding too much *like* Levinas makes thinking *about* Levinas more difficult" (p. 2, emphasis in original).
2  Arguably, most scholars treat the publication of Otherwise than Being, in 1974, as the culminative end of Levinas's contributions. I will argue, though, that the interviews and publications thereafter offer important elaborations, clarifications, and even possibilities for application in the world (especially with respect to issues of justice and politics), *as well as* his own attempts to bring the whole of his work (as perhaps his life) into reflective review. These should be reason enough, if not reason *par excellence*, to examine that work as well.

# Chapter 2

# Philosophy, Psychology, and the Knot of Science

Some readers may already have come across Levinas's name – perhaps you read an attributed quote, or noticed him "name checked" with reference to ethics, "the other," or some phenomenon such as "forgiveness." It is indeed so that Levinas has become quite "popular" of late, in philosophy itself, to be sure, but also in other academic disciplines as wide afield as theology and religious studies, education, literature and literary criticism, nursing, health care ethics, holocaust studies, sociology, and some outposts of psychology.[1]

While invigorated attention to Levinas is certainly to be welcomed, at the same time, there are very real cautions and pitfalls to be aware and wary of. One such challenge pertains to the radical nature of Levinas's philosophy. It proposes a fundamental, foundational, and comprehensive change in thinking what it is to be at the root (radical, thus, its etymology from *radix/c[alus]*, meaning "root"). If one is to pledge fidelity to such thought, any translation and/or application to psychology, or any of a number of academic disciplines which have taken increasing note of his work, will have to contend with just such foundational challenges. One problem, all too often, with such widespread appropriations or applications outside of philosophy, is that the rich complexity of thought is diluted to a violently emaciated version thereof, or is misinterpreted and/or reductionistically misquoted. To the admiring excitement of Levinas's new thought that "makes one tremble," the philosopher Jacques Derrida also laments, however, that

> Levinas's work is in the process of passing, quite late in its history, to the level of facile reference, even communal surety . . . more and more I find tedious and commonplace the expressions "relation with the other" or "respect for the other" . . . "ethics" sometimes plays the same role.
>
> (Derrida, 2003b, p. 31)

Were one generous, some misinterpretations could be "excused" or "understood" – Levinas, after all, is an exceedingly difficult philosopher to read and understand, even for professional philosophers who are not above "getting him wrong." A more pernicious alarm, though, is sounded in attempts to "systematize" or "manualize" his thought in reductionistic accounts which might render Levinas "another plug-in

DOI: 10.4324/9781003315612-2

module in lectures and textbooks" (Harrington, 2002, p. 209), provide "standards" "on whether one's clinical language does violence or not 'according to the work of Emmanuel Levinas'" (p. 209), or provide systematic treatment or research "steps" to follow and "check off" if one was to deem oneself "Levinasian." Psychology seems particularly prone to such attempts, with "empirically validated treatments" (EVT's), "manualized therapies," and stringently procedural research steps and methods being the ruling roost of the day. In a sense, one can understand the seduction to clear plans and procedures, in research or therapy, which may well lessen the palpable pressures about "what to do." Anyone who has trained beginning clinicians, or who would think back on their very first client or patient, might recognize this anxiety about what one says or about how one "does" therapy in the face of the patient's distress. Or whether one's research method and procedure will pass dissertation or publication muster upon its defense or review, given its evaluation against a certain (scientific) procedural rubric. Having an anchor in the form of a manual, steps, or procedures to follow certainly goes a long way towards abetting such uncertainties. The thing about anchors, though, is that it restricts movement into new territories. And the thing about staying in the comfort of a familiar berth is that it tends to tame and subject the "new" or "unsuspecting" to the geography of our bounded understanding. This is one of the key challenges Levinas will pose to us; his work is fundamentally critical of a systematizing order which reduces the one to the procedural law, sacrifices the specific to the general, or presumes to have captured the truth of "the thing itself."

The issue with psychology, however, runs even deeper – beyond the specifics or content of a systematized therapy, research methods and procedures, developmental psychological stages, or organized diagnostic criteria for mental disorders. At issue is also – dare one say it – a *philosophical* concern about psychology's claim to a systematic *science*. Our curricula and our academic practices – even the physical organization of the disciplines at institutions of higher learning – vividly illustrate this tension. Psychology departments are often housed in schools of social science, health science, or natural sciences even, while philosophy departments are most often located in schools of arts and humanities. An undergraduate bachelor's degree in science is as common in psychology as one in philosophy is rare. Even in most liberal arts colleges, where the laudable attempt is to make connections between subjects through interdisciplinary curricula, readings, and learning projects, such connections do not threaten the boundaries of the disciplines themselves. We may be enriched by a trans-disciplinary liberal arts curriculum that navigates across several disciplines but without threatening the fundamental integrity of any. Like the motif of the salad bowl for a multiculturalism of the late 20th century, every ingredient – olives, lettuce, peppers, croutons – maintains their fundamental essences and natures in a togetherness made delicious precisely by the shared space that is nonetheless safe for each component to remain what it "is." And what psychology "is," before anything else, is a science.

As the logos of psyche,[2] the "science of mind" or "behavior," as most introductory textbooks would have it, psychology's interest is *both* that it "is" a science and that the object of its science is human behavior and/or thought (and/or affect or emotion, though that aspect of psyche is often omitted from [scientific] definitions of psychology, an omission not entirely unsurprising as we will see shortly). One of the defining hallmarks of a science is that it is systematic, that it builds and organizes knowledge in an orderly, formal, and structured manner. The alternative appears to be anarchic eclecticism or lawless chaos. But surely, there are, even just within psychology, many different and differing (organized, formal, systematic, and structured) perspectives on what it is to be human and on the constitution, structure, motivation, or operation of psyche. Any personality textbook illustrates this point, listing a variety of divergent and differing perspectives on the nature of the person – all of which are theoretically "organized, formal, systematic, and structured." A common plea from students in most any personality class is "But which one is 'right'?" Which is also to ask, "Which one is 'true'?" Several years ago, I heard a professor respond to a similar question by modifying the old parable of the blind men being exposed to different parts of the elephant; the different theories of personality, he intoned, are all descriptive of a part of the elephant, but as a "young science," our task is to eventually gain a view of the whole elephant, as our techniques and our methods of inquiry become more sophisticated. In such a future, he continued, we will discard older notions and mistakes (his allusive reference to psychoanalysis here was rather thinly veiled) not only to a knowledge of the elephant in front of us but also to the constitutive truth of *all* elephants. Some accounts of psyche are thus considered more or less "valuable," more or less "true," or more or less encouraging of that future where all shall be known. The sorting hat for such value and truth is "science," or rather, a particular – even doctrinaire – perspective on what constitutes such a science.

## The Science(s) of Psychology

It has become almost *de rigueur* to quote Hermann Ebbinghaus's opening statement to his 1908 elementary psychology textbook that "Psychology has a long prehistory, but only a short past" (Ebbinghaus, 1973, p. 3). That is, the questions psychology concerns itself with – subjectivity, motivation, madness, relationships with others, suffering, for example – are not new. Daniel Robinson's pithy comment serves as emphasis: "The subject matter of psychology is as old as reflection" (Robinson, 1995, p. 12). If then, the questions of psychology were ones broached and examined by philosophy since its earliest days, and given that psychology "lived" in philosophy until the late 19th century, what marks this "young discipline's" break from philosophy are less the questions or the subject matter than the manner, method, and means of the question and answer.

### Psychology Is a Natural Science

Origin stories tend to provide an identitary (and as often heroic) account of how something came to be and in the telling as frequently also state or imply how the "new" that came to be is different from the "old" that preceded it. In addition, it is also common for origin stories to contain a statement of fundamental values and of the principles and aims it organizes itself around. For psychology, this story, recounted in every introductory or history of psychology textbook I've come across, involves the figures of Wilhelm Wundt and William James, putative patriarchs of the disciplines who, at Leipzig and Harvard respectively, unshackled psychology from its philosophical dominion. (In 1896, a German newspaper described Wundt and James as "psychological popes of the Old and New Worlds," respectively [Diamond, 2001, p. 2]). We should remind ourselves that both Wundt and James were trained as philosophers – there were no departments of psychology nor psychologists, only philosophers with an interest in the philosophies of science, the self, or perception, for example. Thus, it was, on a blustery day in December 1879, that Wundt proceeded to the third floor of the Augusteum at the University of Leipzig,[3] along with his doctoral student, Max Friedrich. There, Wundt had set up a machine to help his student collect data for his dissertation titled "On the Duration of Apperception for Simple and Complex Visual Stimuli."[4] In a nutshell, the machine was to provide objective measurement data involving the duration of time between when a subject heard a dropped ball hit a platform and his pressing a telegraph key (the difference was one-tenth of a second, by the way). And thus, Morton Hunt (1993, p. 128) writes, "with the first clack of the ball on the platform, the click of the key, and the registration of elapsed time on the chronoscope, the modern era of psychology had begun." Indeed, in quick succession, psychology laboratories were opened at Johns Hopkins University, followed by laboratories in Russia, France, the Netherlands, and England (Chung & Hyland, 2011). In 1903, a mere 25 years after Wundt's experiment, there were already at least 40 psychology laboratories in the United States (Smith, 1997).

The new of psychology, then, was hammered on the anvil of the laboratory. A psychology of experiment and experimentation would replace the philosophical psychology of speculation and contemplation, fashioning itself as it did on the scientific model and methods of the natural sciences, where observation, measurement, prediction, and experimental control was key. It would propose ideals of objectivity and bias-free science, the reduction of phenomena into operationalized and manageable parts, clearly and deliberately defined and circumscribed. It would seek generalized and universal laws, not unlike those for gravity or motion. The mysteries of psyche and self would be laid bare by the assumption of its predictable lawfulness, both in terms of the observable seen and the hidden or obscure which could, like a barometer does with invisible air pressure, bring the self's lawful essence into observable and measurable view.

Almost every introductory textbook to psychology, every student's welcome to the discipline and orientation to the lay and rules of the land, clearly represents the values of the natural sciences. Coon and Mitterer (2014) write that psychology's goal is to "describe, understand, predict, and control behavior" (p. 18), while the immensely popular textbook of Wade et al. (2015) distinguishes psychology from "psychobabble and pseudoscience" by the fact that "it is based on rigorous

research and empirical evidence . . . gathered by careful observation, experimentation, or measurement" (p. 4). Research and publication submissions are scrutinized
for a particular format, for a naturalistic and scientistic "epistemological ideology . . . and exaltation of so-called objective p-values and static research design"
(Clegg & Slife, 2005, p. 66). The American Psychological Association (APA), the
most powerful champion for psychology, and its administrative overseeing body,
unabashedly declares psychology a core STEM (Science, Technology, Engineering, Mathematics) discipline:

> uses the scientific method . . . in order to test hypotheses that lead to creation
> of unique knowledge about human behavior . . . [and uses] . . . state-of-the-art
> scientific instrumentation . . . such as fMRI, electromyographs, robots, virtual
> reality, psychophysical techniques, animal modeling, and behavioral analysis,
> to achieve empirical and theoretical advances.
>
> (APA, 2010, p. 7)

What is true for the field in general is also true for applied spaces, such as psychotherapy, where empirically supported treatments (ESTs) and the diagnostic model
of medicine "institutionalize the values of naturalistic science (e.g. empiricism,
determinism, reductionism, etc.) as the only justification procedures for the mental
health field" (Clegg & Slife, 2005, p. 66). The lab and the randomized clinical trial
remain the heraldic inspiration and marker for psychology, the emancipatory sign
by which it became an independent discipline (Giorgi, 2000).

### Psychology Is a Human Science

A human science approach to psychology, it should be stated unequivocally, *also*
regards its approach as "scientific." However, this version of science takes its inspiration not from the rationalist and empiricist philosophers (such as Descartes and
Hobbes, for example) but from thinkers such as Giambatista Vico, Johan Herder,
Wilhelm Dilthey, and Friedrich Nietzsche, to name a few, all of whom struggled
with and presented alternative paths and insights to the question of how we know,
how a science should set out to know, and why certain ways of knowing are not
appropriate to the study of human beings. Hence Herder, for example, argued that
people were very different in different cultures and different times – their beliefs,
the way they thought about themselves, and the meaning they made about who
they were and what motivated their actions and desires were all shaped fundamentally by the cultures and the times they found themselves in. To seek, then, as
natural sciences do, eternal laws and timeless principles about human beings did
not make much sense; instead, a science of human beings should be of an interpretative sort and take into account precisely those cultures and times in a systematic
and rigorous manner. Similarly, Wilhelm Dilthey, a German philosopher, made a
distinction between the natural sciences (*Naturwissenschaften*) and the human sciences (*Geisteswissenschaften*) (Dilthey, 1977). For Dilthey, the natural sciences

examine phenomena in causal terms; the process is that of *Erklaren*, or explanation (Burston & Frie, 2006) on the basis of explanatory laws, hypothesis testing, experimentation, and quantified findings and data. The *Geisteswissenchaften*, or human sciences, on the other hand, are not about *Erklaren* (explanation) but instead privilege *Verstehen*, or understanding. Culture, history, human volition, and meaning cannot be thought in terms of causal explanation but must be *understood* and demands a qualitative science as opposed to a quantified and reductionist one. In Dilthey's own pithy description, "We explain nature; we understand psychic life" (Dilthey, 1977, p. 27).

It may come as a surprise that Wundt and James, pioneers of psychology as a natural science, are also looked to for their founding roles as human science psychologists. Alongside his experimental "physiological psychology," Wundt *also* proposed a second so-called *Volkerpsychologie* (psychology of peoples, or "cultural" psychology) that would examine "higher" psychological functions which found expression in religion, art, culture, society, and law. These "higher mental functions" could *not*, Wundt was adamant and clear, be studied in the laboratory (Chung & Hyland, 2011; Thorne & Henley, 2001). Instead, this psychology had to be of a descriptive sort and could be studied, for example, through rigorous analyses of folklore, myths, linguistics, and cultural customs (Cole, 1996). Wundt's desire was for this descriptive and complex *Volkerpsychologie* to exist alongside his physiological psychology, the one informing and enriching the other, rendering a fuller picture of human being and psyche. This remains an unfulfilled dream and desire.

William James, similarly, cautioned that a singular focus on experimental psychology would render it "a nasty little subject," excluding everything one would want to know about human being. In the epilogue to *Psychology: The Briefer Course*, an abbreviated version of his influential textbook, James (2001) summarizes psychology (at least the experimental kind):

A string of raw facts . . . [with] not a single law in the sense in which physics shows us laws, not a single proposition from which any consequence can causally be deduced. This is no science, it is only the hope of a science.

(p. 335)

What an indictment and opinion from the pre-eminent psychologist and canonical father of psychology! Morton Hunt (1993) aptly describes James as the founding psychologist *Malgre Lui* ("in spite of himself"), "a distinguished professor of the new science of psychology who denies that it is a science . . . who praises the findings of experimental psychologists but loathes performing experiments and does as few as possible" (p. 144).

There was then, even among these canonical founding fathers of experimental psychology, the notion that "something" about human beings could not be grasped, explained, or accounted for by experimental and naturalistic scientific methods. Human beings operate in the realm of meanings, lived experience, and complex and complicated relationships with self and others such that a simple and reductively predictive formula, law, or generalization misses the very experience of being human. Simply transporting the methods, procedures, and assumptions of the natural sciences, of the sciences that study weather and rocks, or hydrogen and physics, onto human beings runs the risk of missing what is human about human beings. It is, in William James's words, "like seizing a spinning top to catch its motion, or trying to turn up the gas quickly enough to see how the darkness looks" (James, quoted in Hunt, 1993, p. 151).

Again, it is important to stress that *both* psychologies were understood to be scientific but by different methodological means. Given that human being is "different from a 'thing,' it requires an approach and method that can access the positive qualities of humans" (Giorgi, 2000, p. 67). As such, we have to detour to phenomenology and existential phenomenology, so defining of much of the human science psychologies (and as we will learn, of Levinas's work as well). This detour will be brief and much too cursory but hopefully just enough for us to carry on a conversation with our guest, Levinas, who is to arrive shortly.

## Phenomenology, Existential Phenomenology, and Human Science Psychology

As an adolescent in the early 1980s, I remember being fascinated by a television series hosted by the British science historian James Burke. It was called *Connections*, and Burke would present, in an engaging and accessible way, how events and inventions of our day are linked by a series of most implausible and/or forgotten "connections" – for example, between the moon landing and an obscure Napoleonic battle in Italy. (In a summative nutshell, Napoleon's large army prompted a logistical need to feed them, which led to the preservation of food in bottles, then cans, which in turn prompted refrigeration, the invention of the thermos flask, and the technology of sealing air in a vacuum, which directly made possible the V-2 rocket and, ultimately, the Apollo moon landing.) Burke's telling is much more engaging than the preceding example summary, no least because he also delves into the personages, the accidental, fortuitous, and/or uncanny ways different people crossed paths and the history of the times to tell his stories, but the basic analogy stands: that many of the psychological approaches and insights of our contemporary everyday – humanistic psychology and therapy, existential psychology, Gestalt psychology, the personality theories of Carl Rogers, Abraham Maslow, Viktor Frankl, Gordon Allport, Erich Fromm, or Rollo May, qualitative research methods such as interpretative phenomenological analysis (IPA), grounded theory, thematic and hermeneutic analyses, Lacanian and interpretative psychoanalysis, even poststructural or postphenomenological and critical psychological approaches – are all intimately connected, influenced by, linked, or "begotten" by phenomenology and certain philosophical developments of the early and mid-20th century. It is an outsized connection only rivalled by the ease of our forgetfulness thereof.

Although most everyone acknowledges Edmund Husserl's early 20th-century paternity for the phenomenological movement, it bears special mention for psychology that prior to Husserl's groundbreaking philosophical announcement of phenomenology, "proto" phenomenological work was already done in psychology, notably by Frantz Brentano and William James[5], both of whom Husserl acknowledged for their influence and inspiration to his own thinking. There is, in fact, a thread of sorts here, where psychologists and helpers have "done" (and are doing) phenomenology or phenomenology-like things and had/have a "way of doing" in relationships with people as counselors or researchers without the express phenomenological name, necessarily, to brand and characterize what they were or are doing. We suspect that some readers may read here about phenomenology and/ or Levinas for the first time, or be introduced to intricate concepts and theoretical insights while at the same time acknowledging that in some way, they always knew it, or did it, or at least some of it, in some intuitive, inchoate, or spontaneous way.

The story of phenomenology is complicated by the fact that there is no one phenomenology, no singular way to "be" a phenomenologist. An oft quoted observation by the philosopher Paul Ricoeur is illuminating: namely, that phenomenology is really the story of deviations from Husserl, a history of Husserlian heresies (Ricoeur, 1987). Husserl himself wryly commented, towards the end of his life, that in spite of the worldwide movement phenomenology had become and the scores of students from all over the world who studied with him to become influential and even famous philosophers themselves, he was an "appointed leader without followers," even an enemy of the movement (Moran, 2000, 2005).

But let us start with Husserl nonetheless and with the observation that philosophy, like psychology, at the turn of the 19th century, *also* labored under an increasing empiricist and naturalist pressure. The successes of the natural sciences, and the glory of a technology on the victorious rise, similarly presented to philosophy a certain identitary challenge as to its worth, its usefulness, and its historical claim as the "queen of all disciplines." The advances of the great so-called idealist philosophers (like Kant, Fichte, and especially, Hegel), and whose writings were coterminous with the Romantic movement, have all come under dismissive scrutiny and even ridicule. It was into such a philosophical environment that Edmund Husserl entered the fray, questioning the naturalist philosophical assumption of an objective, essential reality beyond the surface of appearance. (For example, beyond the appearance of simply walking around on earth lies the essentially real, which is gravity and which prevents us from floating off into the sky; or for the neuroscientist, beyond the appearance of listlessness and fatigue, there is a depletion of dopamine.) They miss a rather powerful truth, Husserl argues: the thing that appears (the *phainomenon*) – people walking on the surface of the earth or being listless – is not separate or distinct from its essence, but its appearance is the way in which the essence presents itself. Put differently, the naturalistic, scientific attitude assumes an independent, objective world, separate from ourselves, the truth of which can be gleaned by an adherence to particular measurement methods and technologies – a mercury barometer, for example, of which we had a beautifully ornate specimen in my childhood home, a surprise gift to me from my grandmother. Every morning, without fail, my father would peer over his glasses at the barometer, give it a slight tap, and make some pronouncement: "Looks like a fine day" or "It's going to rain." The barometer measures air pressure, the weight of air, simply put, calibrated along measurement intervals; this is the natural scientific explanation for an instrument which, generated by "proper" method and technique, is able to deliver the secrets of an objective world "out there." But this view misses the fact, Husserl argues, that we are "in the world" (most all his "heretic" successors will agree with this, at least), and it is only through and by consciousness that the world and all that appears makes sense at all. Consciousness is not some substance like any other in the natural world but is the fundamental way in which the world appears to us. Hence, for Husserl, the content of consciousness, and the way in which the phenomenon appears to us in consciousness, deserves our deliberate scrutiny. It is an intentional consciousness – oriented outside itself, to the world, to and of something, "a primary openness to what lies outside it" (Davis, 1996, p. 12). The relationship with the object, with the world, takes place within the apperceiving subject, concretely embroiled in life and lived experience. Whereas natural science presumes a view from nowhere, a God's eye perspective, we are not gods; we are in the world and cannot abstract ourselves from the world, where everything we say, do, feel, and are conscious of comes from an always already engagement and immersion in the world. The very weight of air that the barometer measures is the air that envelops a father whose relationship with the object also concedes his relationship with an absent mother; at some point, he told me, "this barometer may be the only tangible thing I ever received from her, and I only received that secondhand through you." We live in a world of meaning, where consciousness is itself "rooted in deeper levels of being-there that precede all sorts of objectifying knowledge and representation" (Peperzak, 1993, p. 16), a fact Husserl's successor, Martin Heidegger, clues us into rather acutely.

If phenomenology is, as we mentioned, the story of Husserlian heresies, then few such heretics are more influential than Martin Heidegger. By his reading, it is no longer consciousness as such that is at the center of our interest and inquiry but human being (*Dasein*)[6] immersed in the world and in time. Ultimately, it is only through Dasein's particularly human way of being that we can gain some access to Being. This is the crucial *ontological difference*, which is that there is a difference between Being and beings – between that which exists and existence itself. There is a difference between me living life and life itself; but the only way to know anything about life itself is to ask me, who lives life, and to study me, as I live life. For Heidegger, then, ontology, the study of the nature of being, has to focus on the meaning of being, and phenomenology has to shift its primary focus there, away from Husserl's consciousness as such. One could say that Heidegger, along with Sartre and Merleau-Ponty,[7] modifies the description of phenomenology's task, which is to emphasize that before there is the thematization of consciousness, our activities and experiences in the world is given by an openness to the world, by a horizon and prereflective givenness within which the understanding and truth of consciousness is possible. Thus, the stage was set for a translation and appropriation of both existentialism and phenomenology into psychology.

The reader will note that the preceding sentence snuck or tucked "existentialism" in alongside phenomenology. Indeed, the astute reader might have spotted some existential "clues" already in references to Sartre, or the occasional lapse or interchange of the term phenomenology or phenomenological psychology with existential-phenomenology. At the risk of a banal simplification, and drawing the ire of all stripes of philosophical purists (and elitists), an elementary argument is that existentialism, of which Soren Kierkegaard is the putative philosophical patriarch, in its focus on concrete existence as it is lived, dovetails well with phenomenology, which provides a rigorous philosophical method with which to study that life. One might continue to argue a certain convergence of existential and phenomenological traditions, notably in the writings of Sartre, Merleau-Ponty, and Heidegger (even as he railed against descriptions of himself as an "existentialist"). A detailed history of the ways existentialism and phenomenology came to psychology falls well outside the scope and space of this book. We will have to be content with sketching broad narrative outlines of such influence and with referrals to other authors who have taken such a task to scholarly heart (e.g. Churchill & Wertz, 2001; Churchill et al., 2021; Giorgi, 1970, 2014). Suffice it to say, though, that the earliest such attempts occurred in different centers and places in Europe, notable examples being the work of Binswanger (1958) and Boss (1963) and the work of the so-called Utrecht school[8] in the Netherlands. Existentialism and phenomenology (of all the Husserlian, Heideggerian, and Merleau-Pontian varieties) thus provided the inspirational font for a new aspirational psychology, whose focus was to be on the rigorous phenomenological investigation of lived human experience in the world as embodied beings in space, time, and culture.

In the United States, concerns with a prevailing positivist and reductionistic natural science psychology took a mostly humanistic turn, the work of Abraham Maslow and Carl Rogers serving as exemplary cases in point (Rollo May being somewhat of a lone existentialist exception). Maybe it is not far-fetched to speculate on the appeal of existential psychology to Europe and humanistic psychology to America in historico-cultural terms. As such, one might argue that for Europe, the aftermath of an absolutely horrific war, where the devastating ruin of cities and families were in plain and reckoning sight, would pressure an existential demand to grapple deeply with questions of life and death, choice and meaning. For America, however, banal and insensitive as it may sound, the war was an economic and cultural boon. Its status as superpower was firmly cemented, and it was confidently on the march. No US city was attacked (Honolulu may be offered as exception, but lest we forget, Hawaii was not a state at the time of the Pearl Harbor attack) such that the horrors of the war, save for soldiers who fought and individual families who lost loved ones, remained quite distant. Socially and economically, the aftermath of the war saw progress and growth of an unparalleled sort. The more "optimistic" and "can do" psychological humanism of actualization and becoming everything one can be, alongside a diminished focus on mortality (a particular existential motivational interest), a valorization of freedom (as opposed to the existential emphasis, alongside freedom, of responsibility for choices), and a fundamental meaningfulness to the world (as opposed to an existential meaninglessness) seemed more culturally and historically resonant. Yet the differences between an American "fourth force" humanistic psychology and a European existential psychology should not eclipse the phenomenological family resemblances, inclusive of a focus on lived experience, and a phenomenal centeredness in self, choice, and agency.

A particular exception on the American landscape, however, was the program at Duquesne University, in Pittsburgh, its influence even gathering to itself the moniker of a movement of sorts, the "Duquesne school" of existential-phenomenological psychology. Besides its philosophical psychological emphasis, and its lonely advocacy for a decidedly existential-phenomenological psychology, its particular innovation was in developing a rigorous phenomenological research method *for psychology*[9] and the integration and application of both existential and phenomenological insights into clinical work and psychological assessment. Indeed, "as the first curriculum in the history of psychology to apply phenomenological methods to the full spectrum of psychological topics" (Churchill et al., 2021, p. 220) and "through its diverse and substantial contributions . . . [Duquesne] has earned the title of the capital of phenomenological psychology in the New World" (Misiak & Sexton, 1973, p. 62). It is an influence that continues to this day not only by its own self-definition and continuing mission but also, more importantly, by the alumni it has produced over 60 years, many of whom have gone on to start academic programs and wield influence in academic departments nationally and internationally.[10] It might not be lost on the reader that this very book issues from my affiliation with this storied department.

To be sure, the psychological translation and appropriation of existential and phenomenological philosophy has not been without challenge and debate, and in the political and scholarly struggles to found a phenomenological psychology within academic institutions, intense disagreements have arisen around just how to "do" phenomenology – what the "correct" method would be or what this or that concept "means." A dynamic we've referred to earlier may also come into play here: the stereotypical distinction between the reflective philosopher pondering the phenomenon by their learned lonesome, as opposed to the psychologist wrestling with the phenomenon in the active excursus into the social and research commons, or working clinically with others whose lives painfully disclose the phenomenon of interest. Differences of opinion seem to matter more – less a simple matter of learned philosophical difference, the psychological stakes seem higher, and the battles perhaps more intense precisely because our research involves others, our results and conclusions sometimes have policy and "real-world" implications, and our clinical and helping responses matter profoundly to the well-being of an other. It is not "simply academic." Here is the rub, though: precisely because it isn't "merely" academic, we have to take special note – as psychologists – of those philosophical differences for the manner in which it becomes psychological ones.

As it is, in broad brush strokes, the inspiration from phenomenological and existential philosophy finds expression in existential phenomenological psychology as an acknowledgment of an existential foundation to human experience (Van Kaam, 1966), a focus on the lifeworld and lived experience, the concrete engagement of human being-in-the-world. As human beings, we are engaged with the world, we are conscious of the world, and we are able to reflect on the world as it discloses itself to consciousness. We are embodied, spatial beings with others and in culture. As such, we are given to language, history, religion, art, and an affective life felt within the body and in space and place. Merleau-Ponty's insightful rejoinder to a certain naturalist science is apropos here: the lived body is not that of the anatomist nor is lived space that of the engineer nor is lived time what the physicist measures on a linear plane (Merleau-Ponty, 1983, 2012). Methodologically, the focus is on description (Giorgi, 1970, 2012), and/or meaning and interpretation (Van Manen, 2016), without the imposition of explanations of the phenomenon before it has been understood or intuited from within by its own terms.

Moran's observation of (existential) phenomenologists with respect to philosophy is also true for psychology:

> extraordinarily diverse in their interests, in their interpretation of the central issues of phenomenology, in their application of what they understood to be the phenomenological method, and in their development of what they took to be the phenomenological programme for the future.
>
> (Moran, 2000, p. 3)

We see such diversity not only in fundamental ontological assumptions but also in areas of contemporary application. Indeed, phenomenology has experienced somewhat of an academic resurgence of late, aggregating around descriptors such as feminist phenomenology (Fisher & Embree, 2000; Shabot & Landry, 2018; Young, 1980), neurophenomenology (Gallagher, 2010; Varela, 1996), ecological phenomenology, and the particularly exciting critical phenomenology (Guenther, 2021; Weiss et al., 2020), to name a few examples. A proliferation of qualitative research methods in psychology – grounded theory, interpretive phenomenological analysis, narrative analysis, discourse analysis, for example – are all rooted in (existential) phenomenology.

## Levinas and Psychology

Existing attempts to bring Levinas to psychology – not many, not nearly enough – all take assumptive issue with prevailing, mainstream views of a naturalistic psychological science. The overwhelming majority of such scholarly articles are to be found in a smallish range of psychological journals some of us have come to know as receptive to "alternative," "theoretical-philosophical," "human science," or otherwise creative and boundary challenging scholarship. These are not, for the most part, the "mainstream" journals most psychologists read; in fact, an electronic search of the heraldic flagship of the discipline, *American Psychologist*, reveals not a single published article on Levinas and psychology as such.[11] In addition to these published scholarly articles, a handful of doctoral dissertations have wrestled with Levinas in/and psychology.[12] (Such dissertations, the reader will notice, were completed at institutions and departments which may attract to themselves a similar portrayal of openness to a human science approach to psychology generally, or allow their students a wider-than-most freedom to engage with theory at the level of the dissertation, outside of the "usual" and the normative.) As for published books, a literal handful specifically and directly frame their projects in terms of attempts at a Levinasian-inspired psychology (e.g. Alford, 2002; Gantt & Williams, 2002; Goodman, 2012; Krycka et al., 2015; Kunz, 1998), while some others spend a sizeable portion of attention to Levinas and psychology, or include within an edited volume some contributions particular to Levinas and psychology (e.g. Freeman, 2013; Goodman & Freeman, 2015; Morgan, 2011, 2019; Orange, 2011). Considering that it has been more than 60 years since the publication of Levinas's groundbreaking text, *Totality and Infinity*, the published record of full-length texts on Levinas and psychology represents, on the average, just about one or two books a decade! Moreover, if one takes into account that the overwhelming majority of these texts were published by a single press (Duquesne University Press, whom readers may recognize as the publisher that introduced Levinas to an English-speaking world), one which no longer exists,[13] it becomes even clearer that there is a pressing lacuna to be entered into and explored.

One is struck, already at the outset and without reading a single word of such attempts to bring Levinas into dialogue with psychology, by *who* leads and/or hosts the conversation. Almost without fail, the psychologists and scholars who have made the attempt were trained in, and/or practice, a human science psychology of a complex, qualitative, non-reductionistic psychology attuned to the uniqueness and experiential of human being and of what it is "to be" (human). Relatedly, one learns that there are centers and hubs of influence which are (and in some cases, have been for a long time) struggling with just what a complex human psychology might mean, clinically as well as theoretically.[14] It is with scholars largely from those universities and departments (Seattle University, especially) where we find the most serious and "prolific" (given the existing few, prolific is a relative descriptor) engagements with Levinas and psychology. One might draw an initial conclusion: that the invitation to Levinas from psychology, thus far, has only been extended by a human science psychology. Having drawn such a conclusion, one may now wonder whether it *can* only come from human science psychology; that is, is there something inherently and fundamentally opposed to a natural science psychology sitting down with Levinas? And if not, what might such a meeting need to be for it to be substantially more than theater or diplomatic grandstanding?

As it is, given its human science psychological issue, the invitation to Levinas is often framed in terms of fundamental shortcomings within mainstream natural science psychology. In its "inebriated" and "greedy" (Cohen, 2015, p. ix) pursuit of a positivistic, natural science assumption, method, and technique, in its "physics envy" (Williams & Gantt, 2002, p. 3), psychology has lost the person, existence, and the things that matter to personhood – like ethics, morality, the good, and indeed, the importance of the other outside of a self-serving, self-contained, actualizing, and individual ego (Clegg & Slife, 2005; Downs et al., 2012; Freeman, 2012; Garza & Landrum, 2010; Goodman, Dueck, et al., 2010; Kunz, 2006, 2012). By its positioning within a natural science model, psychology's manner and method – from the conceptual to the applied – is impoverished and misses the fullness of its promise, suffering as it does from "a crisis of meaning," in large part, the price it had to pay for its mechanistic, reductionistic, deterministic, and egoic practice and pretensions (Kunz, 1998; Williams & Gantt, 2002).

Moreover, and as common, is the accusation that psychology has come to "deify the self" (Kunz, 1998, p. xvii) and to present the interests of the self as its defining concern (Freeman, 2013). The Levinasian fact of the matter, however, is to advance the priority of the other and, even more radically, that the very constitution of the self is by the investiture of the other and the other in me. More hospitable as they may be to Levinas, this criticism strikes close to the bone of human science approaches, such as humanistic and existential psychology especially. By their notions of self-actualization and the freedom of the agentic I, they, too, will be challenged. We will suffice with its mere mention here as we return to this crucial issue in the chapters to follow. A third thematic that a Levinasian turn in psychology highlights is psychology's fundamental allergy to ethics and morality. One would be forgiven a spontaneous incredulity to such an accusation; it seems ethics is ever present in psychology – it is a core component of the licensing exams, continuing education workshops and certifications, and Institutional Review Boards. The ethics code of the APA is almost like a second Moses tablet (the Diagnostic and Statistical Manual [DSM] being the first) to watch over all we do as psychologists and researchers. Quite simply, such universal, rule-bound ethics is not the ethics Levinas has in mind. But even more so, psychological ethics is not intrinsic to the discipline; it does not feature in the conception, at the root, of what it is to be and what it is to be with an other. It retains, to varying individual degrees, an external and imposed hoop to jump through to get the institution's approval for research, a checkbox to tick as insurance against legal liability, having satisfied continuing education requirements, or a chapter to study for licensure and then to return to on occasion, as a check in the rearview mirror, or to rummage for in the glove box. Levinas's ethics "is not grafted on to an antecedent relation of cognition; it is a foundation and not a superstructure" (Levinas, 1987a, p. 56). Contemporary psychology, by this understanding, is "singularly ill-equipped to account for human action in any manner that might preserve its essentially moral character" (Williams & Gantt, 2002, pp. 10–11).

One also notices a sprouting arc of sorts, with the earliest attempts to acknowledge Levinas in psychology issuing from therapists and scholar-practitioners "dismayed by widespread emphases on technique-oriented approaches to psychopathology," those who found, in their clinical encounters, that "the exalted – yet elusive – station held by the uniquely individual face of the other person . . . exceeds diagnostic categories" (Harrington, 1993, p. 4). Indeed, one of the first, if not *the* first, published article on Levinas and psychology was that of Steen Halling (1975), exploring the implications of *Totality and Infinity* for therapy.[15] There is an almost intuitive understanding as to why this should be so, as to why therapists might be the ones to take notice of Levinas first – the demand of the suffering other on us, our responsibility before the other, and the ethical imperatives of the face-to-face relation are after all fundamental to *both* Levinas and psychotherapy. Slavish and dominant adherence to technique, to empiricism without theory or philosophical grounding/acknowledgment, or to the medical model in general misses the fundamental responsibility of the therapist to suffer "with" and "for" their clients (Gantt, 2000), for the therapist to be "traumatized" into ethical response (Orange, 2018). Indeed, broader than the individual therapist, the manner and practice of dominant psychotherapy, it is argued, has lost its soul and fails to adequately address the relational and the inherently ethical in therapy (Dueck & Goodman, 2007; Dueck & Parsons, 2007; Huett & Goodman, 2012; Kunz, 2007; Sayre, 2005; Walsh, 2005). A therapeutic interest in Levinas continues to this day, with much attention from practitioners and therapists (an interest, by the way, that has some parallel in nursing and health care ethics, where some have also turned to Levinas from a frustration and discomfort with the occlusion of the ethical from health care and training in general [examples include Burns, 2017; Clifton-Soderstrom, 2003; Kong, 2008; Lavoie et al., 2006; Nortvedt, 2003; Watson, 2003]).

There have also been engagements with Levinas beyond therapy and to a broader conceptual and theoretical field. Beyers and Reber (1998), Sayre and Kunz (2005), and Williams and Gantt (1998) all challenge prevailing accounts of intimacy, offering a Levinasian reconceptualization instead; developmental psychology is prompted to reexamine its assumptions and its empirical findings with a Levinasian inflection (Bahler, 2015; Vandenberg, 1999), while Davis (1995) takes issue with prevailing "information processing" views of prejudice, proposing attention instead to a view of prejudice informed by the ethical and moral preontological of our very humanity. Goodman, Walling, et al. (2010) and McDonald (2011) explore ways in which Levinas could serve a psychology oriented towards social justice and an interruption of the totalizing effects of oppressive political power in psychological assessments of the raced other. In light of Fryer's (2004, p. 76) assertion that there are important connections "to be made between Levinas and Freudian thought," several authors have attempted to do just that (e.g. Fryer, 2007; Marcus, 2006, 2007; Tallon, 2007; Williams, 2007). Additionally, Alford (2000) brings Levinas and Winnicott into conversation, while Emery (2000) and Cohen (2008) bring Wilfred Bion and depth psychology, respectively, to face up to Levinas. Other areas of interest include ways in which Levinas could help us think politics and subjectivity within a technologically mediated society (Goodman & Collins, 2019), maternal guilt (LeBeau, 2017), the concept of "tolerance" (Skalski, 2017), psychotherapy and language (Fetters, 2015; Severson, 2012), psychotherapy and sensibility (Livshetz & Goodman, 2015), and Levinasian-informed psychological research (Laubscher & Mbuqe, 2020; Rhodes & Carlsen, 2018; Wertz, 2011).

Now, one could ask, in response to the heading, "Levinas and Psychology," what Levinas had to say about psychology. Perhaps another way to frame the question is to ask, having issued an invitation to Levinas: Can we assume that he will accept? After all, we learn that Levinas was quite resistant – perhaps skeptical is a better word – to psychology. There are no sustained engagements in his work with psychology as such, even as comments pertinent to psychology and/or Freud are scattered throughout his oeuvre, functioning more like footnotes or parentheses, somewhat incidental or "marginal" to the body of the work. Having mentioned "psychology and/or Freud," it is, of course, so that whereas Freud is all about psychology, all psychology is not about Freud. One cannot be sure, though, that this distinction is one that Levinas made in any sophisticated sense, given the dominant sway Freud held in Levinas's times, where the easy seduction may well have been to equate psychology with Freud. Moreover, it does not seem as if Levinas read much or any of the relational psychoanalysts whose emphases were considerably more interpersonal than Freud's. One might argue, as Alford (2000) and Rozmarin (2007) does, that such psychoanalytic approaches are considerably "closer" to Levinas than Freud is. Even so, much of what Levinas said on occasion about Freud could also be said about psychology in general.

Before one gets to the specifics of Levinas's broad critical stance, one might call out two positional influences – two instances where the company you keep might be somewhat revelatory of the positions you take. The first is that Levinas's view of psychology, in general, is not altogether different from that of many philosophers: that it does not go "deep" enough, that it "does not get to the root of things, does not reach ultimate significations or ultimate significance" (Cohen, 2001, p. 166). The second influence comes from the acknowledgment that Levinas did study psychology at university, with a professor whom he adored and admired, Charles Blondel. Levinas was thus exposed to a noted and accomplished psychology lecturer but one whose acrimony and distaste of Freud is rather well-known ("a scientific obscenity" [Ohayon, 2006] is one of his more colorful descriptions of Freud). This hostility of Blondel towards Freud, Levinas admits, "made a deep and lasting impression on me" (Levinas, 2004a, p. 65).

In a simplistic nutshell, the core of Levinas's psychoanalytic critique is that it does not start at the root (which, by an early "heads-up" simplification, would be ethics) and as such confuses beginnings for origins (it starts with libidinal desire, but "Before Eros there was the Face; Eros itself is possible only between Faces" [Levinas, 1998a, p. 113]); psychoanalysis gets ensnared in a hamster wheel of its own mythology. In a rather remarkable passage, Levinas writes:

Psychoanalysis is, in its philosophical essence, the end result of rationalism . . . a predilection for some fundamental, but elementary, fables – the libido, sadism, or masochism, the Oedipus complex, repression of the origin, aggressiveness. . . . The fact of their having been collected from among the debris of the most diverse civilizations and called myths adds nothing to their worth as clarifying ideas, and at most evinces a return to the mythologies, which is even more amazing since forty centuries of monotheism have had no other goal than to liberate humanity from their obsessive grip. Still, the petrifying effect of myths must be distinguished from the comfort they are thought to offer the intelligence.

(Levinas, 1998a, p. 31)

For the moment, we will overlook the equation of "forty centuries of monotheism" as humanity's liberating gift (in Chapter 8, we examine charges of Eurocentrism more closely) and focus instead on the narrowly psychoanalytic critique: that psychoanalysis proceeds from reason and as such must employ reason to furnish totalizing reasons. It cannot catch sight of the transcendent "origin" of human being. Now if this quote of Levinas's sounds eerily familiar to psychology students, it is, having been levied by the experimental, natural science, and cognitive behavioral psychological. That Freud is a rot, a pox, on the psychological edifice is because he is not experimental enough, because psychoanalytic concepts cannot be "operationalized" and measured, taken to the laboratory or the randomized trial, and are as such inappropriate to a view of, and desire for, a psychology of the rational and the experimental. Clearly, even as similar words are spoken, the direction is radically different for Levinas. His critique of Freud is that he is not radical enough, that he is *too* rational, whereas the experimentalists say that Freud is not rational enough. A Levinasian psychology, were such a thing possible, might be even more of an abomination to the experimentalists than Freud's.

Perhaps, though, returning to our question of Levinas's response to our invitation, one could argue that it does not matter terribly much what he thinks about psychology. What matters more is what psychology thinks of him and/or his thought. Or/and one could argue that it is precisely because he misconstrues and misunderstands psychology, or that the psychology and psychological demands of our day is not what he responded to, that it is our task to speak to him such that we can convince him otherwise, or demonstrate his thought appropriate to, and for, us.[16] One could also argue, by a poststructural license, that we don't need Levinas's personal blessing – the work no longer belongs to him. The gift of his work is such that it escapes the propriety of his say and becomes an inheritance for us to administer as legatees and executors. There is a terrible and frightening responsibility that accrues to such an administration. One labors under the gaze of the dead, such that our initial question becomes nonsensical – will he or won't he accept our invitation gives way to the acknowledgment that he already and always has.

## Notes

1  The Google Books Ngram Viewer (https://books.google.com/ngrams), which searches all texts in its astronomical database for certain phrases or words, provides compelling evidence for this statement by revealing a steep and dramatic increase in phrases or words related to Emmanuel Levinas, especially from the mid-1980s onwards.

2  Whereas the shorthand of the everyday references *logos* as "the study of" (as in psy*chology*, the*ology*, or soci*ology*), philosophy is more sensitive to its Greek etymology and use, as "ground," "discourse," "word," or "reason." In fact, there, *logos* is often

summoned alongside *nomos* (the suffix of taxo*nomy* and eco*nomy*, for example), which references "law"; hence, astro*nomy* would be the "law of the stars." These terms are more than etymological oddities, mentioned here as passing interest; they are well able to prompt attention to the kind of knowing, the kind of science, we are engaged in or could be (no least, for example, if we complete, from classical philosophy, the triad with *mythos*, a kind of knowing based on value and folk wisdom). Hence, for example, are we really practicing psych*ology* as much as "psycho*nomy*" – that is, are we primarily concerned with the "laws" of psyche (nomos) more so than the "ground" (logos) on which psyche settles into being? And is there place at all, as scholars and scientists struggling with the nature of psyche, for *mythos*? We recall that Carl Jung (and Freud) certainly thought so. Finally, as we will see forthwith, *what* we (should) study – psyche itself (herself) – and *how* she should be approached is not entirely clear either inasmuch as her inheritance is celebrated as either "mind" or "soul" in the accounts two kinds of psychologies give about themselves.

3  This classicist building was destroyed by the East German government in 1968, and an unimaginative, sober university complex was erected in its place. After reunification, extensive renovation and reconstruction began again, in an architectural style that aimed to reference and recall those original, demolished buildings.

4  Friedrich completed his dissertation two years later, in 1891, in so doing claiming the first ever dissertation in experimental psychology.

5  While we do not know if Husserl read W. E. B. du Bois, William James not only did, but was also struck and impressed. Whereas Du Bois's work has, for the longest time, been neglected for its deviation from formal phenomenology (many would also argue a racist component to his omission from the phenomenological canon), a recent, broader understanding of phenomenology has rightly started to accredit him (and Frantz Fanon, for that matter) for what is ultimately an eminent phenomenological analysis of the lived experience of Black people.

6  Technically and philosophically, *Dasein* does not equate to human being, and I might have drawn the ire of "purist" philosophers and "Heideggerrians" here. Beside not wishing to complicate things too much, though, my choice here is also given by Jacques Derrida's quip that whereas *Dasein* is not human being, neither is it anything but.

7  Again, it is worth noting that Sartre and Merleau-Ponty, pre-eminent philosophers both, produced substantial psychological studies, and in Sartre's case, his psychology of imagination and the emotions even preceded his groundbreaking philosophical work (Sartre, 1991, 2000).

8  Kockelmans (1987) provides a good history of the contributions of the "Dutch school."

9  Giorgi remarks that "I was aware that Husserl had developed a philosophical method, but as psychologists we couldn't follow that method because we would end up doing philosophical analyses" (2014, p. 245).

10  Churchill et al. (2021) provide a more comprehensive overview of phenomenological psychology in the United States, as does Wertz (2015).

11  One article by Williams (1992) makes passing reference to Levinas but in the much broader argument of "human agency" and is not about Levinas and psychology as such.

12  A few examples include Hall (2015), Harrington (1993), Hecker (2010), and Yee (2001).

13  This august and influential press was recently shuttered by university administrators as a "budget-cutting measure." Maybe it's best for this sentence to stand alone, without elaboration, like a gravestone marker listing only dates of birth and death in order not to open up the wound to a retraumatizing repetition.

14  We've already mentioned Duquesne University, boasting the longest-continuing history of just such a distinctive psychology department and, until recently, the only APA-accredited human science program in the USA. Just a few years ago, Point Park University, also in Pittsburgh, became only the second APA-accredited human science program.

But in addition to Duquesne and Point Park, psychology departments at Pacifica, as well as Seattle University, West Georgia, Dallas, and Boston College, for example, have all emphasized a human science approach to psychology. Moreover, some individual professors – for example, at Fordham, Brigham-Young, Lesley – while located within a mostly mainstream, natural science department, have nonetheless advocated for, continued to publish, and attracted students to an approach respectfully critical of their work colleagues'.

15  Halling's article appeared in the first volume of the groundbreaking "Duquesne studies in Phenomenological Psychology," a four-volume publication (1971–1983) which remains highly influential to this very day. All four volumes have been digitized and are available at the Philosophy Documentation Center (www.pdcnet.org/wp/).

16  Steen Halling, who with George Kunz founded the human science psychology program at Seattle University – a program which has deservedly become known as the center for Levinasian-inspired psychology and psychotherapy in the United States – relates the story of his meeting with Levinas in Paris. Upon professing his admiration for Levinas's work and telling of his own – as a psychologist – Levinas was reportedly baffled. Why would a psychologist read his work and of what use could his philosophy be for psychology? (Halling, personal communication).

# Chapter 3

# Introducing Levinas

There are several chapters in books, sections of articles, dissertations, and internet resources which all provide some biographical details as to the life (and occasionally times) of Emmanuel Levinas. As I write here, there are also two dedicated, full-length biographies of Levinas, by Marie-Anne Lescourret[1] (1994) and Salomon Malka (2006), as well as a documentary film about his life and work (Ron, 2014). Moreover, whereas Levinas was rather reticent about sharing personal information, some interviews (a good selection of which are published in Levinas [2001b], a text which also contain an oblique and rather strange "autobiographical" meditation called *Signature*[2]) succeed in drawing out valuable comments and reminiscences about a life that spanned the 20th century almost exactly. It is quite tempting to delegate the biographical task to those texts and resources mentioned earlier – it certainly holds expedient appeal in the freedom, then, to devote more time and publication space to the philosopher's work. Doing so, however, concedes a number of assumptions, for example, that the work can stand on its own, apart from the life, that the work is ultimately more "important" to the scholarly project than the life or that the work came to the individual (largely) independent of the historical and political of a time and place. It would, however, be a grave error to succumb to such views: Levinas's work attains insightful meaning with respect to a broader historico-philosophical unfolding, such that Critchley (2002, p. 1) notes:

> the possibility of writing a history of French philosophy in the twentieth century as a philosophical biography of Emmanuel Levinas

as well as that intersection, simultaneously, of the life with

> major historical events, its moments of light as well as its point of absolute darkness.

> (p. 1)

The interest of the psychologist, perhaps particularly so, and the human science psychologist even more so, must demand some acknowledgment of the life alongside the work, the distinction really being a banality of convenience.

DOI: 10.4324/9781003315612-3

We catch sight of yet another disciplinary tension here, between philosophy and psychology. In the introductory chapter, I mentioned that I teach at a university where graduate students in philosophy and clinical psychology on occasion take classes together. I made the point there that the students from those respective disciplines often approached the subject matter with different kinds of questions and sought different kinds of answers or truths, given their disciplinary positions, interpellations, acculturation, and praxis demands. A rather revealing response to the biographical became apparent in another of those joint classes, where mention was made of Heidegger's involvement with, and sympathies towards, the Nazis and German National Socialism. The psychology students not only wanted to hear and learn so much more about this aspect of Heidegger's life, almost for its own sake, but also to actively seek out and wrestle with (possible) expressions of such sentiments in the philosophical work itself. And whereas some of the interpretations and leaps from the life to the work were interesting, some were also frankly quite fanciful and even outlandish. Of course Freud's analysis of Leonardo da Vinci's life and work (Freud, 1964) and Erik Erikson's psychobiographies of Martin Luther (1993b) and Mahatma Gandhi (1993a) are exemplary precedents for such ways of approach. The philosophy students, though, vacillated between bemused silence and uncomprehending frustration; to them, the class was about the work and a close reading of the text – not the man – and it was a futile and fruitless endeavor to bring the two together in the way the psychology students seemed bent on doing. They seemed to take their cue from Heidegger himself, who, as his famous student, Hannah Arendt (1978, p. 297) recounts, introduced his 1924 lecture on Aristotle by remarking that where Aristotle's life was concerned, all there was to say was that Aristotle "was born, he thought, he died . . . the rest is pure anecdote." Philosophy's fault would be that the personality or life experiences of the philosopher matters little or not at all to the philosopher's thought – or more accurately, to a study or understanding of that thought.[3] Psychology's fault, on the other hand, is in a diametrically opposing direction: that the biography and life experience of the individual matters all too much, even "explains" the author's thinking and scholarly positions. In a very real sense, we tend to do what we do in the therapy room, where we bring the biographical to bear on motivation and the dynamics of an action, an utterance, or a present in search of a meaning. It is a vexing conundrum, this: where Heidegger is concerned, how can the theorist of *Dasein*, of care, of being-in-the-world – a theorist who writes so beautifully – also be a Nazi? This haunting question was never answered for the psychology students – perhaps it cannot; but it seemed one that needed to be asked, that needs to be asked and kept alive in its continual asking. Similarly, how is it that this man, Emmanuel Levinas, the theorist of ethics as first philosophy and the absolutely excessive response to the face of the other, is also that man who "survived" the Shoah, while his whole extended family and countless friends did not? But at the same time, how can one presume to know or interpret the bottomless wound of the Holocaust by a psychobiographical statement of its meaning? It is an easy hop, skip, and jump into a violent empathy that claims to "understand," or an arrogant therapy believing in the "resolution" of grief and/or trauma in order for one to "move on."

How, then, am I to introduce Levinas? Especially to that segment of an audience I imagine coming to his company for the very first time in the pages of this book. We will meander around this question for a while before we get to Levinas's story "as such." I beg some indulgence for doing so – I believe it does matter.

A seemingly "easy" and inoffensive tack with which to sail out of this problem of introduction is to simply chart the timeline "facts" of Levinas's life: when and where he was born and died, with some of the presumably, or readily agreed upon, important moments and insights of his life pertinent to his scholarly project. Many authors do so, and truth be told, in the rather strange (hence, the quotation marks) "autobiographical" essay, *Signature*, Levinas seems to do so himself, providing a very short and very terse (one longish paragraph, barely a page) list of already well-known "facts" of his life, a "disparate inventory," which, he says, "is a biography" (Levinas, 1978, 1997). The overwhelming bulk of the essay then proceeds to an overview of his philosophy, with nary a personal or biographical comment there whatsoever. One could easily say that Levinas thus seems to prefer his signature (the title of the essay), that which is proper and unique to him, affixed to his thought, as the autobiographical matter of importance, rather than the biographical personal. And yet there is one sentence, the sentence in fact that breaks or divides the two sections of the essay and which stands alone, a short, one-sentence paragraph of its own. After merely listing the "disparate inventory" of his life, we read this: "It is dominated by the presentiment and the memory of the Nazi horror" (Levinas, 1978, 1997). Everything hinges on this one sentence – one which psychology is particularly well suited to recognize for what it hides as it concedes. Or better still, *that* it hides. But it is also a sentence which psychology is often violently arrogant about, assuming as it does that there is no secret to such an abyssal wound – that it is equipped to understand and, by the swing of its hammer, to deliver blows it assumes "breaks open" when it may simply "break."

It may seem that we are circling excessively around a simple task, sharing background information about Levinas, but in truth, we are already wrestling with questions Levinas would have us ask – of ourselves and our discipline and of our response to him and the other, living or dead. If, for example, we've alluded to the smithy of our psychological craft in terms of reason and understanding, what would it mean or look like if we remodeled our anvils in the direction of the ethical? (When I was younger, I used to watch the television series *Star Trek: The Next Generation* religiously. Even then, I was struck by the "prime directive," a moral principle which governed all interaction with "alien" civilizations and to which technology was subjected such that the first question was not *can* we do it, a question of reason, nor does it *serve us*, an egoic and self-invested question, but *should* we do it, an ethical question.) As for Levinas, even in a book such as this, even if I have never known him personally, even when he is dead, is there not an obligation towards him, a demand he places on me, to speak about him, to "introduce" him, in a way that is careful not to violate him? Perhaps it is clearer now that whereas we have not quite gotten to introducing Levinas, we also already have.

By the word's Latin roots, to "introduce" is "to lead" (*ducere*) "inside" (*intro-*). Not unlike *ducere* in "education," "docent," "conductor," or "doctor," where to lead is to teach and instruct, to show and "cause to know," this chapter is to present Levinas, such that the reader may get to know him from the "inside." We certainly introduce others frequently in the social everyday as well as in our professional lives, from our research and scholarly writings to assessment reports, case and clinical presentations on hospital and clinic wards, or in academic settings where we present invited speakers to an audience by way of an introduction. I remember a particularly cantankerous senior psychologist from my days as a young trainee at a very busy psychiatric institution, who would convene so-called noon ward rounds with an authoritative instruction: "Introduce your cases." I would have seen three or four patients in the morning, whom/which I had to present – that is, introduce – at these ward meetings where psychiatrists, psychiatric nurses, pharmacists, senior psychologists, and allied health professionals such as occupational therapists or physiotherapists were in attendance and where treatment plans were to be decided upon. I had 15 minutes – if that – to introduce (present) the case (person), inclusive of their biographical history, social settings, diagnosis, prognosis, and dynamic formulation (the psychological story, that is, of how and why the person "became like this"). More than 30 years later, I cannot remember a single one of those patients; I cannot recall any of their faces, and while I can remember this or that part of a story, notably the more dramatic or traumatic ones, I cannot place those story fragments with a particular or singular face or history. But I can certainly rattle off many of the phrases and dynamic formulations by which I told whom they supposedly were or "what" they were suffering from ("Several psycho-physical traumas and stressors in Mr. X's history likely predisposed him to develop interpersonal and intimacy deficits and self-medicating behavioral propensities. Given our diagnoses and scaled assessment of the severity of his current psychological functioning, return to premorbid functioning is unlikely but not ruled out, given long-term therapy interventions.") Indeed, in many ways, the case report or ward presentation of a patient followed a rather formulaic, almost "pre-written" script, with codified headings and phrases, allowing us to sometimes simply change or "swop out" names, ages, a few biographical details here and there, cut and paste dynamic formulations or diagnoses from other reports, and pull tried-and-tested turns of phrase from our shelves of stock-ready professional language. What would it be for me to introduce those patients (people) in a different way? What would it be to bring the reader to "face" Levinas, as opposed to "merely" reading about him, or to speak about him to others in a way that also speaks *to* him as we do *about* him? Again, these are not just my questions but Levinas's as well; these are the questions of his project, as it is – or should be – for psychology.

The task of introduction involves an apostrophizing address. There is, firstly, a reading audience I am addressing which, by the desire of most aspiring authors, is a hopefully extensive and broad one. As such, it seems also a rather faceless audience. Even by the delimitation of a particular *type* of audience – scholars or psychologists, say – the very notion of type still suggests a certain generic likeness, a totalizing levelling, to prefigure a Levinasian term. Writing instructors sometimes suggest that, rather than some amorphous audience, one can imagine a specific person – one's sibling or a respected work colleague – for whom one writes as a representative of the audience at large; hence, one's sibling may stand in for a layperson in the field, for example, and one imagines writing to her in a way that is clear and accessible, or one's work colleague stands in for someone somewhat familiar with the field one is writing for such that one can gauge the kind of language or address appropriate to the topic. Yet whereas such a writing "trick" may inject a certain personableness to one's style or provide some guidance as to the writing act and product, one has nonetheless cloned the audience into a sameness of a representative – an erasure of the unique face nonetheless, by the assumption of the same or similar face for all. It seems an impossible quandary, this, one the writer may simply have to live with; other than a face-to-face conversation or a letter addressed to a particular individual, generality and the law of an imagined third (prefiguring another Levinasian term) seems an inevitable given. How am I to face this faceless third in a way that nonetheless desires a unique and individual address – that respects and obliges the individual reader in the crowd? In a later chapter, we examine this issue particularly, for Levinas's notion of justice and our obligations to those we do not know but to whom we are nonetheless obligated. For now, suffice it to prefigure that discussion by responding to my question with the admittedly (at least at this point) elliptical statement that my speech, my address to you, has to be just and has to be proper[4] (as the endnote suggests, proper in the philosophical and etymological sense of "own's own").

One of the ways to be mindful of such proper speech is to recognize that I am conjuring Levinas and thus also addressing him. The model of the eulogy comes to mind, where the speaker addresses a grieving audience at the same time as it does the deceased. Inasmuch as the eulogy permits one to address the dead straight on, it demands an apologetic responsibility. Apologetic in the sense of "a speech in one's defense" because the other is looking at me and even more so because the dead other is without response, looking as s/he does from within and from an elsewhere absolutely otherwise.[5] There is admittedly a certain arrogance in appropriating to oneself an eulogizing honor, usually bestowed or earned by close friendship or familial intimacy, but the Levinasian import is that whatever is demanded of me by those I am intimately close to is also demanded by every other. My response in front of the dead is also my responsibility, singularly, as what I, and no one else, say to the dead person, even if what I say can be said by anyone – even if what I say is where he was born, what he thought, or how he died. It has to bear my signature, my way, if it is to be my introduction, both to those who believe they "knew" the deceased as well as those who feel they did not quite know him "that well," such that they both learn "something new."

Hence, Levinas looks at me, at what I have to say about him, at how I introduce him to you. Derrida's questions about eulogizing speech – "whom is one addressing . . . And in whose name would one allow oneself to do so?" (Derrida, 1999) now provide a rather different inflection to the question of an audience, about whom this chapter – if not this book – is "for," and how it is to step to its task. Perhaps, had I this sense of the patients I introduced at the ward rounds I wrote about earlier, that my responsibility was to tell about them in a way that did justice to them, and sought justice for them, in the form of an apology, which is to say my being able to defend to them what I said about them, as if they were there, keeping an eye and ear on my words, I wonder how my reports would have been different, even as I know that they would have been. I wonder if I would have been able to recall their faces, now, had I faced up to them, then. To sign the work as mine, with my proper name, to designate it as uniquely mine, comes from the demand of the other that I do justice to them, that I do good by them, even if, or especially when, they aren't there or here.[6]

So it is, then, that by introducing Levinas to you, under his gaze, and by the singular manner of my (counter) signature, I happened upon a clearing of sorts – one which surprised me, which is to say seized me, from an elsewhere, a who knows where; not altogether unlike a burning bush or lightning that clears a space, makes space, finding and founding me, as if it was lying in wait for me, making me in and by its making. Therapists and counselors often report such insights which arrive abruptly, seemingly from nowhere which is not no place, from the therapeutic journey and relationship, to be sure, but also not: an image, metaphor, story, or parable by which things come to light or to a different light. For Levinas, and this introduction, it was a line from the Bible and the Torah – Numbers 6:25–26: "The Lord make His face to shine upon thee, and be gracious unto thee. The Lord lift up His countenance upon thee, and give thee peace" (Bible, 2021). This is the priestly blessing, as it is known in the Jewish tradition, or the Aaronic blessing, as it is known in the Christian tradition. Upon some reflection on the appearance of this quote, it does feel proper to the clearing within which to place Levinas's thought and person; it feels proper to the proper name to conjure him with.

In an essay titled *Nameless* (and collected in a book called *Proper Names*), Levinas writes:

Soon death will . . . cancel the unjustified privilege of having survived six million deaths . . . nothing has been able to fill, or even cover over, the gaping pit. We still turn back to it from our daily occupations almost as frequently, and the vertigo that grips us at the edge is always the same.

(Levinas, 1996b, p. 120)

In a sense, the name as commandment, as the Aaronic blessing of peace and the thou shalt not kill, on the one hand, and the absolute transgression of this commandment in the genocidal murder of the holocaust are – I believe – the keys to the course of Levinas's life and work, the mournful prayer of his biography.

\*\*\*\*

Emmanuel Levinas was born in Kovno, Lithuania (renamed to Kaunas after the Soviet annexation and occupation of Lithuania in 1940), on December 30, 1905. (The Gregorian calendar would have it as January 12, 1906, though by a strange consequence of its embattled history, when Levinas was born, both calendars were used in different parts of Kovno; tour guides to the city might relate some version of the joke that the Vytautas bridge at the time was the longest bridge in the world, taking almost two weeks to cross, a quip that plays on the 12-day difference between the Julian calendar used on one side of the river and the Gregorian calendar on the other. Levinas would celebrate his birthday according to the Julian, Western calendar.) History reminds us that Kovno/Kaunas, and that Eastern European swathe in general, was marked by shifting frontiers and borders, of alternating allegiances and monarchic claims; borders were perennially drawn and redrawn between Poland, Russia, the Lithuanian Duchy, Germany, Hapsburg Austria, and even Sweden. And lest one is seduced into a sense of settled finality in the present, it bears reminding that this back and forth continues to this day; the bordering countries of Belarus and Latvia did not exist until 1989, for example, even though they also existed in 1918 and 1919, respectively, while Lithuania itself only achieved independence in the 1990s, even as a Lithuanian identity and/or nationalism traces itself to the 13th century. And as I write here, attempts are underway to redraw borders around Ukraine as Russia wages a bloody war in that country.

Levinas, though, was born into a period of relative calm and peace. Four generations of the Levinas family called Kovno home, comfortably ensconced within a thriving city and a large and active Jewish community. In fact, close to a third of the population was Jewish, paralleling that of the nearby historical capital of Vilnius (Vilna), where the Jewish population at the time of Levinas's birth numbered close to 40% and, by its cultural and scholarly Judaic influence, was well deserving of the moniker "Jerusalem of the East." This influence, however, was not only because of the size of the Jewish population but also – arguably even more so – because of a historical confluence between a rich, confident, and established Jewish cultural and intellectual presence brushing up against a nascent Europeanizing Russia, creatively wrestling with Enlightenment values and culture (Atterton, 2010; Kleinberg, 2019). "The generation of my parents," Levinas remarked, "saw the future of young people in the Russian language and culture" (Levinas, 2001a, p. 24), while at the same time, "the rhythm of Jewish life dominated the rhythm of public life, without it having been necessary to make a special decision" (Levinas, 2001b, p. 26). Levinas remembers his childhood in Kaunas fondly, unable to recall a single instance of anti-Semitism. Yet it is also so that Kaunas was not an "integrated" city – "there was no contact with non-Jews," and whereas there "were no ghettos. . . . Socially Jews lived in a ghetto" (Levinas, 2001b, p. 89).

The reasons for the concentration of Jews in this Eastern European band between Western Europe and Central Russia, stretching from Poland and present-day Lithuania and Latvia all the way through Ukraine to the Black Sea, are to be found in longstanding and historical anti-Semitism and persecution. The Ashkenazim, diasporic Jews from France and Germany, were for the most part already driven out of those countries at the close of the medieval period, if they were not rounded up and killed, while Jews in England were expelled on November 2, 1290, All Saints' Day, on pain of execution. Sephardic Jews, in Spain and Portugal, enjoyed a certain safety and prosperity under Muslim control of those territories, which was, however, all to end by 1492, after the Moors were defeated and the religious fires of the Spanish Inquisition presented justifying cover for an impossible choice: convert to Christianity or leave. Nearly half a million Jews left to join their Ashkenazi kin in Poland, Lithuania, and other parts of the Baltic. By the 1600s, 85% of the Jews in Europe had moved into Eastern Europe.

In 1905, when Levinas was born, though, the Jews of the Baltics enjoyed an unprecedented freedom, such as it was, and though the signs and signals of its ending was already murmured, rumored, and blowing in the wind. We won't go into detail as to the reasons for this "tolerance" other than to mention the constitutional reforms of the revolution of 1905, which granted Jews under the dominion of the Tsar certain political, if not civil, rights. Additionally, reforms of the Austrian Emperor Franz Josef extended religious freedom to all groups in the vast Austro-Hungarian in 1860, while full German citizenship was granted to Jews in 1871. One could also speculate on the effects of even earlier religious, cultural, and economic freedoms enacted by the Polish-Lithuanian Commonwealth and of Prince Boleslav the Pious of Poland. Having mentioned Franz Josef and the foresight of his rule from his seat in Vienna, it also bears some notice that it was nonetheless also there, as his reign came to an end, that the most virulent anti-Semitism took root under Mayor Karl Lueger in fin de siècle Vienna (a radicalizing influence, as an aside, for a young ne'er-do-well who frittered away his parents' modest inheritance to find himself homeless and living in Viennese shelters, eking an existence by painting mediocre watercolor scenes of Vienna; that young man was, of course, Adolf Hitler).

But back to Levinas, as if we ever left. The youngest of three sons, his parents named him Emmanuel after the text of Isaiah from the Hebrew Tanakh, or the Old Testament then – Isaiah 7:14: "Therefore the Lord himself will give you a sign: the young woman is with child and is about to give birth to a son, and she will name him Immanuel" (recalling the line almost verbatim, Matthew, in the Christian New Testament [Matthew 1:23] adds, "which means 'God with us,'" and suggesting Isaiah's prophecy fulfilled). As for Levinas's siblings, we can take some interpretative license by simply reading their names as indicative of that tensive Russo-Baltic-Jewish location: the middle son was named Boris, a "typically" Russian name, while the eldest was named Aminadab, from the Hebrew, meaning "my people is generous." Levinas recalls growing up fluent in Yiddish, Russian, and Hebrew (and possibly also Lithuanian).[7] In fact, the first book Levinas read was the *Tanakh*, or "Hebrew Bible" ("for me the book par excellence" [Levinas, 1985, p. 22]). Hereafter, he often cited the "formative" importance of the Russian classics – Pushkin, Gogol, Chekov, Turgenev, Lermontov, Dostoyevsky, Tolstoy, for example – read in Russian, the language of instruction in schools, as well as the preference of many educated and/or bourgeois Jewish families. Dostoevsky, especially, remained a lifelong influence and love; one quote in particular, from *The Brothers Karamazov*, would be referenced with regularity as a kind of heraldic maxim for his philosophy: "Each of us is guilty before everyone for everyone, and I more than the others" (Dostoevsky, 2002, p. 289). Rounding out a trinity of early influence, as it were, is Shakespeare, especially the tragedies, which Levinas would quote frequently and lean into throughout his life. Given that his father was a book-seller, one presumes he had easier access to these texts than most.

In the series of interviews Phillipe Nemo conducted with Levinas, recorded in the highly recommended little text *Ethics and Infinity* (1982), Nemo asks, "How does one begin thinking?" Levinas responds that "It probably begins through trau-matisms and gropings to which one does not even know how to give a verbal form: a separation, a violent scene, a sudden consciousness of the monotony of time" (Levinas, 1985, p. 21). One could imagine that a war would qualify, and in Levinas's case, as an 8-year-old, World War I. By his own admission, "an element of peace" and a childhood "preserved from shocks" came to a crashing halt "at the end of August 1914 and never ended, as if the order had been forever disturbed" (Levinas, 2001a, p. 25). The eastern front with Russia was particularly tumultuous and bloody, and by 1915, Germany had occupied Congress Poland, Latvia, Lithu-ania, and parts of Volhynia and Belorussia, bringing some 40% of Jews under the rule of the Central Powers.

Caught between a growing anti-Semitism from both German and Russian sides, the position of Jews in the so-called *Pale of Settlement*, that Eastern European strip of land from Poland to the Black Sea, became increasingly tenuous and fraught with danger. In Lithuania, Jews were effectively stripped of any rights to dwelling and space, bringing about a large-scale exodus. This migration included the Levinas family, fleeing from Kovno in 1916 and traveling hundreds of miles across Belorussia into Ukraine, where they settled in the city of Kharkov (currently Kharkiv),[8] nearly 1,500 kilometers from Kovno. Escape from tumult was not to be, though, and in October 1917, the Russian Revolution would inaugurate a new political landscape, the social upheaval associated with this dramatic coup which was to be felt strongly in Ukraine. For the next four years of this "first exile," as Levinas biographer Salomon Malka (2006, p. 8) characterizes it, Levinas continued his high school studies as "one of only five Jewish students granted admission to the school, a reason for celebration in the Levinas household"[9] (Malka, 2006, p. 8).

Levinas would, however, complete his high school career back in Kovno, the result of a "first return" back to the city of his birth in 1920, in the wake of Lith-uania becoming an independent state in the postwar and post–Russian Revolu-tion chaos. Of particular note from the high school years is a growing interest in German culture, leading Levinas, who, as we have noted, was already fluent in Russian, Hebrew, Yiddish, and Lithuanian, to also add German to this list. This facility with German would be crucial to his later discovery of Husserl and the role he (Levinas) played in introducing France to phenomenology. But we are getting ahead of ourselves, at least chronologically, and need to make some mention of Levinas's choice of postsecondary education at the University of Strasbourg in the

French Alsace, where, as a young 17-year-old, Levinas headed towards because it was the closest European city to Lithuania (Levinas, 2001a) and because Germany had already "refused to take [foreign] Jews" in their universities (Levinas, 2001b, p. 85).

Not entirely unlike Kovno, Strasbourg, more so than many other cities in France, also shoulders a history of shifting rulers, monarchs, and governments (the meaning of its name is quite apt: town/fort [at the crossing of] roads). In fact, when Levinas arrived in the city in 1923, it had only been four years that Strasbourg was French again, after the German defeat in World War I. It may not be an exaggeration to state that the city only settled as "French" in the last century, but even then, on the banks of the Rhône which is as often the Rhine, and where Alsation mettissage turns sauerkraut into choucroute. Beginnings are not origins, even though they tend to parade as such. Upon Levinas's arrival in Strasbourg, the city and the region were energized by a postwar French patriotism and a clear sense of an exciting and fresh new start. A small but well-established Jewish community was in place (the Jews of Alsace, in fact, represent one of the oldest Jewish communities of Europe, sporadic pogroms and dispersals notwithstanding). The city quickly became rather prosperous, and scholarship – while not at the level of prestige that was Paris or Lyon – was rapidly gaining in stature and gathering notice beyond the "provincial" stereotype. While it had lost notable German professors and scholars after World War I, the now–French university was able to draw to itself rather prominent faculty and as promising students, the former inclusive of notables like Charles Blondel and Maurice Halbwachs[10] and the latter, of course, counting Levinas and his lifelong friend, Maurice Blanchot, whom we will reference again in the pages to come.

For the young Russian-, Yiddish-, Lithuanian-, Hebrew-, German-speaking Jew arriving from Kovno, the first task was to master French, the language in which, ultimately, all of his later work would be written. Clearly, echoing the words of his grandson, David, "languages were never a problem for him" (quoted in Malka, 2006, p. 21). Levinas enrolled in psychology, sociology, and Latin classes, but philosophy was to be his settled scholarly choice – one which he would later remark he was prepared for by his background in, and love for, Russian literature which "seemed to me very occupied with fundamental things . . . shot through with anxiety – with an essential, religious anxiety – but readable as a search for the meaning of life" (Levinas, 2001b, p. 28). We are reminded that existential psychology, similarly, claim inspiration from several of the Russian novelists, Dostoevsky perhaps chief among them. Within this philosophical sphere, and as a student, the work of two philosophers, more than any other at the time, struck a powerful chord: Henri Bergson and Edmund Husserl. The personal and scholarly connections are more evident for Husserl than for Bergson, whom Levinas rarely quotes in his own work but whose fundamental inspiration and importance he also does not shy away from acknowledging.

It was around 1926/1927, as a senior student, that Levinas discovered Husserl and phenomenology. Keep in mind that Husserl was quite unknown in France at the time, as his work had not been translated into French yet; it was through his facility with German that Levinas gained access to Husserl's thought. Tremendously impressed, Levinas saw in phenomenology an exciting new way of thinking and approach to the questions of philosophy and life, and he proceeded to voraciously devour everything by Husserl he could lay his hands on. What impressed him was both that phenomenology had a rigorous method for reflection and that this way, which emphasized the concrete and the phenomenon as it appeared, nonetheless could reveal what was implicit, dissimulated, and/or obscured from appearance. "There is in this manner a rigor, but also an appeal to listen acutely for what is implicit . . . what is allusive in thinking" (Levinas, 2001b, p. 94). In fact, he was so enthused and excited by what he read that Levinas proceeded to enroll at the University of Freiburg in 1928 to study with Husserl. What two semesters they were! One was the last Husserl taught as an aging, retiring professor (on phenomenological psychology and intersubjectivity) and the next semester, the first to be taught by Martin Heidegger, appointed as Husserl's successor. Of this experience, Levinas quipped, "I went to see Husserl, and I found Heidegger" (Levinas, 2001b, p. 32).

This was Levinas's first exposure to Heidegger, who left him in awe. Firstly, Levinas remembers and comments (as do many of Heidegger's students, including Hannah Arendt) on Heidegger's engaging, captivating, and persuasive lecturing style – by all accounts, he was a consummate, highly effective teacher. But secondly, and indubitably more so, Levinas came to see in Heidegger's critique of Husserl and his elaboration of phenomenology, a position that he agreed with. Whereas Husserl's genius was to create and found phenomenology, Heidegger "made it sparkle" (Levinas, 2001b, p. 156). Heidegger's account of being-in-the-world resonated more harmoniously than Husserl's transcendental idealism, and Heidegger's description of anxiety, being-towards-death, being-with-others, the famous ontico-ontological difference between beings and being, and his emphasis on the finitude and transcendence of *Dasein* – all of these simply captivated Levinas in a way that Husserl could not. Existential (and humanistic) psychology, as we know, likewise find inspiration in the insistence that any science or understanding of human being has to take, as its starting point, the existential and phenomenally centered experience of human being in the world. Heidegger's magnum opus, *Being and Time* (Heidegger, 2001), Levinas would tell Phillipe Nemo much later, and even after the crushing disappointment of Heidegger's political sensibilities were made known, "is one of the finest books in the history of philosophy – I say this after many years of reflection" (Levinas, 1985). In fact, Levinas would credit *Being and Time* as "one of the five greatest books of Western Philosophy."[11]

Drawing philosophically closer to Heidegger, Levinas nonetheless remained greatly appreciative of Husserl's time and mentorship; he actually spent quite some time with Husserl, visiting at his home and even giving Husserl's wife, Frau Malvine, some French lessons in preparation for an upcoming trip to France. In 1929, just a year after his residency at Freiburg, Levinas completed his doctoral dissertation on *The Theory of Intuition in Husserl's Phenomenology* (Levinas, 1995). The dissertation remained deeply respectful of Husserl's thought, notwithstanding swirling Heideggerian doubts and criticisms. (Some scholars argue that this Heideggerian influence can be seen in the doctorate, but they also agree that such influence is implicit and not in the forefront or obvious at all.)

Upon receiving his degree, Levinas moved to Paris in 1930 in what turned out to be a rather auspicious year, both personally and academically (even though the academic importance was not of a kind that promoted or "benefitted" Levinas directly, as I will argue shortly). Earlier, I made passing mention of Levinas providing Frau Husserl with French lessons given a pending trip to Paris. The purpose of that trip was a series of lectures Husserl was to deliver at the Sorbonne, which would serve as the basis for Husserl's book, the *Cartesian Meditations* (Husserl, 1960). Written in German, and carefully edited for publication by Husserl and his assistant at the time, Eugen Fink,[12] the expectation was that it would be published rather quickly in Germany. At the same time, this German text was sent to Levinas for translation into French (recall that Levinas only learned the language a little more than six years earlier). As it turned out, the *Cartesian Meditations* was published in French nearly 20 years before it would be published in German.[13] The reasons for this delay are many, no least of which the growing climate of anti-Semitism which did not take kindly to Husserl's Jewish background.[14] In addition to the *Cartesian Meditations*, Levinas's dissertation was also published, and these two publications in no small measure introduced Husserl and phenomenology to France. In fact, it was Levinas's translation of Husserl that Jean-Paul Sartre and Maurice Merleau-Ponty read, as well as Paul Ricoeur and Jacques Derrida. Ricoeur at one point described Levinas as the founder of Husserl studies in France, and Jean Luc Marion writes that "it must not be forgotten that Levinas would still have been counted as one of the great philosophers even if he had died during World War II, simply by virtue of having done two extraordinary things in 1930" (Marion, quoted in Malka, 2006, p. 39), referring to the translation of Husserl's *Cartesian Meditations* and the publication of Levinas's dissertation on Husserl.[15]

Personally, as well, 1930 turned out to be an eventful year: first, Levinas became a French citizen, a deeply meaningful undertaking for him and the culmination of his sincere respect and admiration for the French Republic and its ideals ("a nation to which one can attach himself by spirit and heart as strongly as by origins" [Levinas, 1978, p. 176]). He also started to seriously court a young Jewish music student at the time from Vienna but as fate would have it, not only from Kovno as well but a neighbor to Levinas from his childhood years. They grew up knowing each other, or at least of each other, but fell out of contact during the turmoil of World War I and the subsequent years of their respective secondary and tertiary studies. Emmanuel Levinas married Raissa Levy in 1932, and they would remain devoted to each other for the balance of their lives together.

At this point, around 1932/1933, Levinas also started working on a book on Heidegger and published an article or two as groundwork for the book – a testing of the waters and his ideas, as it were. It was an exciting time in Paris, culturally and intellectually, an economic depression and political turmoil notwithstanding. And while Levinas, working as he did for the *Alliance Israelite Universelle* (an organization that assisted Jews from "countries where they lived without being recognized as citizens" [Levinas, 2001b, p. 38]), was outside of the rarefied academic and university fray, he nonetheless kept up academic interests, attending the famous soirees of Gabriel Marcel, the Christian-existentialist philosopher and dramatist, and open lectures at the Sorbonne (for example, with Merleau-Ponty and later Jean-Paul Sartre); he sat in on the now-celebrated lectures of Alexandre Kojeve on Hegel (lectures that were also attended by the likes of Sartre, Bataille, Merleau-Ponty, Althusser, and Lacan – in fact, the very lectures that were so decisive in the formation of the young Lacan's thought). Even so, he was never really part of the intellectual "in-crowd" (Gutting, 2001) and certainly not of the creative social excess that frequented smoky jazz clubs or attended masquerade balls with the impressive, eccentric, and often flamboyant literary and artistic set who flocked to Paris in this strange decade, the end of which would so dramatically be marked by the Fall of Paris in 1940. During this time in the thirties, as well, Levinas cultivated a deep friendship with the Jewish philosopher and poet, Jean Wahl, whom we will come across again in the next few chapters.

Hard at work on the Heidegger book, at the beginning of 1933, however, reports started to filter through to Levinas of Heidegger's increasingly open Nazism. Alexandre Koyre, the philosopher of science and a previous student of Husserl's, came to visit Levinas in early 1933 and told him how Heidegger had by now taken to end his lectures with the Heil Hitler salute and how badly Heidegger treated Husserl, his former mentor and friend. Later that year, Levinas would also learn about Heidegger's address upon assuming the rectorate at Freiburg, one that seemed to provide academic cover and justification for Nazism. What was at the level of rumor now seemed publicly owned. Levinas would never complete the book on Heidegger, and from this point on, the articles on Heidegger reveal a wrestling, searching, critical tone – one in which it is as if Levinas wished to find how this thinker of Being can also, so seemingly effortlessly, speak and accept Nazi ideology. Other than the stereotypically psychological seduction to look for such answers in the person, Levinas, in perhaps as stereotypically a philosophical move, turned to the work. At first, and in its most rudimentary form, as early as 1934, Levinas speculated in an article on Hitlerism (Levinas, 1990) that the emphasis on Heideggerian authenticity is a self-centered weakness which opened itself (and Heidegger) to exploitation in the Nazi system, indeed, that the Nazi movement illustrated a manifestation of evil in being which has not been addressed sufficiently in philosophy. We will return to this article in the course of this book, notably in Chapter 8.

At the outbreak of World War II, in 1939, Levinas was called up to serve in the French Army as an interpreter, given his linguistic talents (he was 33 years old). Barely a year later, however, the Battle for France was all but lost. By June 5, 1940, formal French and British resistance started to fall apart, and the Somme was lost in two days; General Rommel was in Rouen by June 9, encircling the Tenth Army to which Sergeant Emmanuel Levinas belonged. The Meuse Front had collapsed at the Battle of Sedan, the Maginot Line had come apart, Calais had fallen, exposing access to the English Channel, and the Seventh and Tenth Armies were forced to surrender on June 18. Levinas became a prisoner of war and was sent to Stalag XI-B, a prisoner-of-war camp near Fallingbostel (halfway between Hanover and Hamburg) in Northern Germany. Shielded from extermination as a Jew because he was a French officer, he was nonetheless assigned to a designated Jewish forced labor camp. There is a pointed instance here of the terrible paradoxes of the German Reich: because he was an officer and a soldier, Levinas could not be exterminated by some treaty and protocol of rights, the Geneva Convention of 1929. These rights, however, were premised on the notion of the human and the humane, but as a Jew, national socialism would question the very ascription of human to Jews such that the rights of humanity or the humane could be scuppered, eventually allowing nothing less than the mechanical eradication of "vermin." Fallingbostel was less than 50 kilometers from the Bergen Belsen death camp, and while Levinas insists "We knew nothing. When rumors reached us, they seemed exaggerated" (Levinas, 2001b, p. 90), a fellow inmate of his, Jacques Laurent, was clear about what they knew and suspected: "We knew about the crematoria," he says, "and when there was fat in our food, jokes were cracked, in bad taste, about where this fat must have come from" (Malka, 2006, p. 73).

Levinas's wife, Raissa, and their young daughter survived the war, largely as a result of the intervention of Levinas's good friend, Maurice Blanchot, who hid them, first in his own apartment and then when it became too dangerous, in the monastery of St. Vincent de Paul, near Orleans. A slight detour is in order here to briefly explore the relationship of Levinas to Maurice Blanchot, celebrated writer, philosopher, and literary critic. They met as students at the University of Strasbourg and were already then the closest of friends. (Malka [2006] reports how someone had scribbled *Doublepatte et Patachon* ["Laurel and Hardy" by analogy] on the back of a photograph of Levinas and Blanchot, presumably referencing both their differences in physical form, as well as the relational intimacy of a deep friendship.) After their studies, both moved to Paris in the very same year but grew somewhat apart, presumably in large part because Blanchot considered himself a "royalist," and his politics took a disturbingly right-wing turn, including statements and associations that were overtly and covertly anti-Semitic. Yet in the immediate buildup to war, and certainly during and after the war, those sentiments and views would swing dramatically to the other side, prompting active involvement in the French resistance, during the war, and clear leftist political sentiments thereafter. Blanchot would come a hair's breadth from execution himself; in the supremest of ironies, the Red Army already lined him up for execution by firing squad on suspicion that he was a Nazi, the consequence of a role he had to play to deflect attention from himself. This incident (which Blanchot writes about directly in a short piece of prose, the English translation of which can be found alongside a brilliant analysis thereof by Derrida, in Blanchot and Derrida [2000]) illustrates a key organizing pivot for this most enigmatic and private of all the postwar French intellectuals and writers: that one cannot experience one's death and that it is utterly presumptive to theorize about one's death, even to say one has only one's death as singular possession. As such, he clearly takes aim at Heidegger and provides an insight to

Levinas, who would agree and take up this criticism to an even greater extent and philosophical detail, challenging in so doing the Heideggerian importance of one's own death to an authentic relationship with being and the self, instead to offer the death of the other, and one's responsibility for and before the demand of the other as constitutive of being and the self.

But while Levinas's wife and daughter survived the war, the rest of his family did not. Upon Germany's expansion of the war eastward, the Russian Army in Lithuania was routed quickly, and on the evening of June 23, 1941, the German Army was on the outskirts of the cities of Kovno/Kaunas and Vilna/Vilnius, the Red Army in frantic retreat. As the Russian soldiers left Kaunas, the upstanding citizens of Kovno, neighbors to the Jews for 400 years, pounced on them and rounded them up, after which a good number were killed and their property and possessions confiscated. All of this before the German Army even entered the city. On the morning of June 24, the mighty German Army rolled into Kovno, and less than three weeks later, all the Jews they could find – 29,000 of them – were corralled and sealed into the Kovno ghetto. In the years that followed, the eastern front would become a staging ground for roving death squads (*Einzatsgrupen*), precursor to the organized extermination camps. Kovno has the vile distinction as the site of one of the first such mass exterminations, on October 4, 1941, when 2,007 Jewish men, 2,920 women, and 4,273 children were selected from the Kovno ghetto, lined up alongside the edge of huge pits dug in advance, and shot. Those that were not killed in this manner would be shipped, gradually, to concentration and death camps all over Europe but mostly into Ukraine. Levinas's parents, his brothers, Boris and Aminadab, their families, and the vast majority of his extended family were all murdered. Over the whole of Lithuania, it is estimated that prior to the war, there were close to 250 000 Jews, a quarter to a third of the population of Lithuania. At war's end, around 90% of them were killed, the most complete destruction of the Jewish population than any other country affected by the Shoah.

Levinas would describe his captivity as "A period frozen in time," and as for his surviving the war, more poignantly, he wrote "Soon death will no doubt cancel the unjustified privilege of having survived 6,000,000 deaths" (Levinas, 1996b, p. 120). References or acknowledgments such as these were extremely rare; Levinas never really spoke publicly about his family's murder, or even the Holocaust in general. In fact, what was true of the public seemed also true in private and the intimate: none of his friends recall him ever speaking to them about the exterminations nor do his children. And while many have argued, myself included, that it is implicit in all that he said, in all that he did, the Shoah was something of such enormity that there were no words for it. The silence of trauma, and the reticence among "survivors" to speak about it, is well-known to psychologists, and the unfortunate model of the Shoah should serve as caution for the banality and violence of any therapeutic talk of "resolution." The psychological task seems, much rather, to find a way of "living with."

After the war, Levinas reunited with his wife and daughter, returning to Paris where he took a position with the *Ecole Normale Israelite Orientale*, a Jewish teacher's college. He was specifically tasked with responsibility for its program of Jewish studies. Levinas published two books, in quick succession – *Existence and Existents* in 1947 and *Time and the Other* in 1948 – which will be the subject of our interest in the chapter that follows this one. Suffice it to say here already that these books were hardly noticed, nor perhaps even understood, and did little to bring Levinas to any scholarly notice, let alone prominence. He was, to all intents and practical purposes and in the eyes of the philosophical elite of the day, little more than a high school principal, an administrative functionary. To be sure, he was invited to deliver the occasional academic talk, notably by his friend Jean Wahl, who was a full professor at the Sorbonne, but save for a few close friends, Levinas was largely unknown as a philosopher in the period between 1945 and 1961. And inasmuch as scholarly publications in one's field are the vehicles by which one gains or sustains academic presence and visibility, Levinas ostensibly had only himself to blame, not publishing anything during this period, at least not in the arena of classical philosophy. The "at least" of the previous sentence should provide a clue to the fact that there is more to the tale than a simple intellectual or scholarly drought.

Indeed, we see this postwar period marked by an intense and serious turn to religious and Jewish studies, specifically the study of Talmud; Levinas "effectively stopped writing philosophy in order to concentrate on Talmudic study" (Critchley, 2002, p. xxi). A most enigmatic and mysterious teacher, a man whose identity and background remained unknown, even to his students, and who went by the name Shushani or Chouchani,[16] served as Levinas's guide and instructor. The scholarly fruits of Levinas's study were a series of lectures and scholarly publications, the most important collected in the texts *Difficult Freedom* (Levinas, 1997), *New Talmudic Readings* (Levinas, 1999), *Nine Talmudic Readings* (Levinas, 2019), and *Beyond the Verse* (Levinas, 2007). Most scholars separate the philosophical work and those consecrated to Judaism, and in many ways, Levinas has done so himself, insisting for example on separate publishers and editors for the philosophical work as opposed to the expressly Judaic or "confessional" texts. Indeed, in response to a suggestion from Phillipe Nemo that his work might be read as an attempt to "harmonize the essentials of Biblical theology with the philosophical tradition" (Levinas, 1985, p. 24), Levinas expressly and categorically denies this as his aim or project at all. Yet one can see the temptation of Nemo's question – by Levinas's philosophical emphasis on transcendence and infinity, by the widespread characterization of his work as bringing Jerusalem to Athens (Derrida calls him a "Jew-Greek"), by his own statements and writing proposing a transcendent truth that both religion and philosophy aim at, is it small wonder that some (e.g. Janicaud, 2000, most prominently) are suspicious of a religiosity, if not religion, parading as philosophy? Several authors (e.g. Meskin, 2000), after all, argue that "several traditional Jewish sources play a vital role in Levinas' *philosophical* writings" (pp. 79, emphasis in original). But the accusation or claim also runs in the other direction. Levinas's Talmudic scholarship is anything but "traditional," and we agree with Cohen (2007), thoroughly inflected by his philosophical training and reading.

One could, therefore, as easily ask a variation of the foregoing question: whether the Talmudic studies are not philosophy, parading as Jewish study. This no least because in spite of his upbringing within a household that followed Judaic ritual, celebration, and practice, Levinas did *not* study Talmud or Talmudic commentary (Moyn, 2003) in his youth. As such, he comes to the tradition late, nearly 40 years of age already, after extensive study in philosophy and as his radical philosophical ideas are already germinating, budding, and developing apace.

The chicken-and-egg tension of the Jewish studies and the philosophical aside, there is also some debate as to the Talmudic exegetical itself. On the one hand, is Levinas attempting to create a "Vilna on the Seine," to borrow Friedlander's (1990) memorable book title which vividly illustrates such desires, if not attempts, to bring an old tradition, way, or truth to a new setting? On the other hand, there is the image of the new, of a fresh and inventive translation or application of the old to the demands of the new – an image that also carries with it the suggestion of a certain break from, or with, the old. Scholars such as Annette Aronowicz, in the translator's introduction to *Nine Talmudic Readings* (Levinas, 2019), seem to nudge us into thinking of the Talmudic readings in this manner. Still, others have characterized the Jewish writings "political" and "communal" (Bernard-Donals, 2005; Eisenstadt, 2019), arguing that – in contrast to the philosophical writings – they are more "certain" (Bernasconi, 1998), concerned with an interest in the social and questions of politics, community, and society. But there is a rather interesting additional approach to the Jewish writings, offered by Moyn and which – maybe not surprisingly to a psychologist – is worth entertaining. The turn to Jewish studies, Moyn writes, seems "a bridge of longing," an expression of a longing, "creatively and constructively, for a past that they never themselves possessed and that they imagine as much as they recover" (Moyn, 2003, p. 340). I would add that given Levinas's clear assertion of the importance of the Shoah to this interest in Jewish studies after the war coupled with his own oft stated reference to the Jewish writing as "confessional" that the psychological of trauma and loss may yet provide the dynamic qualification within which Moyn's suspicion finds credible possibility. For all his genius as a teacher and mentor, Shushani also represented "the embodiment of a chain of tradition associated with his childhood, his parents, his family, and his community in Lithuania, all of which was lost" (Kleinberg, 2019, pp. 444–445). As such, the question of which it "is" – translation or resurrection or politics or nostalgia – is not necessarily important, as in any event, it would be all of that and more. How much of the early spiritual and attitudinal Jewish upbringing, within a specific time and place, informed his draw to the questions of philosophy, how that philosophy in turn informed his reading of the Talmud, the extent to which the experience of the Shoah prompted the Jewish "turn," or how then that return circled back to the philosophy that came thereafter? These are questions that are ultimately unanswerable in the manner of an accounting ledger and the definitives of demarcation lines. The political scientist may be able to privilege the civil rights politics of Martin Luther King Jr. or Mohandas Gandhi, say, over their religious practice or beliefs as such, but doing so has to acknowledge more than a mere selectivity of the message given the interest of the messenger and the presumed demand of her audience; it also has to concede a calculation without answer, an unsettled account.

In the chapters to follow, we will try our best to avoid the temptation and dilemma that either reads the philosophical writings through the religious, on the one hand, or that reads the religious writings through the philosophical. Whereas we will make mention of connections and cross references as appropriate, our focus on the task – Levinas and psychology – will be the compass with which we hope to steer through these muddied waters. In this chapter, given its task to sketch an outline of the life, avoiding mention of the Jewish studies would amount to a betrayal.

Levinas's philosophical obscurity was to change with the publication of *Totality and Infinity* in 1961 (an English translation was published in 1969), a text which presented unquestionable bona fides as a major player in the philosophical canon. Levinas was offered a position in the academy, at long last. Well into his 50s, he accepted a position as Professor at the University of Poitiers, where he stayed until 1967. Hereafter, he moved to the newly established University of Paris-Nanterre, working alongside luminaries such as Paul Ricoeur and Jean-Francois Lyotard, as well as an "up-and-coming" young scholar in sociology, Jean Baudrillard. It bears mention that Nanterre was at the center of the famed French student uprising of 1968. Even before the events of "May 68," which would halt the economy and push France to the brink of a wholesale civil and political revolution, students at Nanterre already protested and occupied administration buildings in March of 1968. The pressure on faculty to choose sides, or express positions in a time where complicated ambiguity was not tolerated, was palpable – especially at Nanterre, so central to the broader movement. Levinas's response, though, remained philosophically measured and personally distanced (many would say uncommitted and/or reactionary).

In 1973, Levinas accepted a position at the prestigious Paris IV (or the Sorbonne as most readers would know it), and whereas he was only there for three years – he retired in 1976 – Levinas was immensely proud of this high honor. It was also here, in 1974, one year after his appointment to this celebrated university, that he published what some consider to be his magnum opus, *Otherwise than Being, or Beyond Essence*.

In the manner of a timeline of sorts, it is worth mentioning that the first extant application of Levinas's work to psychology was published in 1971 (Steen Halling's, *The Implications of Levinas' Totality and Infinity for Therapy* [Halling, 1971]), preceding the first book-length philosophical examination of his thought in English (Edith Wyschgrod's excellent *Emmanuel Levinas: The Problem of Ethical Metaphysics* [Wyschogrod, 1974]) by a good three years.

After his retirement, Levinas remained active, giving talks and interviews and overseeing new, revised, and/or collected editions of his various philosophical and Talmudic writings. He lived to see and enjoy even greater and growing recognition; from the early to mid-eighties, "questions of ethics, politics, law and democracy were back on the philosophical and cultural agenda and the scene was set for a reappraisal of Levinas's work" (Critchley, 2002, p. 3), such that in the nineties, "the floodgates opened . . . not solely in philosophical circles, but also in departments of literature, religion, psychology, political science, and on and on" (Morgan, 2019, p. 1). As his popularity and presence grew, it also unfortunately became increasingly more difficult, and finally impossible, for Levinas to participate in public talks and lectures, as he was battling an increasingly relentless Alzheimer's disease. Levinas died on December 25, 1995, a year after his beloved Raissa. Levinas had lived for almost the duration of the century, and writing at its close, Critchley makes a rather astute summation: "It now looks as if Levinas were the hidden king of twentieth century philosophy. Such are the pleasing ironies of history" (Critchley, 2002, p. 5).

## Notes

1 Lescourret's biography, unfortunately, has not been translated into English and is only available in French.
2 *Signature* was also published in Levinas (1978).
3 I am aware that this is a somewhat caricatured difference. A philosophy student may point to Nietzsche, who stated powerfully that every philosophy is but "the personal confession of its author and a kind of involuntary and unconscious memoir" (Nietzsche, 2003, p. 37), or Derrida, who writes that "a man's life, as unique as his death, will always be more than a paradigm and something other than a symbol" (Derrida, 1994, p. xv). But these kinds of philosophers are either exceptions or, as in the case of Derrida (who was as famously reticent about sharing personal details), complicated by the acknowledgment that biographical truth, and the excess of a life, is important but also that it is not necessarily to be shared or circulated. The secret is the fraught, unstable, and fundamentally incomplete and perpetually deferred domain of the wholly individual.
4 In philosophy, and particularly that of Levinas and Derrida, considerable value accrues to the word "proper" and, particularly, the proper name. From the Latin *proprius*, it is one's own, what is particularly, uniquely, individually, and singularly one's own. It is clearly related to property, proprietary, and private (*pro privus*, for the individual, own's own). We are in psychology's wheelhouse here, given its interest in subjectivity and that which is "proper"/unique to one.
5 Jacques Derrida, who delivered the eulogy at Emmanuel Levinas's funeral, eloquently presses the same or similar point. "Often those . . . who make themselves heard in a cemetery, end up addressing directly, straight on, the one who, as we say, is no longer, is no longer living no longer there, who will no longer respond . . . This is not necessarily out of respect for convention, not always simply part of the rhetoric of oration. It is rather so as to traverse speech at the very point where words fail us" (Derrida, 1999).
6 In a recent class (on diversity and difference), a white student remarked that when she is with her African American friend, she always speaks up when she notices or suspects even the hint of racism. To which her African American friend replied, "But do you speak up for me when I am *not* around you, like when you are with your family for Thanksgiving or Easter?"
7 Urban and middle-class Jews tended to privilege Russian and Yiddish over Lithuanian, which was associated with "peasants" and rural, lesser educated folk (Critchley, 2015). Levinas's facility with Lithuanian remained a question, though he did write, in 1933, very early in his career, an "odd little text" in Lithuanian (Levinas, 1998b), the only extant record of his writing in that language.

8 So much hangs on a vowel: the Ukrainian spelling of Kharkiv (and pronunciation – har-kiv), after independence, as opposed to the Russian (Kar-kov). Similarly, Putin's Russia continues to refer to Kiev as Kee-ev, while for Ukrainians (and the West, recently), it is Kyiv (K[r][ji]eev).

9 In a phenomenon so sadly characteristic of reform (or the promise of reform) followed by backlash (Obama followed by Trump), the Tsarist statutes of the early 19th century, granting Jews new civil rights and especially access to education and Russian schools, were met with anti-Semitic retaliation. Such was the pressure on the Tsarist government that the Ministry of Education decreed a *numerus clausus* ("closed number") for Jews in the Pale of Settlement, limiting access to education – between 3% and 10%, depending on one's location. That Levinas's acceptance was a cause for celebration is bittersweet for the knowledge of many other deserving students denied such education. It is also noteworthy that, while not a national (federal) decree, *numerus clausus* practices were in place for Jews in the United States during this same period and especially among the so-called Ivy League universities of the Northeast. Later, as a precautionary way out of legal jeopardy, Yale University implemented an ingenious (or ingeniously devious) way to restrict the admission of Jews, namely, legacy admissions. Other prestigious universities would follow the Yale model soon. Where Blacks were concerned, the practice was less *numerus clausus* than *numerus nullus*.

10 In addition to Blondel, a psychology professor ("who was very anti-Freudian"), and Halbwachs, a sociologist, Levinas singles out two philosophy professors, Henri Carteron and Maurine Pradines, whom he lauds as embodying "all the virtues of the university . . . true men, who are unforgettable" (Levinas, 2001b, p. 29). One can reasonably suspect, and Levinas confirms, that some (or much) of his antipathy to Freud was the result of Blondel's strong mentoring influence ("It is due to him, no doubt, that I have remained outside of psychoanalysis to this day" [Levinas, 2001b, p. 86]).

11 The other four being Bergson's *Time and Free Will* (Bergson, 1960), Hegel's *Phenomenology of Spirit* (Hegel, 2018), Kant's *Critique of Pure Reason* (Kant, 2007b), and Plato's *Phaedrus* (Plato, 2002).

12 Eugen Fink would rise to scholarly renown himself as a noted philosopher and phenomenologist, albeit in later years of the Heideggerian variety.

13 Levinas (and Gabrielle Pfeiffer's) French translation was published in 1931, the German version in 1950, and the first English translation (by Thomas Dorion Cairns, who also studied with Husserl) in 1960 (Husserl, 1960).

14 Born to a Jewish family, Husserl converted to Lutheran Christianity in his 20s. Given the Nazi understanding of Jews in *racial* terms, Christian baptism and/or conversion did not erase or diminish one's essential (genetic) status as a Jew.

15 Sarah Bakewell, in her outstanding book, *At the Existentialist Café* (2016), relates the moment when Raymond Aron told Sartre and De Beauvoir about Edmund Husserl and this new philosophy called phenomenology. De Beauvoir recounts that "Sartre turned pale upon hearing this" and rushed to the nearest bookshop, telling the bookseller to "give me everything you have on phenomenology, now" (Bakewell, 2016, pp. 3–4). He tore open the book he received "without waiting to use a paperknife, and began reading as he walked down the street" (Bakewell, 2016, p. 4). That book was Levinas's dissertation, *The Theory of Intuition in Husserl's Phenomenology* (Levinas, 1995).

16 Mystery certainly surrounds the figure of Monsieur Chouchani. Another of his famous students, Elie Wiesel, writes that "even if all his disciples, everywhere, were to begin speaking about him – and nobody else – we would not know more about who he really was, about what shadows he fled or sought, or the nature of his power and torment" (Wiesel, 2011, p. 124). Disheveled and unkempt, M. Chouchani would appear and disappear at different times and places in the world – quite literally – for stretches of time, sharing an undisputed genius with those who studied with him. While no one knew

where he came from, where he went, what his name was, how old he was, how he managed to live and travel as he did, what everyone who came into contact with him did know and acknowledge was his unsurpassed and singular genius – from Jewish studies (he could apparently cite the Torah, Talmud, and Zohar by heart), to religious studies in general, to nuclear physics and mathematics. "This was no ordinary man." Shushani died in Uruguay in 1968, and his gravestone (which Elie Wiesel paid for) reads, "The wise Rabbi Chouchani of blessed memory. His birth and his life are sealed in enigma."

# Chapter 4

# The Early Work

As we turn to a closer engagement with Levinas's writings and thought, and particularly as scholars and practitioners from the social scientific and helping professions, we must acknowledge that the texts we examine here are not quite the "usual" or "expected" ones within the extant literature; very few of those who have invited Levinas to psychology and the social sciences have paid much, if any, attention to *Existence and Existents* (Levinas, 2001a) and *Time and the Other* (Levinas, 1987b), the so-called "early work" (published in 1947 and 1948, respectively) and the focus of our attention in this chapter.[1] One could certainly argue for the "early" descriptor by the simple fact of chronology but not unlike the ambiguity attendant on "phases" or "stages" of life (When exactly does young adulthood end and midlife start, or midlife end and late maturity start?), if time was our only yardstick, we would run into difficulty marking such "periods" definitively. We make the distinction, instead, by a thematic shift in philosophical focus to a sustained and deliberate emphasis on ethics which marks the publication of *Totality and Infinity* (Levinas, 2013), the subject of our next two chapters. Indeed, the explicit characterization of Levinas as the pre-eminent philosopher of ethics and the demand of the face of the other derive from *Totality and Infinity* and the texts that follow subsequently. Of these important concepts and arguments, there are no explicit mention in the early texts.[2]

Inasmuch as the psychological yield – such as it may be – of the early work has largely lain fallow, the tasks of this chapter consequently become, firstly, to introduce the reader to some of the main ideas and insights of this early work and, secondly, to explore the possibilities of such work for psychology. Thirdly, though less explicitly stated as such, this chapter will also lay the groundwork for an argument that will become more evident as we grapple with the so-called later work of *Otherwise than Being* (Levinas, 2004b), namely, that there is then a certain return, where the later work assumes greater meaning only from our having wrestled with the earlier. As such, it is not simply a matter of some continuity but also "a kind of call and response between the early and late work" (Critchley, 2015, p. 47).

DOI: 10.4324/9781003315612-4

## *Existence and Existents* and *Time and the Other*: Some Background

Published a mere year apart from each other, in 1947 and 1948 respectively, both texts, upon publication and even up till the recent past, had very little impact on established scholarly and philosophical thought. In the foreword to the English translation of *Existence and Existents*, the philosopher and eminent Levinas scholar Robert Bernasconi characterizes the book's reception and impact by invoking David Hume's now-famous description of his own tome, namely, that it "fell dead born from the press" (Bernasconi, 2001, p. vii). As for *Existence and Existents*, so, too, for *Time and the Other*.

However, we also concur with Bernasconi on both the following counts: that "Existence and Existents remains indispensable for understanding both Totality and Infinity and perhaps especially Otherwise than Being," but also that "it has its own intrinsic interest" (Bernasconi, 2001, p. viii). This is also abundantly true for *Time and the Other*. Llewelyn (1995) in like manner notes that with "hindsight," the early works hold so much in reserve, it is as if they "are produced with the later masterpieces in view" (p. 4). Were we to add that these texts provide the horizon for a psychological anthropology, we have reason enough to commit them to closer scrutiny.

The overwhelming bulk of *Existence and Existents* was written while Levinas was incarcerated as a prisoner of war. We've already mentioned, in the previous chapter, that the temptation to hold the text as mirror to the personal experience is frustrated by Levinas's refusal to name or reference the experience in the text. There is no easy or evident correspondence to be had, which is not to say there isn't any but perhaps that we have to work a little harder at it.[3] The same is true for *Time and the Other*, which grew out of a series of lectures, hosted by Jean Wahl,[4] the philosopher and poet and good friend of Levinas's. Wahl, who was a professor at the Sorbonne at the time, felt frustrated that "nonacademic discourses" and "nonconformist intellectuals" could not find as widespread a platform within the halls of the Sorbonne, certainly not to the extent that he desired. Hence, he started the *College Philosophique*, which was to provide a forum for just such conversations and gatherings: "It was a place where intellectual non-conformism – and even what took itself to be such – was tolerated and expected" (Levinas, 1985, p. 55). *Time and the Other* is the result of a series of four lectures Levinas delivered at the College Philosophique in 1947.

One might be tempted to think these two texts by some chronological linearity, the one building on the preceding or taking up where the other left off. As a matter of fact, one of the final chapter headings for *Existence and Existents* is "on the way to time," and one would be forgiven the assumption that *Time and the Other* is the logical conceptual installment to follow. The truth of the matter, or a "better" way to think the relationship, though, as with all of Levinas's work, is of a "deepening." Whereas *Time and the Other* revisits some of the themes of *Existence and*

*Existents*, this recircling or restatement is not a matter of "mere" repeating nor is it a simple new installment of thought, another cumulative or additive level to a rising Levinasian edifice. One of the keys to reading Levinas is to forego such an image or expectation; more apt is Derrida's observation and characterization of Levinas's work (Derrida, 1978) as the same wave incessantly beating on the shore, but each time, it is also a different wave. Or Critchley's characterization (via Isaiah Berlin's story) of Levinas as a hedgehog "who knows 'one big thing,' rather than a fox, who knows 'many small things'" (Critchley, 2002, p. 6). Each time there is a deepening, a facet or nuance one glimpses anew or differently or which opens another aspect of the one wave or thought. Perhaps not altogether unlike the expression of love in a long-married couple, where each gesture of that one big thing is/was both the same and different, a fastening and a loosening at the very same time, which is also to say a certain deepening over time.

## To the Texts Themselves

Up until the publication of *Existence and Existents*, with a few minor exceptions, Levinas's writing on Heidegger was largely devoid of sustained or explicit criticism and challenge. With *Existence and Existents*, however, the very first paragraph will state unequivocally, "a profound need to leave the climate of that philosophy" (Levinas, 2001a, p. 4).[5] We read this oft quoted and powerful statement as an overdetermined one but proceed (at least expressly) as Levinas does, by focusing on the philosophical departures from Heidegger.

To do so, it is worth reminding ourselves of Heidegger's ontological difference, between beings and Being, between that which exists and existence itself. Hence, and by its extension in existential and humanistic psychology, we are given an understanding of the features of existence – such as our inescapable mortality or our freedom to choose – within which each individual, each being, wrestles with the meaning of their existence uniquely. Whether our psychological inspiration is via Carl Rogers or Abraham Maslow, Viktor Frankl or Rollo May, the therapeutic and psychological theoretical stance of a deeply personal centeredness in a particular life that nonetheless also transcends us, as individuals, is common to all of them and issue in a particular way from the philosophical bedrock of the Heideggerian ontological difference.

Levinas also starts from this distinction between "that which exists, and its existence itself" (Levinas, 2001a, p. 1) and acknowledges the Heideggerian insight and complication of the inseparability of *seiendes* (beings, and in Levinas's rephrasing, "existents") from *Sein* (Being, or in Levinas's terms, "existence"). As being-in-the-world, we've already mentioned that existence and the existent are not separable into variables, and any access to the meaning or "truth" of existence, moreover, is always through the existent. It is a truth that is prone and party to rather personalized distortion. Hence, the scrupulous researcher would consequently be wary of any utterance or truth about existence, hobbled as it may be by "contamination" bias, or distraction of the participant analyzing its participance right in the embroiled midst of its participation. The psychologist and therapist are similarly on the lookout, their whole task being to help peel away such "prejudices" in order for the individual to live a more "authentic," "actualized," "reflexive," or "insightful" life. There is no god or "pure" messenger to relay an uncluttered, unfettered truth of Being, or existence in general, separate from existents who "inhabit" it. The question of Being in general seems unanswerable, at least in any definitive sense.

Yet it is precisely this impossible question of Being which Levinas will nonetheless address and tackle. And he will up the stakes considerably by reversing the Heideggerian insight – that is, that anything we can say about Being has to come from, and through, beings concretely being-in-the-world. Levinas clues us to his intention in the original French title of his book already, contra Heidegger, to instead move in the opposite direction, *from* existence *to* existents (the English translation – *Existence and Existents* – does not quite capture this sense of movement "from" and "to," evident in the French, *De l'existence a l'existant*). We can wonder, already, if existential and humanistic psychology, for example, relies on Heidegger's fundamental ontological insights upon which to construct a theory of the individual-in-the-world, and Levinas is about to issue a challenge to those fundamentals (without us even knowing what the challenge is, save that "before" there is being-in-the-world, "there is" ["some thing"]), how might our psychological anthropology change or need to be adapted? *If* it does or has to, that is.

### The Il y a, or "there is," and Hypostasis

For all the (true) assertions that the meaning of existence for an existent is located in the relationship of the existent with existence (conceding, Levinas reminds us, that the descriptor "relationship" is an analogy because existence is not a thing, is not a substantive to have a "relationship" with), "there is" something antecedent and prior to this "relationship"; there is "bare existence." As an imaginative thought experiment, consider "all beings, things and persons, reverting to nothingness" (Levinas, 2001a, p. 51). What happens then/there? What would "pure nothingness" be? Levinas answers his own question: "something would happen" (p. 52), something will remain even if it is not some thing, even if it is a silence which is not no-thing. This "something" is indeterminate and impersonal (as in the form of the verb "it rains," what is designated is an impersonal action, a "happening" without author). "This impersonal, anonymous, yet inextinguishable 'consummation' of being, which murmurs in the depths of nothingness itself we shall designate by the term *there is*" (Levinas, 2001a, p. 52, emphasis in the original). The "there is," or *il y a* in French, is "being in general."[6]

The "there is" is an exceedingly elusive and slippery thought – Bernasconi notes that "Levinas can barely say even what it is not" (Bernasconi, 2001, p. xii), which goes some way to explaining its "inherent impenetrability" (p. xv). "Thought experiences a kind of vertigo" is how John Sallis (Sallis, 1998, p. 154) puts it, while Sean Hand and Varakakukalayil offer that the il y a "cannot be intelligibly understood" (Hand, 2009, p. 31), as it "cannot be conceived in the common categories of our thought" (Varakukalayil, 2015, p. 285). Yet to the extent that an inability to explain a "strange" feeling of unease as darkness settles over our camp in the woods does not make the feeling any less real or "true," we might use this recognition as a foothold into what Levinas is reaching for here. Indeed, Levinas himself uses a similar "example," likening the "there is" to the experience of night, which "invades like a presence" (Levinas, 2001a, p. 52). As night "nights" (Llewelyn, 1995), it is neither something nor no-thing; an absent, impersonal presence, the darkness of night envelops, permeates, "invades," and submerges one. Moreover, and quite importantly, like night, there is something menacing about this indeterminate presence of the *nothing* before which there is no withdrawal or hiding and that suffuses everything. In this enveloping absence, there is a sense of presence, the menacing possibility of something that lurks or of "things that may go bump in the night."[7] It is the experience of a scary silence that accompanies the child left alone in his or her bedroom after the adults have shut the door for the night (Baumgartner, 2005). Truthfully, it is the formless impersonality that is most distressing – a fact not lost, for example, on masters of the horror movie genre, where one is more scared and anxious in the *anticipation* of the monster or killer's appearance, from "anywhere," than when s/he/it actually appears and we now have a form to respond to. The "there is" gestures to an impersonal, anonymous, and undifferentiated existence without existents. A conceptual analogy might also be found in the Biblical nothing before creation, or the silent expanse of space where there is no-thing but not nothing. "There is" a certain "fullness of what is empty" (Davis, 1996, p. 23), a fullness "of the nothingness of everything" (Levinas, 2001a, p. 53). Now:

> To be conscious is to be torn away from the there is, since the existence of a consciousness constitutes a subjectivity, a subject of existence that is, to some extent, a master of being, already a name in the anonymity of the night.
>
> (Levinas, 2001a, p. 55)

Consciousness is about the emergence of a figure (a prototypical or "evolving" I) from the anonymity of the "there is." Imagine a popular cinematic image of a dense fog from which a figure emerges, from which a form materializes, as if the fog somehow produces and births the figure, not entirely identifiable as of yet but taking form. As it does so, it interrupts the anonymity and impersonality of the fog, of the fact that "there is" just fog. A figure emerges from the il y a, but it is not yet an "I"; it is not conscious(ness) yet but its beginning.

This emergence, "the passage going from being to a something, from the state of verb to the state of thing" (Levinas, 1985, p. 51), Levinas calls *hypostasis*. A simpler description of hypostasis would be the dynamic of becoming-a-subject, "where an existent is put in touch with its existing" (Levinas, 1987b, p. 51). The "first moment" of this dynamic, though, is still before every act of understanding. Returning to our movie image, we make out a figure, a beginning to take shape, an apparition for which, and to which, this first recognition brings no understanding, no consciousness yet of the shape in any categorical manner. Is it human? What is it? It has shape, even materiality, but we do not know it, as it does not know itself, or of itself, save that it has form (a vessel/body). It is the second before, or alongside, understanding, a certain wakefulness that is not (yet) understanding – the instant before consciousness even as it is also the advent of consciousness, a localization of consciousness and self in anonymous being. I imagine it concretely as that moment one is startled by an alarm into wakefulness; one wakes up but is not yet awake, as one unthinkingly reaches out to hit the snooze or off button on the alarm – awake but not quite. One glimpses here what will become an important insight and which we will return to in greater detail: the importance of the body to our being a subject. In fact, one is a bodily subject "first," and it is through the body that the subject as self is constituted. "There is not only a consciousness of localization, but a localization of consciousness" (Levinas, 2001a, p. 65). It is only through corporeality that the I can say the famous "here I am" of Levinas's later work (put differently, the body of the early work is indispensable to the ethical of the later).

Returning to our example, there is a moment, somewhere between flailingly and unthinkingly reaching for the off button on our alarm, neither awake nor asleep, where we nonetheless "wake up" and become conscious of our surroundings, the day ahead of us, and our sense of who we are. This instant is an inst*ance*: it is a moment, outside of time, that inaugurates an instance, in time. The noun and the verb are indistinguishably implicated, their "separateness" notwithstanding. Such is the instantiation of consciousness: an instant and instance whereby existence is accomplished. The existent takes a position in the *il y a*: there is a base from which consciousness arises and a subject is affirmed. This hypostasis (which Levinas defines as "the upsurge of an existent into existence" [Levinas, 2001a, p. 25]) suspends the *il y a*, as a being arises on and from the ground of the "there is" and assumes both being (existence) and this particular being (the existent), exercising in so doing a certain mastery over the fatality of Being. It is by this second or subsequent moment, speaking as one does of "moments" for the sake of explanation only, that the apparition is recognized as a distinguishable form; "that by which a being is turned toward the sun, that by which it has a face, through which it gives itself, by which it comes forward" (Levinas, 2001a, p. 31). The "I" is this appropriation of existence, an existent who masters existence in consciousness but carries the weight of existence by the same act and movement. Put another way, whereas one "escapes" the indeterminate horror of existence in consciousness, one never does. Consciousness is not the vanquishing victor whose victory is the instantaneous, isolated, summary killing of a foe but rather, the price of victory which inaugurates the burden of rule, the labor of sovereignty and relation in the world, a weight to be carried and from which there is no escape.

### Solitude and the Body

From the undifferentiated, anonymous, and indeterminate *il y a*, there emerges a subject, a substantive, which, in its breaking from existence, attains consciousness of itself as existent ("which" becomes "who"). Its self-recognition as a differenti-ated entity is to be aware that the work of the existent is existing (Hutchens, 2004). This indissoluble unity between the existent and the work of existing is a solitude; it is by existing that I am alone. Even as I am surrounded by others, I am not the other, and I cannot exchange my existence in any way for, or to, another: "One can exchange everything between beings except existing . . . to be is to be isolated by existing" (Levinas, 1987b, p. 42).

Now consciousness of existence prompts two "realizations": of a certain "virility and sovereignty" (a feature Levinas says the existentialists have neglected in their seeming emphasis on solitude as despair and abandonment) by which existence is "mastered" and, secondly, of its existence as a material "enchainment." The exist-ent cannot detach itself from itself; one does not exist as a "spirit, or as a smile or a breath of air" (Levinas, 1987b, p. 56) but has a body, a materiality, by which one is encumbered and for which one is responsible. As such, inasmuch as it has freed itself from the there is, and has the freedom of agency and mastery, as a "free being (it) is already no longer free, because it is responsible for itself" (55), because it's very identity as a differentiated existent is bound by the materiality of its embod-ied existence – "I am forever stuck with myself" (Levinas, 2001a, p. 85). This is, however, not the encumbrance of a tomb or prison – materiality is at once and of necessity wholly imbricated in the freedom of hypostasis. Consciousness – "the freedom of the Ego" – and materiality "go together" (Levinas, 1987b, p. 57). More-over, the materiality of the body "remains an *experience* of materiality" (Levinas, 2001a, p. 69) and "the condition necessary for any inwardness. It does not express an event; it is itself this event" (Levinas, 2001a, p. 70). Hypostasis consequently "bears the mark of corporeality because it is through the body that self is consti-tuted" (Ciocan, 2009, p. 10).

Already in 1934, shortly after Hitler came to power, Levinas wrote about the elemental connection of the body in a short article, *Reflections on the Philosophy of Hitlerism* (Levinas, 1990). Western philosophy, since Socrates, has seen the body as a tomb, an obstacle to overcome, an inferior encumbrance to reason and mind (Ciocan, 2009). Yet Levinas asks, Isn't it so that the body is more familiar to us than any object in the world and, more than that, that we "affirm ourselves in the unique warmth of our bodies long before any blossoming of the Self that claims to be separate from the body" (Levinas, 1990, p. 68)?[8] The body is fundamental to the sense of identity, to the awakening of ourselves to ourselves; it is never the case that we relate to ourselves or the world without a body to which we are concretely and irrevocably yoked. "To be truly oneself," then, is to become aware of this "ineluctable original chain" of the body to consciousness (1990, p. 69).

### Getting Out of Existence/Transcendence

Up until this point, the story is of solitude arising from the hypostatic tear from the there is, enchained by materiality (which is both the fact of a body and the material needs of the body for survival) and with the weight of existence as a brute fact.

This heaviness of Being is a suffering, by the etymological notion of the word (from the Latin, *sub* [from below] + *ferre* [to bear]) as something I carry and bear, made even more acute by the recognition that this work of existing is mine, alone, and that I have to do so by the bonds of the materiality of space and the corporeal. I cannot, like the gods, flit effortlessly between worlds or assume different material or spiritual forms to suit my needs or desires. But I wish I could, as everyone who fantasized about being a "superhero" or possessing a "superpower" can attest to. Perhaps this explains the popularity of such movies, catering as it does to this very fundamental desire – to escape this solitude and enchained existence, to transcend it. The existent wishes to escape the brute weight of existence; it wishes to reach elsewhere, to a transcendence beyond solitude, a salvation.[9] It wishes to escape the solitidunous I bound to itself, to flee from "the brutality of existence" (Critchley, 2015, p. 49) and "to get out of oneself, that is, to break that most radical and unalterably binding of chains, the fact that the I [moi] is oneself [soi-meme]" (Levinas, 2004b, p. 55).

We should emphasize this point and do so with a particularly psychological ear. To get out of existence (philosophers like to phrase it thus) is also to get away from oneself (psychologists might prefer this phrasing and so does Levinas, actually, wishing as he does to "glimpse wherein [ontological] solitude can be exceeded" [Levinas, 1987b, p. 41]). From the beginning, the self includes the need to leave itself (Llewelyn, 1995); from the beginning, identity is disordered, fractured by its recognition of itself as conscience/psyche and body and of existence as that which demands alteration to what also remains the same. Put differently, "identity is always being changed by the process of being self-conscious and yet what does the identifying does not change" (Hutchens, 2004, p. 44). The self can never come to complete self-determination, and even more so when we meet the other, in due course, who will completely upset any fantasy of fulfilled self-sufficiency.

Now having mentioned the desire to transcend existence and having conceded a certain "virility and sovereignty" that comes with the hypostatic emergence of the existent, how does the existent attempt such escape given the powers of consciousness and the self? We've organized such *attempts to transcend existence*, to get outside of ourselves, in the next section, starting with a false start, the seeming escape of death, followed by more promising avenues of potential escape. In the end, however, all of these will ultimately turn out to be insufficient, "preparatory" at best for the arrival of ethics and the other in *Totality and Infinity*. But we proceed as we do in life, where false starts may end up as lessons in and of life and, as such, never quite abandoned for their persistence, if not necessity, to the discovery of the true.

## The Dead End of Death

Even though Heidegger is not mentioned by name, it is rather obvious that Levinas's dismissal of death as possibility for transcendence is in conversation with Heidegger, for whom Dasein is a being-towards-death. In the existential psychological appropriation, the recognition of our mortality and the nothingness of death gives rise to an existential anxiety. In the face of such anxiety, we can either attempt to flee from the truth of our mortality, losing ourselves in distractions, or we can recognize death as a motivational "condition of possibility" for Dasein to come to its "ownmost" and "authentic" essence. It is precisely because we do not have forever that we are pressured to live each day as if it is our last, to live fully in the present and make the meaningful most of every moment. "Being-toward-death" enables Dasein to project and live its possibilities, to confront this unbearable prospect of death in an elemental care (*Sorge*) that provides meaning to its actions. Indeed, it is only a finite, mortal being – one who must die – which can have a future (Peperzak, 1997), as it is within the horizon of its finitude that Dasein can have projects.

This is not the case for Levinas for whom we do not flee death as much as existence: "Is not the fear *of* Being just as originary as the fear *for* Being?" (Levinas, 2001a, p. 5). The horror of existence is in the recognition of a "condemnation to perpetual reality, to existence with 'no exits'" (p. 58), of being "backed up against Being . . . of being riveted to Being" (Baumgartner, 2005, p. 53). There is no escape from Being, no ability to "stop the music," even in suicide (Marcus, 2008). A quote from his friend Maurice Blanchot makes Levinas's point:

> Just as the man who is hanging himself, after kicking away the stool on which he stood . . . rather than feeling the leap which he is making into the void feels only the rope which hold him, held to the end, held more than ever, bound as he had never been before to the existence he would like to leave.
>
> (Blanchot, 1973, p. 36)

Moreover, whereas the music may end for an individual, who would know nothing about its ending, the music itself does not; after any individual death, existence itself continues. (We are well served reminding ourselves of Hamlet's dying words: "things standing thus unknown shall live behind me . . . Oh, I die Horatio" [Hamlet, 5.2.371/380].) The person who commits suicide knows this and often leaves a note in recognition thereof, makes a last telephone call, leaves a memento from life, or chooses a place to die where life had meaning (which is also to hope against hope that by this choice, death would as well). Death is not the possibility of impossibility, as Heidegger would have it, but the impossibility of possibility. "What is important about death is that at a certain moment we are no longer *able to be able* . . . the subject loses its very mastery as a subject" (Levinas, 1987b, p. 74). It is true that I can anticipate my death, which "is a power, but what I anticipate is precisely my impotence, my definitive disempowerment" (Hofmeyr, 2012, p. 466).

It is not, however, just that the ego is dissolved by death and that its powers and abilities cease; as such, its alterity, the alterity of death, cannot be a basis for transcendence, as there is no subjectivity to survive it. It is also that the ego/subject cannot know death, cannot experience its own death. Although death is of an absolute alterity, a mystery, it is not transcendence because the ego cannot survive it, has no sense of it, and cannot retain itself in it. Death is the unknown and can never be "my" death, as I cannot experience it.[10] The existential notion of death as one's "ownmost" (whereas I can sacrifice my life for another's, that other will still die; I cannot die their death for them to the same extent that only I can die mine) is challenged by this insight that there is no way to claim death as one's own because we cannot know the instant of our deaths as a subject in life and conscious experience. Because we are "no longer able to be able" (Levinas, 1987b, p. 74), death is an event we cannot assume. While death is certainly in the order of alterity, the question of transcendence is of a relationship with what is wholly other without losing my subjectivity. In death, while wholly other, I am also no longer a subject, no longer an existent; I've been absorbed by it. Hence, death provides no exit from life: "To be or not to be is not the question where transcendence is concerned" (Levinas, 2004b, p. 3).

## Nourishment as Escape

A seemingly more promising possibility of escape or "salvation" is through nourishments – through what we "live from." We will return to this rather innovative contribution of Levinas's when he expands upon it in *Totality and Infinity*, in the direction of "enjoyment." For now, it suffices to say that whereas comportment of care is instrumental for Heidegger (the world is an ensemble of tools), for Levinas, "prior to being an ensemble of tools, the world is an ensemble of nourishments" (Levinas, 1987b, p. 63). By means of an example, one could argue that the bicycle I rode to work this morning is like the Heideggerian hammer, a tool and means to a project, goal, or will – say a decision to exercise and lose weight. For the most part, to continue in a Heideggerian register, when the bicycle works well, I don't have occasion to notice my dependence on the tool; it is when the instrument breaks down, as when I get a flat tire, that I realize my hierarchical dependence on the tool. Levinas, however, turns this argument on its head and says whatever the ends are, I *enjoyed* the ride this morning, I *lived* the ride. To be sure, I recall crossing a bridge over the river, the light bouncing off the metal struts and the bicycle tires humming to my pedaling, my legs and body one with the bicycle, in a moment that was completely mine; I recognized my *independence*, that is to say my ability to take the other, the bicycle and bicycling, into me, into my experience, into my enjoyment as nourishment for my life. It is living life as a living *from*, as a happiness of the moment and *not* as the finality of losing weight. This is a sheer and utter egoism, of a singular I in the world, cycling over some bridge, or sloppily eating an orange, or sighing contentedly as I down an ice-cold beer on a hellishly hot day; it is a sheer love of life, an essential nourishment, a primary happiness. "It is perhaps not correct to say that we live to eat, but it is no more correct to say that we eat to live"— that is, we are in "a relationship with an object. . . . Characterized by enjoyment [*jouissance*]" (Levinas, 1987b, p. 63). Contra Heidegger, the things we live from are, therefore, not "means of life" (the mechanisms by which we live), nor "goals of life" (air as life, for example), nor "tools or implements" (Heidegger's famous hammer springs to mind) but always involves *enjoyment* inasmuch as existence is always adorned, or "embellished," as a happy independence.

It turns out, though, that the path to transcendence is not quite to be had through nourishment either. Ultimately, the distance from the object is bridged; it becomes incorporated into the self and loses its alterity in the process of enjoyment. The refreshing glass of cold beer on a hot day is enjoyed in its difference and distance from me, but in the process of slaking my thirst and enjoying my enjoyment, the cold beer becomes me. The loss of oneself in enjoyment, an ecstasy (from the Greek ek-stasis, literally, "standing outside oneself" – *ek-* [out] + *histanai* [to place]), comes to an end, the other has been incorporated and/or disappears, and one returns to oneself and the fact that one must exist (Purcell, 2006). If death does not offer transcendence because I lose my subjectivity in the relationship with it, then nourishment is not transcendence because the otherness of the object is not retained in the relationship – it is subsumed to become my energy, or disappears in the enjoyment of my enjoyment. Nourishment, too, cannot quite afford a path out of existence, even as it hints towards a certain "forgetfulness of self," as a "first abnegation" to pass through.

## The Mastery of Reason and Knowledge

As with nourishment, reason and knowledge illumes an object in a way that subsumes the alterity of what is other than me. There is a distance between me and the object of knowledge, a mystery, say, of the sun and moon, or a certain illness and malady. But reason and knowledge are often able to master such mystery, to illume the object in understanding. As it does so, the light of this illumination remains as if it came from me; the object retains none of its "strangeness," its alterity, in that its transcendence is made immanent. Even a divine carriage that draws the sun over the firmament daily, or some bewitching fiend whose curse causes me to break out in hives are already ways of understanding, and as knowledge draws everything into the law of universality. By its mastering powers of reason, the existent finds itself again in solitude. It is a solipsism which is the very structure of reason, as nothing can be on its outside: it is the very nature of knowledge to bring objects and phenomena to understanding and the law – "knowledge is always an adequation between thought and what it thinks" (Levinas, 1985, p. 60). Knowledge does not surmount solitude but consummates it.

Some years ago, my family spent some time in the South African bush. Growing up, I did this frequently and have learned over time to identify certain behaviors, tracks, or dung of various animals – an experience I now readily shared to the questioning delight and disgust of my children, who did not have this experience growing up as they did in the United States (from "So this is elephant dung, and you say it's fresh, so they must be close. Wow!" to "Ewwww, he is picking it up and smelling it!"). On one particular occasion, however, I was stumped. I had no idea about a certain track, clearly preserved in a muddy patch just outside our camp. Unbeknownst to me (because we usually prohibit or restrict telephone use in the bush), my pubescent son had whipped out his telephone, took a picture of the track, and performed a reverse image search on some wildlife website. "It's a wild dog, Dad," he proclaimed proudly as he pulled up a picture of what a wild dog looks like. I remain conflicted about this postmodern and virtual moment: On the one hand, it was good to know. I had new mastery, a new skill and power with which to bend the world to my knowing grasp. On the other hand, conversation was foreclosed and came to an end – the alterity and mystery of the other and not knowing had been overcome, had been subsumed by reason and knowledge. While nourishment incorporates the object of enjoyment into the me, with reason and knowledge, the alterity of the other is obliterated in immanence and universality. The "light of intelligibility" comes from me, and "in this sense knowledge never encounters anything truly other in the world" (Levinas, 1987b, p. 68). This, too, is not an avenue for transcendence.

## Exiting by Need/Work

By the sovereignty of consciousness, and the material dictates of need, the existent tills and works. By the weight of existence, the existent toils, invents tools, and uses them to the ends of its needs. At this early juncture, the importance of work is related primarily to the way in which the weight of existence comes into relief as pain and effort: "the one who works not, eats not" (Levinas, 1987b, p. 68). By labor, one reaches into the world to grasp and subdue. In *Totality and Infinity*, the matter of labor is revisited and masterfully expanded, and while we will have to wait some for that revision, a trailer preview is that labor attempts to ward off the threat of the il y a in possession and enjoyment, to work over the land and craft and collect things in an attempt to reserve a future of enjoyment *and* forestall one where peril may lie in wait. These attempts, too, however does not allow an escape from existence. If anything, it emphasizes our material and corporeal rootedness in it.

## Exiting through Eros

All the avenues or possibilities for escape seem, in one way or another, to revolve around the question of "the preservation of the ego in transcendence" (Levinas, 1987b, p. 77). In death, the self ceases, while in nourishment, knowledge, and labor, the ego's subsuming mastery is such that it returns to itself, without alteration from the encounter with what is other to it. In the erotic relationship, however, the loved other is not taken into the self and in "desire for the other, one is taken out of oneself" (Perpich, 2001, p. 42). The alterity of the beloved is not like that of things in the world. In love, the relationship with the loved other is neither of knowledge nor of mastery or possession; it is "neither a struggle, nor a fusion, nor a knowledge" (Levinas, 1987b, p. 88). "Love does not dissolve distance, but rather infinitely preserves it" (Ciocan, 2009, p. 15); the loved other remains a mystery. Moreover, love springs not from need but from desire, and as desire, it is never satisfied but deepens as the desire is slaked. There is always a wanting for more and a more which is not mine to make as an activity but to receive from the other as it is given, as it is gifted. Some of Levinas's most beautiful and lyrical lines can be found here, as in "Love is not a possibility, is not due to our initiative, is without reason; it invades and wounds us, and nevertheless the *I* survives in it" (Levinas, 1987b, pp. 88–89, emphasis in original).

The mode of Eros in the world is the caress, which is not grasping or touching. The caress does not seek out mastery, as the grasp does, and while it is a sensation, it does not seek sensibility; in fact, it does not know what it seeks and is always as of a future and an anticipation. In the caress, "the hand loses its instrumental meaning and its mastery" (Moyaert, 2000, p. 36), and to touch the other is also to be touched by the other. This is one of the few instances where Levinas references Freud, by noting that whereas Freud's libido seeks pleasure, the significance of this pleasure against the backdrop of what it is to be is not questioned. As such, Levinas maintains that Freud misses the mystery of the future.[11]

For the most part, however, we mistake the erotic relationship. Generally, we understand the relationship in terms of possession and knowing the other or we think it in terms of a fusion. I attended a marriage ceremony recently where the bride and groom lit a "unity" candle, each with their own separate candles. The minister intoned that they each came with their own, separate candles to light the one candle with one wick because they had now "become one." Both the existentialists and Levinas would groan silently, I imagined. I was also reminded of notions of possession in phrases from the formulary, such as "I take you to be my wife" or "Now you are mine, and I am yours" (or from a more "conservative" wedding formulary, where the priest addresses the bride and tells her, "You belong to your husband as your husband belongs to God. You will honor and obey him as he honors and obeys God").

For all its promise, though, the erotic falls short and cannot be the model for transcendence, as the ego "does not *become other*" (Perpich, italics in original, p. 36). The erotic meeting is of equals, of the dialogal, whereas the developing other of transcendence will represent a fundamental asymmetry, of an other with "height," who will disturb my self-satisfied existence to the core. Moreover, erotic and romantic love is a sealed-off world, a world of just us, which is an isolation from responsibility to others who are not us. The erotic relationship comes close to transcendence but does not quite settle the account. However, it does provide an opening for what – at least with respect to the early work – does, fecundity as the birth of the child.

## Exiting via Fecundity

It bears mention, lest those familiar with Levinas accuse me of hagiographic omission, that Levinas's descriptions of Eros and fecundity has come under criticism for its supposed sexist overtones (Eros, for example, is presented as the "feminine" and fecundity in terms of the birth of a son). We examine such criticisms closely in Chapter 8. For now, we proceed simply with a theoretical description of the transcendence of Eros which makes possible an actual concretization of transcendence, through fecundity, and in the child. With the child, Eros exceeds the couple.[12] The question one should keep in mind is, How can an ego remain itself even as it becomes other than itself, transcends itself? For Levinas, the child is a relationship "with a stranger who, entirely while being Other, is myself, the relationship of the ego with a myself who is nonetheless a stranger to me" (Levinas, 1987b, p. 91). The ego has become other to itself while retaining itself.

One of my sons was only a few months old when my father, his grandfather, passed away. He never knew his grandfather. In the years since, the way in which my son resembles his grandfather – not just in looks and build but especially eerily also in mannerisms, gait, and comportment – is uncanny. And as I grow older, my siblings remark how I am resembling the father they remember. This is not simply about genes or a biological accident; it is about the realization and perpetuation of obligation (Beyers & Reber, 1998), about a "future beyond my own being" (Levinas, 1985, p. 70) and "being able to escape the closure of your identity and what is bestowed on you toward something which is not bestowed on you and which nevertheless is yours" (p. 70).

It is entirely understandable that the reader, at this point, will want more. The notion of fecundity as transcendence seems a rather powerful point, but it is also disappointingly short and not developed much further in these early texts. Truthfully, hereafter, it is not developed much at all: with the publication of *Totality and Infinity*, the parental relationship is no longer the prototypical model for transcendence in alterity; ethics and the face of the other emerges to take center stage. If nothing else, though, we see here how Levinas grapples with the desire to leave being without leaving, to transcend being within concrete finitude and enchainment.

## Some (Initial) Psychological Implications from the Early Work

"All this talk about escape!" a psychology graduate student remarked somewhat exasperatedly in a recent class. Her comment betrayed precisely the question and concern with what this all means for psychology and to her as a therapist in training. Truth be told, the question may be one for others as well, a point Dianne Perpich makes when she notes that while "escape" may have been a "watchword" of Levinas's day, in our time, it may "appear . . . as an odd and uncompelling problem" (Perpich, 2008, p. 37). One might even interpret the urgency of this desire in culturo-historical terms, as a consequence of a *mal de siècle* ("world weariness," a word Levinas uses himself in his essay *On Escape*) wrought by World War II and its aftermath. The argument would assume a gulf between the world of Levinas's day and ours, an assumption which is a literal truth, of course. However, in the midst of a lingering worldwide pandemic, a resurgent cold war alongside several hot ones, all with global ramifications, a society wracked by the possibility of erupting gun violence in any school and any commons, and the apocalyptic specter of a climate catastrophe, "world weariness" may well be much less of an "uncompelling problem" to our present. Indeed, the cultural psychologist or socially minded psychoanalyst may read and understand the global rise of authoritarian, fascist, and neo-Nazi sentiments and leaders, as well as the increasing popularity of religious nationalisms precisely as attempts at meaning in the midst of a threatening, uncertain, weary world – as "escapes from freedom," in the sociopsychological understanding of Erich Fromm's (1994), for example, or the ego-psychological defense of the group, as Freud or Bion (Bion, 1989; Freud, 1989) would have it. Levinas's questions are metaphysical, ontological, and existential; they challenge (and may even provide) a certain psychological anthropology such that all this "philosophical" talk about escape has sociological, political, and psychological import, after all. If we can accept a metaphysical and/or ontological desire for transcendence, for escape from being, the displacements of such desire and expressions of refuge are squarely within psychology's concern – as Freud's theogeny or William James's varieties of religious experience already attests to or as the transpersonal peak experience may or the seductions of cults and religious fundamentalists, even the attraction and seduction of conspiracy theories.

Hence, it is precisely at the level of such "fundamentals" that, we argue, the neglected "early work"[13] may be illuminating. Moreover, inasmuch as Heidegger and phenomenology, generally, is an inspirational bedrock for existential-phenomenological psychology and humanistic psychology, Levinas's challenge to Heidegger is also, *ipso facto*, a challenge to some of the core assumptions of these very psychologies.

### Solitude and the Heroic Struggle of/for Existence

Much of existential and humanistic psychology proceed from the recognition of existential solitude. "Only you can live your life," "only you are responsible for you," or even the ready-to-hand social media YOLO response – "you only live once" – are all familiar and everyday expressions precisely of the idea that we, alone, shoulder a responsibility for and to ourselves: to live the most meaningful and "authentic" life for ourselves and to do so by the existential freedom of choice and the agency of our will.

Moreover, in order to do so, authentic Dasein needs to foreswear the inauthentic ways of the "they" (*Das Man*), the "herd," and the everyday. I realize all too well that "Heideggerians" will take issue with the preceding statement: they might offer that one is always "being-with" and that all possibilities for meaning and authenticity are available to us only by the they, that the "world of Dasein is a *with-world* [*Mitwelt*]" (Heidegger, 2001, p. 155), and that authenticity is not a private, isolated, mental operation (Holt, 1999). That is, while one can experience material solitude (the factual solitude of Robinson Crusoe or Henry Thoreau, for example), absolute ontological solitude is not possible; one is always *mitandersein*, with other people. The self (of Dasein) is never alone, even when s/he is; others insinuate themselves in memory, desire, or in our modern virtual world by means of the prosthetics of presence.

And yet for all this talk about being-with, the climate of Heidegger's description leaves one with the clear sense that the other, albeit theorized as an ontological structure for Dasein, practically "plays no role in the drama of being or in the existential analytic" (Levinas, 1987b, p. 40). Existence, for Heidegger, remains "a movement from the inside toward the outside" (Bernasconi, 2005, p. 107) and the message of *Being and Time* is of a relation with an impersonal everyday, with "the they," the crowd, "the mass that surrounds and suffocates me" (Critchley, 2002, p. 12). Ultimately, authenticity and an existentially meaningful and full life comes from the individual struggling in their own solitary way, heroically and resolutely, with their being-in-the-world and in the face of their own pending mortality and the resultant existential anxiety that prompts them to live each day meaningfully as if it was their last – yolo, after all. We recall Sisyphus struggling with his rock, heroically and alone. We have to imagine him happy.

Even the transpersonal psychologists, who some may argue propose a difference – that the self becomes most itself by forgetting itself, or letting go of itself, in a transpersonal peak experience – nonetheless still proceed from the individual who takes this ecstatic experience into its own actualizing journey. The transpersonal experience is absorbed into actualizing insight, such that one can become "all that they can be." As such, it is not Levinasian transcendence. It bears acknowledgment, though, that whereas transpersonal psychology fails a Levinasian litmus for its retained focus on the sovereign self, and the way in which the ego dissolves the alterity of the transpersonal experience by its actualizing incorporation into the ego, it succeeds in catching a glimpse of the Levinasian message in its emphasis on the nature of the experience as embodied sensibility, outside of reason and will. Similarly, when transpersonal psychology says that the experience overcomes one, without notice or warning, it is closer to Levinas than when it says, as it also does, that the experience can be primed, with mindfulness exercises, for example. Of course, we are focusing on the contours of the experience and not on its content or prompt, which also signal a difference in emphasis from Levinas: for the transpersonalists, it is that of nature, beauty, the aesthetic, and not necessarily (even though, less frequently, it may) the human other.

Levinas does not forget or contest individual struggle. In fact, he will say that the existentialists themselves (at least the philosophical ones) tended to focus too much on the despair and abandonment of the existent in existence, in so doing neglecting the sovereignty, pride, and virility of the existent (which the psychological existentialists and the humanistic psychologies [especially], on the other hand, tend to reify to the neglect of the despair). Sensitive, then, to "all the themes of the Romantic and Byronic literature and psychology of proud, aristocratic and genial solitude" (Levinas, 1987b, p. 55), Levinas's crucial difference is in the source and materiality of our solitude. Given by the bodily enchainment of an I to a self, even before there is thought, the fact of identity – of an I that can say I, to paraphrase Derrida – is the materiality of a bodily self emerging from the anonymity of the il y a but from which it cannot escape. As the "indissoluble unity between the existent and its work of existing" (Levinas, 1987b, p. 43), existence is a weight, a suffering.

I sometimes refer to Viktor Frankl (1963), who acknowledges much more deliberately how his experience in the concentration camps informed the eventual existential psychology he ends up with. For him, what the camps revealed was naked existence, and what naked existence revealed was the existential thrust to meaning, even in the midst of the most horrific suffering. The trajectory is of a heroic embrace of one's freedom in the world, to make meaningful choices. Levinas, too, mentions that the camps revealed naked existence and "an exceptional present" dictated by "a new rhythm of life" (Levinas, 2009, pp. 201–203). But what Levinas discovers there is horror. The there is. For Levinas, there is a fundamental, hypostatic solitude, deeper and "prior" to anything the existentialists have theorized (the argument of the early work) and that the escape from that solitude is in the other, also in a way that is deeper and prior to anything that has been theorized (the argument of *Totality and Infinity*, which we turn to shortly).

### Being Towards Death

We've marked Levinas's core objection to the Heideggerian (and existential psychological) being-towards-death. If the motivational anxiety arising from mortality is replaced by the horror of "the condemnation to perpetual reality, to existence with 'no exits'" (Levinas, 2001a, p. 58), what might some of the psychological implications be for this shift?

A response from my own clinical work springs to mind immediately, from a fairly extensive exposure to depressed and suicidal patients. I daresay most therapists who have worked with depressed and suicidal patients will concur that even when the patient or client says, "I want to die," what they are really saying is "I want to stop living." They wish for this life to stop, and to die is but the vehicle they embrace to escape life; they wish to flee their enchainment to the suffering weight of existence. That life will go on without them, this the suicidal person knows. While they cannot know what awaits them in death, they wish that there is no suffering there, albeit at the cost of being able, of knowing anything. As such, the suicidal person mourns, preemptively, such that the tears of suicide are not (only) for the sadness of life as it is (also) for the inability to carry it. "You feel that life has no meaning" is different from "you feel that life is too heavy for you to carry." The emphasis on the patient's desire to leave existence (as opposed to die), as with a sensitivity to the sensibility of the body (which we return to later), effects a fundamental shift in the psychologist's attitude towards the patient. We tend to focus on cognition, reason, the spirit, and the gift of life, such as it is – and the heroic impetus to struggle as Sisyphus did. But in the process, we lose the importance of suffering in the body, of fatigue and insomnia, of the crushing weight in one's bones, effected as it may be by the desire to leave life as opposed to enter death. Yalom, an existential psychotherapeutic flag bearer, notes that suicide offers a certain relief from the terror of death in an act that "permits one to control that which controls one" (Yalom, 1980, p. 122). But there is no control of death, by Levinas's reading; the attempt is much rather to control life by flipping an off switch – an attempt that we've already shown is impossible. The horror is not of death but of life, which we suffer.

The pain of solitude, of existence, is, therefore, not a function of anxiety and nothingness but instead the pain of suffering (in the physical pain and effort of work and the materiality of a body needing to satisfy needs, as well as suffering from the proximity to death). Pain makes one aware of one's inability to escape from existence, and to suffer is to find oneself a stranger to oneself; one desperately wishes to escape the experience of suffering, to not be the person who suffers, knowing at the same time how impossible that wish is for the enchainment of our selves to ourselves. Whether in the physical suffering of torture or the experience of loss of a loved one, say, the wish is not to be this person who suffers, who buries a dead child, whose fate this suffering is. It is the operation of a person who has become a stranger to themself.

## Rooted Embodiment

There has been renewed attention, of late, to embodiment but only after a long period of neglect. Indeed, the separation of soul/mind and body runs like a golden thread through the whole of Western philosophy and religion. In Western philosophy, and at the risk of banal oversimplification, one pole of thought is of the body as an obstacle to be overcome – it "restrains the wings of the spirit or the soul and threatens to confine rationality within the nets of nature and biology" (Critchley, 2015, p. 37). On the other end, the body's importance is highlighted only when it breaks down. In this view, the body is a tool, an instrumentality that comes to the fore for Dasein when it breaks down – a thoroughly Heideggerian move thus. Of course, there were exceptions to this characterization, Merleau-Ponty (2012) being an exemplary case in point, as is Frantz Fanon (2008), for whom the Black and colonial body upends Western ontological assumptions (including that of Merleau-Ponty).[14] Such exceptions notwithstanding, the overriding plot of the Western philosophical story is one where the body is minimized or ignored, in stark contradistinction to Levinas, for whom our bondage to the body is the very advent of consciousness and subjectivity.

Within psychology, one sees again a startling divide between natural science and human science approaches to the importance of corporeality and the body. Whereas human science approaches have paid some attention to the body and materiality, mainstream and natural science psychology, has, for the most part, kept lockstep pace with the larger philosophical omission (except for the last several decades, a localized resurgence which we will explain shortly). Rigorously scholarly appropriations of Merleau-Ponty's thought into an embodied existential phenomenological psychology (e.g. Simms, 2008) and ecopsychology (e.g. Adams, 2023), the theoretical and psychotherapeutic innovations of Eugene Gendlin (1982), and all manner of "body work therapies," unfortunately inclusive of the faddish and outlandish, attest to some corporeal and material attention within human science psychology. Still too little and still on the fringes but attention nonetheless and often serious attention at that, which may provide some compensatory solace. The sidelines of human science psychology, however, are matched by the wholesale erasure of the mainstream naturalistic. Until rather recently.

In natural science psychology, an almost complete dismissal of the body has recently been challenged from "within"; there has been a flurry of activity in the last two or so decades around what has come to be called "embodied cognition" (Barrett, 2017; Barsalou, 2020; Casasanto, 2013). At first glance, such attempts seem remarkably promising, even to the point of crossing the divide between the two psychologies, several embodied cognitivists, for example, drawing inspiration precisely from phenomenology and Merleau-Ponty as they also twiddle and tune their neuroscientific knobs and instruments within a thoroughly natural scientific laboratory. The organizing assumptions of embodied cognition, that cognition or features of it, is shaped by the body, constituted by it, and/or integrated into it, and as such is broader than the brain and/or abstract representation, is certainly one that the human sciences can get behind, support, and agree with. It certainly delivers a blow to Cartesian dualism and one that smarts all the more because it is delivered from within the family, so to speak, as opposed to some weird and wayward human science outsiders. The rub, however, is in its application and narrow(ed) focus. The seduction to narrow perceptual claims, cognitive operations, and the body and mind (as opposed to body and world) impoverishes its promise.

Levinas's message is a radical one and one that comes even before any phenomenological claims. For him, "all dualism between the self and the body must disappear" (Levinas, 1990, p. 68), as the body is the very event of being (Levinas, 2001a) and enchainment to the body "the essential aspect of its humanity." Consciousness arises not from a positing as such, or only, but also from a position, from a place and a space – a concrete setting and localization. The body in space, even as we acknowledge an inwardness and an expressiveness, "does not express an event; it is itself this event" (Levinas, 2001a, p. 70). In sensibility, the body "transforms the impersonal trembling of the il y a into the personal affair of the body" (Cools, 2005, p. 65). It is a relatedness to self *before* language and thought as an unthinking primordial link to the there is.

> To be truly oneself does not mean taking flight once more above contingent events that always remain foreign to the Self's freedom; on the contrary it means becoming aware of the ineluctable original chain that is unique to our bodies, and above all accepting this chaining.
>
> (Levinas, 1990, p. 69)

The parent whose child complains of a sore tummy reaches out to stroke and rub it. It is a consoling caress, focused not so much on a promise to end pain or suffering as much as a concrete attention to the instant of bodily discomfort, which she transports elsewhere by touch and proximity. One could thus imagine a psychology that sees the body woven into systemic social relationships; that acknowledges an anonymous dimension to the body, impermeable to consciousness, a self that does not sit in the body, like a pit in a peach (Eva Simms, personal communication,

February, 2023), but *is* the body and its relationship in space, time, and the social; that acknowledges a perspectival and lacunary knowledge (the self as body is not completely transparent to itself but "sees" from a specific point of view); and that acknowledges the body does not end with the skin but is entwined with the world (Eva Simms, personal communication, February, 2023).

### Rethinking Existence as Gift

As helping professionals, and particularly those within the existential and humanistic psychological orbit, we tend to pay homage to the Heideggerian notion of Being/ Existence as gift. On the surface, indeed, the Heideggerian notion of "es gibt" (as "there is") corresponds to the il y a; it may even be considered nothing more than a simple translation of the term, from the German to the French. But as "an original and binding act of donation" (Davis, 1996, p. 22), *es gibt* (as "it gives")[15] is an act of generosity where Being is given and gifted to Dasein for its care and concern. The extension into psychology is seen in the imperative to live life "authentically" or "purposefully." That is, by the courage of reflexive knowledge of self and the freedom of responsible and meaningful choices, we come to actualize ourselves as beings-in-the-world for whom being is a caring concern. Life, existence, and/or Being is a gift which we honor by purposive, agentic, aware, and courageous actions.

There is, in Levinas's il y a, none of this mood of donation or gift. Levinas's il y a is impersonal and has no concern for the existent – it is existence without existents. Quite laconically, and pointedly, Levinas remarked that "no generosity which the German es gibt is said to express showed itself between 1933 and 1945" (Levinas, 1978, p. 181). If Heidegger's es gibt serve as the backdrop for the Dasein of possibility and power, Levinas's il y a is the ever-present reminder of the limits of the existent's power, "a 'not yet' of possibility" (Sealey, 2013, p. 436). Even more, the il y a contains a certain horror; a menace and insecurity arises from one's absolute exposure to the indeterminacy of existence. "The rustling of there is . . . is horror" (Levinas, 2001a, p. 55), and "rather than the generosity of a radical Giving, il y a is the name of a dark and chaotic indeterminacy that precedes all creativity and goodness" (Peperzak, 1997, p. 3). Existence, or Being, is not a gift but the experience of an undifferentiated, indifferent, enveloping, "malignant world, not because it bears any cruel intentions, but because it is a world viewed from nowhere" (Correia, 2018, p. 96). "Not grace but gravity characterizes the *il y a*, like the weight of the chains that bind one to existence, as Levinas was held in the *Stalag*" (Llewelyn, 1995, p. 24). Enchainment "appears in the form of suffering and invites us to escape . . . to get out of oneself, that is, *to break that most radical and unalterable binding of chains, the fact that the I is oneself*" (Levinas, 1982, p. 55, emphasis in original).

Moreover, for Heidegger, Being shows itself in understanding, preontological as it is, whereas for Levinas, Being is experienced in sensibility and as a breakup of comprehension. As sensibility (an insight that will gain much greater currency in later works), the ego is "swept away" by the disintegration of the divide between "outside or any inside" (Levinas, 2001a). Being is not understood as much as suffered/carried. For Heidegger, Being is the source of meaning and intelligibility; for Levinas, it is a heaviness and weight, the desire from which it is to escape (Ciocan, 2009). Heidegger writes, moreover, that "so long as Dasein exists, which means the factual possibility of an understanding of being, 'is there' being (*"gibt es" Sein*)" (Heidegger, 2001, p. 212, emphasis in original). Hence, the meaning of Being is disclosed by Dasein, given that es gibt (it gives), but without Dasein, the question of Being is meaningless. Clearly, for Levinas, the "there is" *is*, with or without the existent. Again, existence is a weight, a certain weariness, experienced not by thought as much as sensibility – not unlike nausea, shame, insomnia, and horror which are visceral reminders of our bodily captivity and which we do not choose as much as experience. Existential psychology catches a glimpse of this insight in its ontological proposition that "life is hard" and that it takes courage to live. But for Levinas, this is less principle than condition, and the heroic existentialist and humanistic features of the lone individual overcoming existence in authentic or actualizing struggle is patently absent.

The importance for a psychological anthropology and an ontological basis for psychological thought is crucial. For example, as Cohen (2005, p. 110) presents it, Freud "posits libidinal drive but does not explain its ontological origins." Put another way, what motivates the Freudian desire? Existential psychology does heed such ontological motivations but falters for the inspiration of such principles in a "preontological." One could imagine a "Heideggerian" psychological trajectory of the egoic hero, an individual striving to make the meaningful most of his or her individual life in the agentic exercise of selfish freedom ("selfish" is not necessarily used derogatively as much as literally), operating as it does in response to an existential anxiety given by its "ownmost" death. The world is mine to master, even to overcome, as motivating imperative to becoming all that I can be, to finding "my place in the sun" (an excerpt from a quote by Pascal, which Levinas will use as epigraph to *Otherwise than Being* and which I beg the reader to "store away somewhere," as it will reveal itself to greater significance as we proceed). A "Levinasian" trajectory, on the other hand, fractures the ego from the start by its enmeshed and enchained bodily rootedness and (as we will see in the middle and later work) by its motivating formation in the other. The world is mine to grasp only to the extent that I am grasped by it. What matters is not my place in the sun or my death as much as it is the other and the other's death, by which I realize my freedom and by which transcendence is wrought. These statements are, of course, not quite explicated in full yet, both by myself and by Levinas in the early work, but they serve as pointer to the implications of a psychological ontology which would have to be thought differently if we are to take Levinas seriously and which we will continue to circle around and chip away at as we proceed.

### The Fractured Self

There is a clear duality or opposition for Levinas between the I and the self (*moi* and *soi*). As these terms are in common psychological use, some clarification is in order. For Levinas, the ego (*moi*) is consciousness, the intentional subject, while the self (*soi*), on the other hand, is a non-intentional subjectivity, almost. The ego is the autonomous and active subject, aware of its identity and consciously laboring in the world; the self is exposed to the world as a passivity and vulnerability, a relational openness to others and as the "viscous double" of the ego. Truth be told, beside this distinction, Levinas does not provide much of a structural or dynamic exposition; one might argue that that would stereotypically be the task of psychology, really.

It is also worth noting, though, that Levinasian subjectivity is not of a unified subject at peace with itself but is always already split. This is not simply by means of a simple ego and self-distinction. Whereas the I is freed, or frees itself, from anonymous being and is "occupied with itself" and "mired in itself," it is by the material encumbrance of the ego to the oneself that it is never "at home" or "at peace" as such. "Matter is the misfortune of hypostasis" (Levinas, 1987b, p. 58):

> In the identity of the ego (moi), the identity of being reveals its nature as enchainment because it appears in the form of suffering and it is an invitation to evasion . . . the need of going out of itself . . . to break the most radical, most irremissible enchainment, the fact that the ego is itself.
>
> (Levinas, 1982, p. 72)

Identity can never be "whole" or "come home" to itself: "any interiority, upon which one might rest the potential of internal peace, is already an interiority compromised by disruption" (Sealey, 2010, p. 108), already "a function of the very structure of my identity" (p. 109). "One's self is from the start the need to leave oneself . . . Its unity is a disunity" (Llewelyn, 1995, p. 11). If the Western story is of human being as a "thinking thing" – a Cartesian *res cogitans* – it has neglected and missed the "bodily thing" that human being is, as it has the "ethical self-for-the-other." The implication of the existential and humanistic perspective is of the self as sufficient onto itself. Its neglect of the body (and the other) is to valorize reason, spirit, and will as heroic overcoming. Levinas turns all this on its head, saying that dissatisfaction and disquiet is at the heart of subjectivity, that the very enchainment to the body and to existence in suffering prompts a desire to escape, the only possibility of which is in the other (the subject of the next three chapters).

Beside these initial suggestions, there is more, much more, that psychology can attach to in the early work. We have not, for example, explored the ways phenomenological research psychology could benefit from the early work and the exquisite phenomenological analyses of fatigue, indolence, shame, nausea, and/or insomnia. Even as he is concerned with the ontological significance of these phenomena, as opposed to their psychological meaning and structure ("it is not phenomenological to *the end*" [Levinas, 1987b, p. 67, emphasis in original]), Levinas's descriptive analyses are exemplary models of phenomenological scholarship. They are worth reading, also because such descriptive analyses are largely absent from the later work. The point to emphasize is that whereas Levinas's move to transcendence indicated the so-called postphenomenological or marked some kind of exit from phenomenology, he insists on reaching that side without going "outside" the limits and experience of finite being. If the other is decidedly not a phenomenon as much as an enigma, it is the phenomenological struggle that ultimately reveals its limits for the enigmatic beyond. There is much more we are neglecting, both in terms of the work itself as well as the possibility of psychological appropriation and use, but we will have to soothe ourselves with the return of some of those themes and issues in the waves that are the other texts we are to consider and/or the reader's own exploration.[16]

## Readying for *Totality and Infinity*

Towards the end of *Time and the Other*, we start to see the emerging shape of ethics and the other, a glimmer of the landscape that *Totality and Infinity* will populate. It is worth noting again, as does Bernasconi (2005), that in these early works, Levinas was not looking for ethics but transcendence, and yet, "when he discovered the meaning of transcendence, it turned out that it was indeed ethics" (Bernasconi, 2005, p. 101). In a sense, ethics is the concretization of transcendence. At the end of *Time and the Other*, even as the other now figures in a way that it hasn't quite before, the transcendence Levinas finds there is not quite ethical yet: it is ontological (Giannopoulos, 2019). If Levinas attempts to surpass Heidegger's "ontological difference" between Being and being, it will be in this very difference, in this breach of being, that the other person will appear to turn ontology into ethics. Without the other, existence remains solitary, without exit or escape (Purcell, 2006), indeed without time or a future.

The early work presents subjectivity as an essential solitude, an ego emerging from the il y a, realizing its power and sovereignty to engage with the work of existing, even as it does so under the weight of existence and in suffering. It seeks reprieve and escape in enjoyment, love, and toil and is a sketch of the ego as existing for the "subject alone, alone due to the very fact that it is an existent" (Levinas, 1987b, p. 67). Much of this early conception will be reworked, even taken back. But what is not returned to but never retracted or modified to any great extent is the il y a, which Levinas will call the "morceau de resistance" (the most important part of the whole) of his early work. In *Totality and Infinity*, the lonely rumbling of the there is will be pierced by the face of the other.

## Notes

1   Even as they were the only ones to be published in book form, Levinas also published a number of influential and important essays and articles during this "early period." The interested reader would be well served exploring some of those as well, especially *On Escape* (1982/1935), *Reflections on the Philosophy of Hitlerism* (1990/1934), and *Is ontology fundamental?* (1989/1951). The latter is an excellent preparatory reading for the student about to tackle the imposing *Totality and Infinity*. In some ways, one might even characterize it as a yoke of sorts between the early and so-called mature works.

2 Again, however, let us retain a healthy suspicion of quick divisions and categories lest we run the risk of losing a certain continuity, or being deaf to an echo that may sound across the oeuvre. A messiah need not be named to be foretold.

3 Jacques (2017), for example, argues that the conditions of captivity progressively erode subjectivity to the extent that the prisoner is left with a glimpse, if not an experience, of just that impersonal existence which is the centerpiece of *Existence and Existents,* the "there is." By this insight, one could argue that even as Levinas says nothing directly in this book about his time in the camps, everything he says is also about life in the camps.

4 Wahl in fact studied at Freiburg with Levinas in that strange year that had them attend Husserl's last formal class and Heidegger's first. They most likely met there for the first time (Moyn, 2005). Wahl had already completed his dissertation, under the direction of Henri Bergson (whom we've mentioned was also profoundly important to Levinas's thinking), and was well on his way to a successful academic career. Wahl's story makes for quite remarkable reading, a few dramatic highlights of which include a daring escape from Paris during the war (being Jewish, albeit secular and nonobservant, he could not retain his position at the Sorbonne), across several German checkpoints, to a remote location in Bayonne, close to the Spanish border. He would make the return journey to Paris when the Vichy government reopened schools and universities to hold lecture meetings in a hotel room with his students (as a Jew, he was still excluded from teaching), where, eventually, the Gestapo arrested him, having gotten wind of this arrangement. It is said that Wahl laconically remarked, "It will not hurt to say that we are studying Heidegger," which they were. Wahl was interred, and tortured, at La Sante prison from where he was sent to Drancy, which some readers may recognize as the staging ground for Klaus Barbie's deportations to Auschwitz. Wahl escaped from Drancy, again in dramatic manner. While incarcerated, Wahl was appointed as a faculty member of the New School in New York (an attempt mostly to save European and Jewish academics), which led to his name being put on a list of prisoners to be released; however, this order came on the same day that another list appeared which his name was also on – a list of public enemies to be shot. In the confusion between which list to follow, Wahl was spirited away by strangers in the trunks of cars and an empty butcher's cart, wrapped in meat sacks, to finally sprint across a field for two miles in order to catch a ship from Marseilles to Casablanca and then onwards to New York. After the war, Wahl returned to his position at the Sorbonne and started the College Philosophique. An inspiration to many (Derrida was Wahl's research assistant, for example, and Deleuze his protégé), Wahl's influence is vastly underrated and underappreciated. Consider that Wahl delivered a lecture in 1937, which Levinas attended, about subjectivity and transcendence – a lecture which Levinas simply called "the famous lecture" and which in some ways set the stage for Levinas's entire project. Schrift and Moore (2017) provide an excellent introduction for English speakers to Wahl's work.

5 *Existence and Existents* also takes issue with several key insights of Husserl and phenomenology, generally. For our purposes, however, we omit attention to that engagement, focusing instead on Heidegger more closely, notably given his closeness to existential psychology and existential phenomenology. As such, the forceful language of this oft quoted sentence must concede more than an abstract, theoretical, and philosophical difference. Heidegger's Nazi sympathies, the ill treatment of his (Jewish) mentor, Husserl, and his silence on the Nazi treatment of Jews had by now become common knowledge among his students and colleagues. The psychologist must and will read this statement of Levinas's as an overdetermined one. Furthermore, If *Existents and Existents* heralds a need to leave Heidegger, *Time and the Other* articulates an even more ambitious desire, to "break with Parmenides" (p. 42), which is to break with Western philosophy as such (Parmenides is considered the "father of Western philosophy").

6  For many commentators, the il y a is Levinas's most outstanding contribution of the early work, and even as he rarely refers to it by name or explicitly in his later "mature" work, it remains foundationally true for him. On several interview occasions, asked why he never returned to the il y a again, the response was of a sort that indicated it as a given, a foundational truth established and no longer in need of further elaboration.

7  The source for this common phrase is often given as a poem, from 1909, which gives expression, precisely, to this menacing character: "From ghoulies and ghoosties, long-leggety beasties, and things that go//bump in the night, good Lord, deliver us!" (Noyes, 2016).

8  It is worth noting that this passage was written more than a decade before Merleau-Ponty's seminal work on embodiment, *Phénoménologie de la perception* (Phenomenology of Perception), was published in 1945.

9  As with Derrida, Levinas will often use words that seem strange at first sight or even contrary to everyday usage. This is occasionally the consequence of a translator's choice, to be sure, but more often than not, the word is deliberate for its etymological meaning or as in a dictionary, the second or third "alternative" meaning other than the common or everyday one. Inasmuch as "salvation" might qualify here, its meaning as *salvare* – to save – might offer some insight – that is, how the existent is to be saved, or save itself, from the weight of existence.

10 Whereas we are not focused on it, given our particular emphasis, death is an important pivot for Levinas in the promulgation of time and the other. Death is never present, is never now – if it was, I no longer am. I can master the now, grasp the present in action, but death is always of a to come, a future. The future, like death, cannot be grasped and is always a surprise in spite of its anticipation in the present. But inasmuch as one cannot enter into a relationship with death in the present, the other as wholly other, like death, is what we can enter into a present relationship with. As futurity becomes an element of time, it only does so in the gap between present and future, a gap that can be accomplished in the face-to-face with the other. "The other is the future. The very relationship with the other is the relationship with the future" (Levinas, 1987b, p. 77); hence, the book's aim is realized to demonstrate how time is of the other and not the achievement of the lone, virile existent.

11 One can take issue with Levinas here and argue that he misreads Freud or have not read enough of Freud. For example, libido is but a component of Eros's energy and certainly not the whole as Levinas implies. And if one brings Thanatos onto the scene, an argument can even be made for Thanatos in terms of the il y a, or the elemental, as this pull to nothingness that persists as a motivation for existence, rather similar to Levinas's double burden of existence.

12 The inevitable question is of those who do not have children. Whether Levinas thought a response as clearly in 1947 as he did in 1985, where the quote is from, may be open to debate but is offered as such nonetheless: "It is not necessary that those who have no children see in this fact any depreciation whatever; biological filiality is only the first shape filiality takes; but one can very well conceive filiality as a relationship between human beings without the tie of biological kinship" (Levinas, 1985, pp. 70–71).

13 Whereas our claim of neglect still holds true for psychology, we've noticed an uptick of attention to the early work in philosophy in the last few years and especially for the recognition of the relationship and links to the later, specifically *Otherwise than Being*.

14 We return, all too briefly, to Fanon in Chapter 8.

15 If the non-German speaker enters the phrase "it gives" followed by "there is" into an electronic translator, they may find it rendered – in both cases – as "es gibt"! Things are, though, more complicated. Borrowing an example from a colleague, Eva Simms (personal communication, December, 2022), one could say in colloquial German, "*Es gibt heute Suppe*," which means "There is/there will be soup today." One could also say,

"*Hier gibt es doch noch Blauwale,*" which means "There is/are still blue whales here" (even though you may not see them). One could argue, in a generous reading, that the Heideggerian es gibt has the quality of a transcendent beyond being, but there is none-theless a clear sense of donation and a resultant indebtedness of Dasein as such – the it (es) which gives (gibt) is being itself.

16 Salanskis (2010) provides an elegant description of *Existence and Existents* (which I would also apply to *Time and the Other*): "This little book published in 1947 is quite surprising, not least because in some mysterious way it is not a 'little book' at all. When you read it just for the fun, you feel exhilarated by the speed and the far-reaching beauty of what you discover. And you only feel frustrated when you realize, shortly after, that you forgot almost everything . . . Then you understand why you were not able to keep the information in mind. . . . It is an encyclopedic essay" (Salanskis, 2010, p. 51).

# Chapter 5

# Totality and Infinity
## Indictment and Promise

*Totality and Infinity* (Levinas, 2013) is without doubt the cornerstone text from which Levinas's distinguishing reputation as a "philosopher of ethics" is derived. If the previous chapter painted an anonymous "there is" from which an I emerges by hypostasis into a burdened, riveted existence, *Totality and Infinity* sets out first to explore how the I "works toward interiority, separation, and autonomy" (Capili, 2011, p. 680). As such, Levinas's characterization of the text, as "a defense of subjectivity" (Levinas, 2013, p. 26), makes intuitive sense. There will be a twist in the tale, though, a disturbance in the primed expectation to think subjectivity in egoic terms, as the Odyssean journey of a sovereign and independent self. Levinas's argument will unfold to demonstrate that the self is a function of the other, "founded in the idea of infinity" (p. 26). We'll proceed deliberately to that plot's unfolding.

Having mentioned ethics and its powerful appearance here in a way it did not in the earlier texts of the previous chapter, it is worth noting that *Totality and Infinity* is the text other disciplines (education, nursing, theology and religious studies, communication studies, as well as psychology, for example), seeking some or other form of translation or application of Levinas's thought into their own professional and academic fields, seem to rely on most. One could also say it is Levinas's most "popular" book, if with popular we mean quite simply most read or "bestseller." Another perspective on "popular" might also be read in the (seemingly) light-hearted comment of a colleague's when I asked him about his teaching emphasis of *Totality and Infinity*: "No one has read or heard of *Existence and Existents* or *Time and the Other*, and no one can understand *Otherwise than Being*, forget about teaching it. At least with *Totality and Infinity*, I have a fighting chance of ending the semester with the same number of students that started it."

Regardless of how we understand *Totality and Infinity*'s importance to interdisciplinary translation, there is the real danger of a certain migratory ruin; the radical thought proposed in this bold and daring text is often tempered (or violated) in appropriative translation. Selective concepts or insights are exploited out of context, while its nuanced complexity is frequently trivialized into some banal humanism or heroic empathy or worse still, "practical" "how-to" suggestions. We are not arguing for some elusive or elitist purity. The very project of this book is precisely

DOI: 10.4324/9781003315612-5

one of translation and migration, of selective appropriation, and of blurring, cross-ing, or even erasing disciplinary boundaries; but the hospitality of welcome has to show respectful fidelity to that which arrives. To demand that the stranger on our shore learn our language and assimilate to our ways, or to appropriate the stran-ger's arrival to our own ends without putting ourselves in question, without being questioned, is not to welcome at all but to colonize, to oppress, and to betray the generosity of our invitation. It is to mold and make the other into our image, into the same, which is in fact the very *j'accuse* of Western philosophy and knowledge systems levelled in the book itself.

Let us proceed carefully and deliberately, then. And let us set the scene first before we open the text to the promise of its riches – in a way heeding the advice of the most accomplished hosts and event planners, who will say that the most successful gatherings are those which have carefully been prepared for well in advance of the guests' arrival and the band striking up the tune to mark its com-mencement. The event starts long before it does.

## Totality and Infinity: Gathering the Text

Given the landmark importance of this book, it may come as somewhat of a surprise to readers that it was initially rejected for publication by the prestigious French publisher, Gallimard. We've mentioned before that Levinas was outside the aca-demic mainstream; in fact, he had pretty much resigned himself to a nonacademic career (Moore & Schrift, 2017). Recall that in the late 1950s, when Levinas wrote *Totality and Infinity*, he had been a teacher and school principal, an administrator, for a little over 30 years already – well outside the rarefied halls of the French university as well as that peculiar (and quite enviable, I confess) French adulation of the intellectual.[1] Yet while Levinas was certainly not part of the academic in-group, he stayed in touch – as best he could – with the intellectual and philosophi-cal developments and debates of the day. Perhaps more than any other, though – at least to all practical and material intents – it was the person of Jean Wahl (whom we've already come across in previous chapters) who provided a sustained connec-tion to the academy. A frequent visitor to the Levinas home, Wahl was already an accomplished professor of philosophy at the famed Sorbonne, a valued friend, and an intellectual sparring partner and sounding board.

After *Totality and Infinity* was rejected for publication, Wahl reached out to his dejected and disappointed friend, offering an alternative to Levinas's threat to rip the manuscript to shreds (Malka, 2006): defending it as a thesis for his *Doctorat D'Etat* instead. Thus, it was that Levinas, already in his mid-50s, well beyond the age for most scholars taking this examination, faced up to a committee of philosophical luminaries to defend this thesis, the rejected manuscript of *Totality and Infinity*. In addition to Wahl, the examining committee included Gabriel Marcel, Paul Ricoeur, Georges Blin, and Vladimir Jankelevitch.[2] Of everything that was said at that doc-toral defense, the prescient first and last words arguably belong to Wahl, who wel-comed the committee, saying that they were there "to evaluate a thesis about which other theses will be written" (Malka, 2006, p. 153). It was Levinas's success at the *Doctorat* that paved the way for the publication of *Totality and Infinity* in 1961 and Levinas's entry, late as it was, into the French university system. That the book was dedicated to Jean Wahl and his wife, Marcelle, makes considerable sense for the debt of friendship and academic mentorship Levinas felt owed to them.

Many commentators and professors present the text to their readers and students with a trigger warning of sorts – almost like the caution or mandatory public announcement of danger on cigarette packages. The warning is that the text, important and groundbreaking as it is, is also tremendously difficult and challenging, even for those students and scholars steeped in philosophy and/or familiar with its disciplinary grammar. I will add to that choir, and similarly proceed to acknowledge the daunting difficulty of the text, but certainly not in the manner of a caution to keep out or keep away – quite the opposite. If there is some similarity to the notions of addiction and danger of the cigarette warning, this is a fulfilling addiction to the radical danger of the good. Even so, by the wisdom of forewarned being forearmed, it behooves us to examine, briefly, what about the text makes it so challenging.

Firstly, the book is densely written, as well as liberally reliant on metaphor and allusion; added to which Levinas often uses language and terms in a novel manner, against the grain of the usual and expected. Words and terms we think we know, or are familiar with – the face, desire, infinity, ethics, for example – will be put to creative use (the face is *not* the signified referent of everyday usage, though it also is, or could be!), or in some cases, used in terms of an "earlier" etymological meaning, or to denote the second or third "alternative" meaning of a word in a dictionary definition. Right at the beginning of the text, for example, Levinas writes that "The true life is absent. But we are in the world. Metaphysics arises and is maintained in this alibi" (Levinas, 2013, p. 33). One might be inclined to respond to the word "alibi" in terms of its everyday understanding, as an excuse or defense, as in "What's your alibi?" or "Do you have an alibi for the night of the crime?" The sentence certainly works by this understanding – "metaphysics arises and is maintained in this '*excuse*,'" which is to say this reasoned articulation of a certain motivation, of a certain position, within the tension between the competing truths of the absent true life and the fact of our worldliness. One could also, however, add the etymological meaning of the word to alibi – alibi meaning "elsewhere" – so that the sentence, reread as "metaphysics arises and is maintained in this '*elsewhere*,'" opens up another layer of meaning and understanding. Now quite straightforwardly, metaphysics comes from "elsewhere," beyond the material to nonetheless haunt our lives, "here below." There are numerous such instances in the text, and my advice is often if you think you know the word, but it does not quite feel or look "right" in the sentence or if it just "feels" as if there can be "more there," to go back to a descriptive or etymological dictionary – often that is enough to open thought to an excess, to more than is apparent or revealed.

Part of the reason Levinas uses words in such peculiar and novel ways pertains to the fact that his goal is no less than to upend and reconfigure a philosophical tradition, and to do so, the grammar and conventions of traditional philosophical discourse often will not do (Mensch, 2015). As psychologists and helping professionals, for example, we sometimes write reports about patients – to colleagues in the field, insurance agencies, or the courts, say. We write those reports in a generalized and uniform way, using terms understood and agreed upon for their meaning within the discipline. We also know, though, that those reports don't come close to describing the experience of the patient's pain or the course of therapy. For that, truth be told, a poem might be more appropriate, attempting as it does to express what falls outside of language and commonality. Levinas's struggle is not necessarily to express the specificity of an individual's experience; he is still working within a broad philosophical regimen and system. But he is similarly faced with the fact that his "new," his "otherwise," has no language, or the words that it does have are inadequate to the phenomena he wishes to describe – transcendence, infinity, an unknowable elsewhere, absolute alterity and difference, for example. Hence, he has to invent a new language, and he has to make words do what they would not ordinarily. (Describing his own similar desire, Jacques Derrida provides a beautiful image appropriate to Levinas's aim here; Derrida says he aims to write like a rider on a horse directs it to dressage. Whereas such surprising and uncommon movements do not ordinarily happen in the everyday, the horse is clearly capable of it and, on occasion, may surprise itself [and others] by its occurrence – whether by all of an accident, an inspiration, and/or a cultivation by the rider.) Having referenced Jacques Derrida in parentheses, we may as well linger with him some more, for a beautiful, sinuous, and winding quote (referenced in the endnote)[3] with which he describes Levinas's project in *Totality and Infinity*. It is not uncommon, Derrida says, for a philosopher to announce the end of philosophy, to boldly charge that everyone before got it wrong. But it is precisely by such challenges and new questions that philosophy has a future; by announcing the death of philosophy, paradoxically, is opened the possibility of a philosophy to come. In this regard, "the thought of Emmanuel Levinas can make us tremble" (Derrida, 1978, p. 91). There is a lesson here for psychology, as an aside. We do not quite announce our disciplinary deaths (except when we crucify Freud, perhaps) as philosophy is wont to. In fact, quite the opposite – we revel in the youthful virility of our discipline in a way that borders on arrogance or omnipotent delusion. But psychology's virility may well be a function of its sterility – like a eunuch, who rises to power and is powerful by the mark of his castration. Like youth, it often presumes to do and know everything, even that which, echoing Donald Rumsfeld, it does not know it does not know.

The implications of Levinas's new and radical challenge to thought also extends to the organization of the book. Browsing the table of contents, one might presume a clear and neat organization into divisions and sections. The arguments in the book, however, are not as neat or linear at all. Honestly, it is rather "unsystematic." Sections will revisit themes from earlier ones and/or present them in different contexts; conclusions will be presented without the argument, which may come later; analyses seem to have a provisional character; and terms are used differently in different contexts and sections. Moreover, terms are often opaque, or cryptic, when they make their first appearance. To illustrate the latter, a striking example is the first time the word "ethics," this crucial and fundamental term, appear in the book: it is simply "dropped" in the sentence "*ethics is an optics*" (Levinas, 2013, p. 23), which is not explained or expanded upon at all. "Ethics is an optics" What on earth could that mean? Let us reiterate and emphasize: this is not because Levinas is not a systematic thinker or because he is unable to present a linear or systematic argument. Listening to or reading the transcripts of interviews about his work would dispel such a suspicion out of hand, as he is supremely clear, systematic, and organized in his responses there. But the manner of the text's presentation is part and parcel of its message; the text performs the message, if you will. It is like this spiraling said, which invites a response and new said, such that there is never a last word. Indeed, for Levinas, this is the very heart of teaching in general, which has to proceed through conversation (from the Latin *conversare*, which is to take turns; to turn with [*con*] an other, as in a dance). As long as the conversation continues, what is said is not the last word. There is a new speaking, questions are raised and answered, and the person who utters something can come to its defense upon the response to it; it is not defenseless like the words of a printed text. As in a conversation as well, a term, a concept, a thought can be held to the light of different angles and times. All of this is what Levinas aims for in a written text, such that – it is clear – the text is not to be read in a linear manner, from a to z, nor with the expectation that one will "get it" upon the first, or even subsequent, reading(s).

Moreover, as if the task is not difficult enough, another consequence of the attempt to reconfigure the Western philosophical tradition is that Levinas assumes some knowledge of that tradition without spelling it out. A familiarity with the history of philosophy, and especially the works of Husserl and Heidegger, are assumed and taken for granted. This is a particularly challenging assumption and demand for psychologists and nonphilosophers who may not have been exposed to the language, concepts, and tradition Levinas assumes without too much mention or explanation. Whereas we will provide pointers to that tradition, we will provide just enough background for his writing to make sense.

In the preceding chapter, we tarried some with the title of the text we examined there. We do the same with *Totality and Infinity: An Essay on Exteriority* – as pithy an encapsulation of the project as it obscures the project by its somewhat enigmatic phraseology. Imagine, if you will, walking into a bookstore in the sixties or early seventies – even today – and simply by looking at the titles on the spine of the books, you see *Totality and Infinity: An Essay on Exteriority*. What would you think the book is about? The words are certainly familiar; you have a basic sense of the meanings of infinity, and as a psychologist, you even have a conceptual sense of exteriority. As for totality – well, one can form a reasonable suspicion as to what it might mean. But together, joint and juxtapositioned, what might this title mean or signify? We venture being stumped is more the rule than the exception.

On the one hand, and quite simplistically, as a preview of sorts, Levinas will characterize the whole of Western philosophy through the notion of totality, against which he will argue an infinity or transcendence that has been suppressed by that tradition (Peperzak, 1993). The very same can be said about psychology. So without "knowing what it is, necessarily," Western philosophy – this love of wisdom, this search for truth – will be characterized by a certain manner, a certain way of knowing that is of a totalizing sort and which, as a consequence, neglected and oppressed and marginalized another kind of truth, another kind of "knowing," namely, that of transcendence, deriving/arriving as it does from infinity. As another heads-up, Levinas will also use the terms the same and the other to characterize, and at times, to stand in for, the terms totality and infinity; hence, totality and the same are linked, and infinity and the other are linked. Additionally, he will concretize these terms so that totality and the same find expression in a monopolistic ego, an interiorizing I, while infinity and the other are revealed in the human face of the not-I person, exterior to the self. The title, then, would signal a project that examines totality, the same, the egoic I, on the one hand (an examination that is familiar to Western knowledge systems, including psychology, and in fact the stock, trade, and hallmark of Western knowing), while on the other hand, there is infinity and the transcendent other, exterior to the self (a story and examination which is not familiar to Western knowledge systems and has in fact never been fundamental or central to serious inquiry).

Even an examination of "and" in the title is instructive. Truthfully, some of the most accomplished scholars sometimes fall into one or two traps. Some characterize the text too harshly as opposition, as if it is really totality *or* infinity, as if Levinas is proposing a substitution of totality by infinity. That is, we have gotten it wrong by our totalizing emphasis, which we need to replace now with infinite transcendence. In the opposition of "heaven and hell," say, one has more value than the other, and our lives – it may be argued – are more meaningfully informed were we to focus on the rewards of heaven than the punishments of hell, for example. Others, in a second move, go to great lengths to say it is not the one or the other, it is totality *and* infinity, and you cannot have the one without the other; the one needs the other and the other needs the one. The danger of this argument, pressed deliberately to the order of a caricature, is in the temptation of equivalence; in saying that the "and" equalizes, one may be tempted to assume them qualitatively similar in the sense of an opposite – black and white, man and woman, light and dark, I and thou. They are alike by some unifying term by which difference or alterity can be adjudicated; hence, length distinguishes short and tall or luminescence light and dark. This is not what *Totality and Infinity* is about at all. As is so often the case in Levinas's writing, even the simple and seemingly apparent holds much in reserve and overflows its presentation. The "and" here, in *Totality and Infinity*, is *not* of equivalence *nor* is it a statement of opposites; it is of terms wholly different and exterior to each other yet joined asymmetrically by, and in, experience, space, and time. As in air and sea, maybe, or sand and oxygen – two seemingly completely different terms, but nonetheless *one in the other*, as "and." As it is, these completely different terms are really unrepresentable, as is the relationship between them, but we only have recourse in language to the impoverished option of an "and."

Finally, the oft neglected phrase after the colon ("An Essay on Exteriority") presents another sticky wicket, to perform a similar obfuscation in plain sight by deliberately using a metaphor we assume largely unfamiliar to a North American audience. If this is to be an essay on exteriority, of that which is exterior to us (infinity, the other [person]), what are we to make of Levinas's early insistence in the very first few pages that this is a book, above all, that will be "a defense of subjectivity"? How is an essay on what is exterior to us simultaneously a statement, a defense, of whom we are as subjects and of subjectivity itself? Before we tackle this question head-on, or rather, in order to tackle this question, let us first circle around it, perhaps to size it up strategically, as a wrestler would in the moments before contact and direct engagement, precisely to ensure "better" contact and engagement. As such, we identify some fundamental notions developed and/or addressed in *Totality and Infinity*, both for its usage in psychology and for the ways Levinas will trouble such usage.

## Transcendence

Levinas's interest in transcendence was already apparent in the early work, examined in the previous chapter, as this wish to surpass and reach beyond the physical and material circumstances of existence to "something other than ourselves" (Levinas, 1982, p. 3) – a desire, that is, to escape from being. We saw the movement of this reaching elsewhere, from the early articulations of need, nourishment, work, and knowledge as possible attempts at transcendence, to articulations of Eros, fecundity, and the birth of the child. Now in *Totality and Infinity*, transcendence will receive the fullest account yet, indeed as the very mark of our existence, located outside of ourselves (exteriority), in the other person. In ethics. In a sense, and echoing Bernasconi (2005), Levinas arrives at the shores of ethics, which "was not his starting-point, nor what he was aiming at, but was what he found at the end of his journey of discovery" (p. 35). Put differently, inasmuch as Levinas's interest was in the meaning of transcendence, what he found was that meaning to be ethics.

The anthropological and religio-spiritual archive provide ample descriptions of a human yearning for a transcendent beyond as well as the godly riches of that beyond, promised to human being here below, provided s/he meets certain thresholds of conduct and character. Whether Valhalla and Folkvangr, elysian fields or Hades, the communion of the ancestors, heaven or hell, the vision quest world or nirvana, there certainly seems to be some thematically consistent touchpoints to this desire for a transcendent world beyond, as well as some linkage of that or those worlds to the real of an existing present in this world. The narrative plot seems built around the tension that there is, firstly, a (world) beyond, the (non)location, description, and content of which we've either inherited from some timeless, authorless past or which we can only imagine, wish, or intuit from the words and visions of a prophet or the enlightened and extraordinary testimony of some inspired traveler claiming wisdom or experience of both. Secondly, access to this beyond is available to us by a particular means and manner: from the infinite distance of a heavenly paradise or karmic return, to the somewhat closer community of a shining city on a hill, or the even closer and individually enveloping possibilities of transcendence in a blade of grass or the soul of the white ant.[4] Yet for all its distance, the question of entry to that beyond is nonetheless a continually pressing one for the concrete and experiential everyday: "Where or how in the world might we find transcendence within experience?" (Richardson, 2014, p. 359) or "How should I live in the world in order to experience transcendence?" In many ways, stripped to its fundamental core, these are the questions running through the whole long story, whether that story is of Valkyries, Greek ideal forms, bodhisattvas, vision quests, or all kinds of travelers to Damascus, struck by an experience and insight not of this world. As questions about experience and about concrete behavior in the world, these are eminently psychological questions, notwithstanding the discipline's seeming pretense that it is not. It behooves us, therefore, as we proceed, and as we open ourselves to Levinas's challenge, to remind ourselves of just how we, in psychology, tend to view this issue and these questions.

## Psychology and Transcendence

There are clear disciplinary differences to the question of transcendence as a focus of study. Theology or religious studies may approach transcendence with a view to the role of the divine therein and anthropology or sociology to the organization thereof within cultural and social life and practice. For psychology, the framing of transcendence in terms of desire already renders it of importance, quite simply and fundamentally. But in addition, given its interest in the individual and the self, the question of the self transcending itself, of self-transcendence, must be within the locus of its concern, even if this means modifying the broader, more stereotypical philosophical interest; rather than the imagined "philosophical" question, "What is transcendence?" the psychological question would become "What is self-transcendence?" or "What/How is it for the self to transcend itself?" A keen reader may register a philosophical objection here: "How can you ask about self-transcendence without asking about transcendence, one of the key terms of your inquiry?" To which psychology might reply that it is a false challenge, as there is no removed, disembodied meaning to transcendence, which can only show itself through the self reporting on itself. We believe both statements true, as we imagine Levinas does and whom we will see traverses this stereotypical disciplinary squabble quite adroitly. As a philosopher, he is certainly interested in thinking the meaning of transcendence, but he is as, and sometimes even more, concerned with transcendence as a feature of the concrete, lived everyday.

Not altogether surprisingly, the manner of psychology's interest in transcendence – including that it is interested in the first place – falls out quite markedly along the prior distinction we've made between psychology as a natural science and psychology as a human science. Thematically, we can identify three broad approaches to self-transcendence. The first stance is really one of dismissal and denial. A mainly naturalistic position, this view historically holds that psychology has no traffic with such experiences, as they are, firstly, not available to rigorous experimental study and fails the rubric standards of scientific predictability, measurability, replicability, observation, falsifiability, or experimental controls. Relatedly, by the early association of the transcendent experience with religion, mysticism, or spirituality, the clear feeling was that the experience, even if it did "exist," belonged in the ambit and bailiwick of religion, history, or anthropology – *not* psychology. Because the phenomenon cannot be formulated in naturalistic scientific terms, it is "essentially considered out of bounds, beyond the purview of science" (Freeman, 2014, p. 323) and, by extension, beyond the purview of psychology which fashions itself a science. Moreover, inasmuch as the experience, even if it did exist, is not "normal," "typical," or "characteristic" of human being, gesturing more towards the abnormal, the psychotic, the hallucinatory aberrant, and the dysfunctional extraordinary, there is no real need to study it specifically, as there is ample theoretical precedent for the explanation of abnormality. It may be good and well for theology to believe that a burning bush can speak in the voice of God, but to the clinical psychologist or psychiatrist who hears reports every other day of God speaking through light fixtures or by adopting the form of a squirrel or a cat, the truth of God's audible voice is more accessibly that of pathology and misaligned neurotransmitters. Even the psychologist whose client may be the creative genius who produces his most resplendent work in moments of blinding "transcendence" is also the client who happens to cut off his ear and ultimately kills himself. But we also don't need imaginative and imaginary Dutch artists to make our argument; we can simply open our DSM-5s, where some of the features of the psychologically transcendent experience have been codified symptomatically as depersonalization/derealization disorder, an admittedly more subtle extension of the Group for the Advancement of Psychiatry's (1976) description of mystics as suffering from borderline psychosis. There are, of course, attempts to distinguish the psychotic experience from the transcendent, as we will see later; the point here is simply that there is clear precedent for psychological agnosticism vis-à-vis (self) transcendence for the aberrant and the messy limits of its borders and for policing those borders to prevent smuggling the divine or the "nonpsychological" in through the back door, so to speak.

Recapitulating the dual psychologies narrative, the second thematic approach to transcendence occurs within human science psychological approaches and in fact threads to the patriarchal beginnings of that divide, notably with William James (1982), whose seminal lectures on *The Varieties of Religious Experience* (1982) provides one of the first imperatives for psychology to take transcendence seriously. The well-documented experiences of mystic and religious experiences suggest, James argued, that "normal waking consciousness" is but one kind among others, which we, as psychologists and scientists, are beholden to examine in order to provide a fuller account of human being and experience. We can follow, from James, this human science interest for the rest of the century through the existential psychology of Viktor Frankl (1964, 1965), the humanistic and transpersonal psychologies of Abraham Maslow (1968) and Ken Wilber (Wilber et al., 1986;

Wilber & Wilber, 2000), and in some fashion to the current positive psychology of Seligman and Csikszentmihalyi (2000) as well as the wildly resurgent contemporary interest in psychedelic therapy (e.g. Pollan, 2019).

In his description of the "peak experience," and the later proposition of a transpersonal "stage" beyond that of self-actualization, Abraham Maslow invokes the notion of transcendence quite directly. Hearkening back to William James's descriptions of the mystical experience, as well as his own,[5] Maslow first decouples the experience from religion; it is in fact available to all, everywhere, and need not involve a religious component whatsoever. Rebranded as the peak experience, these are intense, transient, unexpected experiences of deep joy and very strong or deep positive emotions akin to ecstasy, a deep sense of peacefulness or tranquility, feeling attuned to the universe and oneself. These experiences are automatic (passive) in that they surprise and "overcome" one and may arise from involvement in any number of activities – athletics, sex, listening to music, viewing art, being in nature, traveling, smelling the ocean, cookies, freshly cut grass. Fully absorbed in the experience, senses of time and space are distorted; one's embodied anchor is lost in an "out-of-body" experience, devoid of distress or anxiety, free of fear or uncertainty, and involving "unifying cognitions of objects in-the-world in relation to self-as-processes" (Maslow, 1968, p. 71). The memory of the experience is lasting, detailed, and held to be dear and intensely meaningfully, no least for the gift of a feeling of deeper knowing or profound understanding, difficult or impossible to describe adequately in words (i.e. it has an ineffable quality). The sense of self is expanded beyond the ordinary definitions and self-image of the individual personality, allowing a comprehensive, felt "knowledge" (experience) of a fundamental connection, harmony, or unity with others and the world. For Maslow, such experiences demonstrate the pinnacle of consciousness and optimal states of human functioning. They allow a reflecting mirror of sorts to what is possible for the actualizing individual – "the peak experience is an inner glimpse of self-actualizing potentialities, like opening a door to a room full of hidden treasures that one did not know existed" (Sollod et al., 2009, p. 414). The experience is consequently an inherently positive experience, a source of growth and development towards the "real me." These are not dissociative or pathological states; they are precisely integrative, positive, and without distress to self or others and, by the qualities described earlier, are patently and obviously distinguishable from the pathological by its wholly health-enhancing consequences and possibilities.

It is from this experience that Maslow would elaborate and extend his already popular theory of actualization to suggest a superordinate and final level of development – that of the transpersonal need for self-transcendence as the pinnacle of human development, one where we come to the highest knowledge of self, paradoxically by "losing" the self (well, temporarily). The "self" which is transcended is an egoic constellation of roles, images, and ideals we've been socialized into believing whom we "are" or how we need to be in order to be accepted and respected, even loved; it is not the same as one's "true" or "actual" nature and essence. One can easily see how various strands of ecopsychology would find this attractive as self-transcendence opens one to the experience of a deeper nature, one "centered in the cosmos rather than in human needs and interest, going beyond humanness, identity, self-actualization, and the like" (Maslow, 1968) towards "an expanded range of human experience and potential . . . a spectrum of states of consciousness including true 'higher' states and even enlightenment or liberation" (Walsh & Vaughan, 1980, p. 8). The foundational premise of transpersonal psychology, as the *Journal of Transpersonal Psychology* suggests, is its concern "with the study of humanity's highest potential, and with the recognition, understanding, and realization of unitive, spiritual, and transcendent states of consciousness" (Lajoie & Shapiro, 1992, p. 91).

We may already state, categorically, that this is not the transcendence Levinas has in mind. It is neither ecstatic nor mystical, not divine or supernatural. It is not exceptional and rare as much as it is common and of the everyday. More fundamentally, even, transcendence is not to be found within the egoic terms of the self finding itself, actualizing itself, or coming to integrating wholeness in the humanistic psychological view that the "realization of the self through transcendence is actually a form of self-fulfillment" (Conn, 1998, p. 324). Just the opposite: transcendence is wrought by the other, external to me, and comes to fracture the self, questioning and challenging its integrity. Peace, tranquility, and harmony are decidedly not the terms by which the Levinasian transcendence is characterized; much rather, it is an "allergic," "heavy," weighty, demanding, arresting recognition of a demand for the self to respond in order to be. For all its pretension to a trans-egoic position, the transpersonal remains trapped in the ego's return to itself; in the movement back to itself, supposedly wiser and more complete now, it remains that the ego simply set out from itself to return, like Odysseus to Ithaca. Levinas's figure, instead, is Abraham, who wanders interminably and for whom home is a promise, an always to come.

In contrast to the transpersonalists and humanistic psychologists, existential psychologists seem closer to Levinas. Viktor Frankl, for example, sees self-transcendence as a constitutive characteristic of human being. Always concerned with "meanings in the world" and with "others in the world," being human is essentially to be directed to something other than itself: "The essential self-transcendent quality of human existence renders man a being reaching out beyond himself" (Frankl, 1969, p. 8). In making meaning of its world, human being consequently is always and fundamentally oriented towards its other, towards meanings and relations that transcends the self-interested ego. Frankl's disagreement with humanists would be that "human existence is essentially self transcendence rather than self actualization . . . .. self actualization cannot be attained if it is made an end in itself, but only as a side effect of self-transcendence" (Frankl, 1963, p. 175). Yet whereas the existentialist psychologists come closer to Levinas in their assertion of transcendence as an ontological feature of existence, it falters in the privilege it accords to the egoic individual making meaning, grasping meaning, coming to knowledge as it subdues the world (inclusive of the other) in authentic living. As such, transcendence *belongs* to the self and is *essential* to human being, an *immanent* component of itself (Freeman, 2014).

A third position in psychology is that of positive psychology (Seligman & Csikszentmihalyi, 2000). By its focus on "the good life" and "positive human qualities," transcendence is a central component of such an emphasis; indeed, it is regarded as one of the "overarching virtues that almost every culture across the world endorses: humanity, justice, temperance, and transcendence" (Seligman et al., 2005, p. 411). In a sense, positive psychology positions itself as an extension of the humanistic, transpersonal, and existential psychology focus but within a natural science empiricism. As such, it aims to "do for psychological well-being what the Diagnostic and Statistical Manual of Mental Disorders . . . does for the psychological disorders that disable human beings" (p. 411), to correct the absence of "a cumulative empirical base" (Seligman & Csikszentmihalyi, 2000, p. 7), and to serve as bulwark against the unscientific "new age" quackery of crystal healing, aromatherapy, and all sorts of like deceptions, fads, and "hand waving" (Seligman & Csikszentmihalyi, 2000).[6] Transcendence and self-transcendence was now to be measured, researched in the laboratory and by means of predictive models, statistical equations, and experimental control groups. An explosion of scales to measure transcendence or aspects of transcendence is the result, for example, scales (such as Jackson and Marsh [1996]) to measure Csikszentmihalyi's (1991) notion of "flow" (a state of absorption in a task where the self seems to fade away, only to "reemerge" after the task's completion, all the richer for it), to measures of "self-transcendent positive emotions" (such as awe, love, gratitude, compassion, or mystical experiences), or scales for the transcendent or sublime experience of beauty, or nature, to measures of transcendence as developmental, gerontological achievement or mindfulness ability/skill. In a review of various research and evaluation methods for self-transcendence, Kitson et al. (2020) list close to 50 (!) such scales. Sometimes research also involves structured laboratory settings where "prompts" are provided to approximate the experience (for example, "viewing awe-inspiring images" and then measuring "awe" via such scales [Yaden et al., 2017]; or watching a short movie as "mood induction" stimulus for the measurement of self-transcendent compassion or altruism [Westermann et al., 1996; Yaden et al., 2017]; or in "double blind, between groups, cross over design with an active control" [Yaden et al., 2017, p. 6] studies, where participants were administered the psychedelic substance psilocybin, and the reported experiences were evaluated in terms of meeting criteria for "mystical experiences" and, hence, for supposedly experimental and scientific conclusions about "mystical experiences" [Griffiths et al., 2006]).

A related and parallel trend to the one earlier derives from the technological advances of neuroscience and the resultant scramble often common of a new hammer, which is to hit everything in sight with it. Revolutionary advances in brain scanning and imaging technologies, as well as neurochemical research, have led to an explosion of attempts to "see" transcendence in the brain, "find" the "God gene" in the body, and "locate" the phenomenon without on its throne within (Hamer, 2004). Yet while Hamer's (2004) "god in the brain" is essentially the neurotransmittal of VMAT2 proteins, Comings et al. (2000), Mandell (1980),

Ham et al. (2004), and Lorenzi et al. (2005) found "other genes . . . to effect self-transcendence, including those influencing the 5-HT1A, 5-HT2A, 5-HT6, and Dopamine D4 receptors" (Garcia-Romeu, 2010, p. 37). Still, others find a supposed association of transcendence and "out-of-body experiences" with parietal functioning (Azari et al., 2001; Blanke & Arzy, 2005) and, in general, "by inhibiting the superior and inferior parietal cortices, regions responsible for modeling bodily and self boundaries" (Yaden et al., 2017, p. 8 in online); then there are "positive relationships" and feelings of self-transcendence, which involve neuropeptides oxytocin and arginine vasopressin (Heinrichs et al., 2009), and/or the vagus nerve, which "is activated during self-transcendent positive emotions like awe, compassion, gratitude, and love" (Kok et al., 2013; Porges, 2007). We could go on – positron emission tomography (PET) evidence for the involvement of the dorsal raphe nuclei, the neocortex, the hippocampus (Borg et al., 2003), or the parietal lobe (Urgesi et al., 2010; Azari et al., 2001) – but there is no need to belabor the point any further: for every supposed reductionistic correspondence, there is a competing other, and for every seemingly objective relationship, the relationship turn out to be either a minor one or but a fractional one. The folly of these ingenious men and women of La Mancha is satirized well by Carl Zimmer (2004), who retitles Hamer's (2004) book where he claims to have found "the God gene" as

A Gene That Accounts for Less Than One Percent of the Variance Found in Scores on Psychological Questionnaires Designed to Measure a Factor Called Self-Transcendence, Which Can Signify Everything from Belonging to the Green Party to Believing in ESP, According to One Unpublished, Unreplicated Study.

(Zimmer, 2004)

The dream persists, though, and recapitulates a continuing hope of someday, with better and even more sophisticated technological advancements, to find just that place in the brain, for example, to induce transcendence, "perhaps eventually, through noninvasive brain stimulation" (Yaden et al., 2016).

There simply is no "single, valid, reliable measure" (Garcia-Romeu, 2010) for self-transcendence, no single cortical or genetic throne, and no quantifying key with which the secrets of transcendence, like gravity at 9.8 meters per second, can be unlocked. But even if one could "explain" it, as neuropsychologists have love, in terms of "the firing of dopamine and oxytocin" (Gorelik, 2016, p. 287), these aren't explanations – or worse, causes – at all; the release of dopamine and oxytocin over the synaptic gap hardly explains what love (or transcendence) "is" and provides even less of an understanding thereof as people live and experience it. Somehow positive and neuropsychology don't quite "get it." Their frustration with their wildly varying findings is never quite understood in terms of the phenomenon itself or as an attempt to do the impossible, which is to quantify what cannot be quantified. Much rather, it is for them a function of the necessity for "better" research instruments, "more research," or developing and "validating" even more measurement instruments, "better" operational definitions, "better" validation procedures or item pool statistics, more prevalence studies, descriptive epidemiology, analytic epidemiology, multifactorial models of antecedents and health outcomes of the transcendent experience, and specialized investigations of the transcendent experiences in specialty areas such as "neuroepidemiology, psychiatric epidemiology, and geriatric epidemiology" (Levin & Steele, 2005, p. 98). In the explosion of reductionistic research and scale attempts, transcendence has become everything and nothing. It has been a personality trait, a motivation, a value orientation, a psychological state, a developmental achievement, a transient emotion such as awe, a mystical experience, a skill and competence to be cultivated, a focused activity (Kitson et al., 2020), but at the same time, none of those is what it "is" nor what it is to experience transcendence.

Levinas's transcendence is none of the ones mentioned earlier and radically challenges them all.

### Need and Desire

Hofmann and Nordgren (2015b), in a substantial anthology of *The Psychology of Desire* (which counts some of the most eminent psychologists and researchers among its contributors), introduce the text by asking us to think about what we did the last couple of hours. They then proceed to speculate that chances are we had a desire "of some sort, be it for delicious food, a freshly brewed cup of coffee, a quick 'surf' on Facebook, or for someone else you simply find 'irresistible'" (Hofmann & Nordgren, 2015a, p. 1). In this sentence lies the fundamental, banal, and utter mistake of mainstream psychology. When it has not reduced desire to neuroscientific differences in excitation, tension reduction, regulation systems, neurotransmitters, or as "wants and urges . . . intricately linked to motivation, pleasure, and reward" (Hofmann & Nordgren, 2015a, p. 5), it has systematically confused need and desire.

For Levinas, desire is to be distinguished from need, its most customary association. Need implies a consciousness or sense of what has been lost so that the desire for the lost is a nostalgia, "a longing for return" to the way things were and/or could be. Fulfilling a need is to fill a void; it is always directed to a satisfaction. Need is that which is lacking or which makes an achievement incomplete or that which we long for, having fallen from it. When I say I need something, I am expressing a lack that requires filling – either in the sense of a consciousness of a lack (hunger) or a reminiscence of something I once had (money and fame) and now no longer do; I have a nostalgic sense of what I lost and want to recapture, like Odysseus longing for (and "needing to") return to Ithaca. Need for Levinas will be a movement of interiority, a descent into oneself by which one establishes an individual identity – by which one attached one's own truths to the world. Even those psychological approaches which espouse a more nuanced and complicated understanding of desire – approaches such as that of Freud and Lacan, for whom desire is a cornerstone of the theory – even there, the notions of lack, of a void to be filled, or of an internal and interior dynamic by which desire serves the self, are nonetheless evident.

Need can be satisfied, at least theoretically. Levinasian desire, however, is not satisfied. It cannot be satisfied. As is the case with love, or "goodness – the desired does not fulfill it, but deepens it" (Levinas, 2013, p. 34). Its purpose is not that of fulfillment: there does not come a time when one says to a partner, for example, "I've now been satiated with love," "I've been satisfied," or "Of goodness that I've had 'enough' or been good 'enough.'" The act sustains itself in a deepening and continuing perpetuity. This is desire, "that which is always infinitely beyond us" (Kunz, 1998, p. 42). Whereas need can be thought as a movement inward, to the satisfaction or wants of an ego, metaphysical desire is a movement outside oneself, where truth is the property of the other.

One could make an argument for "different" kinds of desire; I have just slipped "metaphysical" into the previous sentence, a precedent one might say for qualifications such as sexual desire or for desire as all kinds of hopes, wishes, and longings befitting the dictionary definition of desire. Levinas is not particularly helpful in helping us sort out such particular complications: beyond saying "most of our desires," at least of the kind "we speak lightly of as desires satisfied," are not pure – they "resemble metaphysical desire only in the deceptions of satisfaction or in the exasperation of non-satisfaction" (Levinas, 2013, p. 34) – he does not make the fine distinctions a skeptical psychologist might insist upon. Yet it is precisely here that the psychologist can both accept the Levinasian metaphysic *and* expand or describe its path through the psychological ontological and epistemologically psychological. For example, if we were not so parochially partisan, we could bring Freudian fantasy and phantasy to conversation with need and metaphysical desire. We could say that the metaphysical desire for transcendence, which is to say the other, is the non-sited site for subjectivity, the energy of a primordial ethical unconscious, were we to use such language. From such a beginning, phantasy, as unconscious wish and desire, as well as fantasy, the conscious mental of the daydream or conscious longing, are energized by metaphysical desire. In such a reframing, the argument for phantasy as arising from an ethical unconscious dovetails well enough with Levinasian metaphysical desire for transcendence, but even fantasy and need, *even* in the extreme reduction of fantasy to ego and need to biology, could *still* retain a relation to alterity and to exteriority (in fantasy, as the proximity of the other-in-me [which we explore in the chapter on *Otherwise than Being*] and in need to the separated I reaching into the world through nourishment and possession [which we continue to explore in the next chapter]). Metaphysical desire, as the desire for the absolutely other, an other that "is not 'other' like the bread I eat, the land in which I dwell, the landscape I contemplate," nonetheless cannot "dispense with acts" (pp. 34–35). We are, I believe, eminently positioned as psychologists and helping professionals to help Levinas with these acts he does not theorize and which desire cannot do without, provided we heed his caution, to think those under the breath of the ethical, such that "these acts are neither consumption, nor caress, nor liturgy" (p. 35). We "experience" desire "in ways that precede, and reside beyond, the categories that we produce to explain them" (Clegg & Slife, 2005, p. 69).

## Totality and Infinity, Same and Other

We've made some mention already of the way these terms are deployed but wish to revisit that terrain by linking it to psychology more explicitly. Recall that totality, for Levinas, is the characteristic way in which Western philosophy has operated, as an ontology which brings everything into knowing submission, into totalizing systems of knowledge or understanding. Psychology is squarely aligned with this philosophical characterization. However, whereas natural science and mainstream psychology exemplifies this desire (!) for universal laws and essences to psyche in spades, even human science orientations (such as humanistic psychology) are nonetheless still prone to the seduction of universal motivations (such as the self-actualization tendency) and psychic conditions. Moreover, as with Levinas's characterization of philosophy, so, too, with psychology, where the totalizing violence of such a uniform and lawful universalism derives its energy from reason, logic, and categorical thought (the purview and achievement of the ego). The consequence of such universalizing knowledge is to flatten difference into the same. We do so by the use of third terms and "mythologies." The Oedipus becomes a theoretical dynamic by which everyone struggles, universally, and once one "is" a paranoid schizophrenic, everything else is smelt by that categorical fire into the shape of the understanding term. Any "excess meaning, identity, or essence beyond, or other than, what the conceptualizing mind bestows in the act of capture" (Williams, 2007, p. 683) is lost by assimilation into the totalizing law by its reduction into something known, something categorizable – the same. Hence, every other is essentially just like me (Alford, 2000). Stripped of "surface" differences, such as skin color and looks or "contaminating variables" of culture, class, and geography, we are fundamentally "human" – the same.

The totalizing same of Western philosophy derives its power from the sovereign power of reason, the ego. Western philosophy and psychology, arguably even more so than philosophy, have emphasized the self-contained and individual ego. Of course, the irony is that whereas the term is Freud's, his was also to point out the chink in the ego's armor – to demonstrate more than any other that the ego is not master in its own house. And yet it is also Freud's belief that "where id was, there ego shall be," that insight leads to cure, and that the other of the unconscious, once known, will lead to a stronger ego, which is to say a "better" self, a more functional, integrated, even moral and "healthy" self. This is also true for Jung. Hence, even here, among those who did question the supremacy of the self-reliant individual, there is still an individualism and self-interest, a self-reliance and isolated autonomy which, while not entirely in lockstep, marches alongside a general egocentric psychology. But the danger is "if we start with ourselves, we end with ourselves" (Loewenthal & Kunz, 2005, p. 1); "the ego remains stuck within the totality of the horizon that it defines and within which it takes its pleasure" (Faulconer, 2005, p. 51).

This privilege accorded to the ego and totalizing ontology which renders difference into the categorical and lawful same has banished and marginalized the other, the "knowledge," desire, and experience of infinity, of what is other than us, wholly exterior to us, and nonreducible to categorical knowing. Levinas will rupture the rule and the law of such totalizing, self-centered regimes.

## Ethics and the Ethical

We've made some passing mention of psychological ethics as a codified list of rules and/or guidelines for permissible and indicted behavior. The rather legal allusion is deliberate – much of the list of rules carry legal weight – and is grounds for legal prosecution and sanction. The ethics code and the law share the characteristic of the universal (totalizing) law, the same for everyone, everywhere. The ethics code is a reasonable, reasoned, rationally argued document. But "when ethics is rooted in reason, the fundamental question of reason – the question of certainty – overshadows the fundamental question of the ethical – the question of right" (Williams, 2005, p. 8).

Levinas has no interest in a normative ethical theory. By his own admission, "My task does not consist in constructing ethics; I only try to finds its meaning" (Levinas, 1982, p. 90). For him, ethics is responsibility, "the essential primary and fundamental structure of subjectivity" (p. 95). Ethics is not something one does or practices, it is what one "is"; it is not knowledge or reason, but the "reason" one can *be*, to begin with. It is a responsibility prior to commitment. The ethics code and all kinds of prescriptions, guidelines, and admonishments on how to act morally and ethically are all ontological, egoic, expressions of a responsibility that is more elemental and primordial, as the very constitution of subjectivity itself. Ethics is not an obligation or response "mediated through the formal and procedural universalization of maxims . . . ethics is lived in the sensibility of an embodied exposure to the other" (Critchley, 2002, p. 21). We continue to ride this wave in the next chapter.

## Notes

1 There is a fair measure of irony here in that the spark for much of the intellectual flames and heroes of the day was provided years earlier by Levinas himself, as we've mentioned earlier, by his translation and introduction to France of the works of Husserl and Heidegger.
2 Also scheduled to be on this already illustrious defense committee was Maurice Merleau-Ponty, who suddenly and unexpectedly died from a stroke just one month prior. Consider that Merleau-Ponty, at the time of his death, was 53, two years younger than Levinas.
3 "That philosophy died yesterday, since Hegel or Marx, Nietzsche, or Heidegger – and philosophy should still wander toward the meaning of its death – or that it has always lived knowing itself to be dying . . . that philosophy died one day, within history, or that it has always fed on its own agony, on the violent way it opens history by opposing itself to nonphilosophy, which is its past and its concern, its death and wellspring; that beyond the death, or dying nature, of philosophy, perhaps even because of it, thought still has a

future, or even, as is said today, is still entirely to come because of what philosophy has held in store; or, more strangely still, that the future itself has a future – all these are unanswerable questions. By right of birth, and for one time at least, these are problems put to philosophy as problems philosophy cannot resolve" (Derrida, 1978, p. 79).
4 An astute reader may suspect some allusive reference to Walt Whitman (*Leaves of Grass*, 2019) and Eugene Marais (*The Soul of the White Ant*, 2017). They would not be wrong.
5 Lest we forget, Abraham Maslow was trained as an experimental psychologist (his doctoral dissertation was with Harry Harlow, whose "monkey studies" on attachment are groundbreaking, cruel and ethically controversial as they nonetheless were for their treatment of animals). Maslow famously writes about his Damascus experience, upon witnessing the birth of his child, as "the thunderclap that settled things . . . I was stunned by the mystery and by the sense of not really being in control, I felt small and weak and feeble before all this . . . anyone who had a baby couldn't be a behaviorist" (Maslow, 1977).
6 One of the most accessible, summative, and even scathing critiques of such a departure for positive psychology is that of Taylor (2001). Not only has most everything that positive psychology is "about" been said already, it has been said more elegantly and with more nuance and sophistication by those very theorists positive psychologists seem to ignore or demean. Moreover, the criticism of a lack of research support is only "true" from an understanding and valorization of experimental, positivist, and naturalistic research.

# Chapter 6

# Totality and Infinity
## Order and Ordination

This chapter follows the broad itinerary of *Totality and Infinity* itself, with an examination first of the egoic I, the "same," followed by an exploration of the other, notably in terms of "the face." Though he arranges the text chronologically in terms of the I at home in the world, to be followed by the I's meeting of the other, it is in fact a story with a radical twist – almost like a murder mystery where all clues or common sense unfold so as to suggest a certain suspect or culprit, only to be thrown a curveball at the end, when all is revealed. The spoiler alert for *Totality and Infinity* is that it is in fact the other that comes "first," responsible for the I as such in the first place and "originally." But let us pretend to be naïve readers, with no knowledge of the plot twist, and follow the text as it is presented.

## The Same, or the I in the World

Many existing attempts to bring Levinas to psychology hone in quickly, in my view too quickly, on the other and the admittedly radical implications of the "face" for psychology. In doing so, it often misses the rich descriptions of the ego in the world, from which I propose much can be learned. The quite innovative notion of enjoyment, for example, or the unique meaning of the dwelling is no less important for psychology to take note of and to wrestle with as a prompt for refashioning and questioning itself.

Let us not start with the I in some abstract way, Levinas would say. Let us not proceed or begin with some Oedipal scene or Cartesian "I think." Instead, we recognize the I in concrete relationship to a world, fundamentally embodied (as we have seen already), materially in space and place. This is an "atheistic" I, by which Levinas means an I that is free – free in the sense that it masters its world, has an internal life, uniquely its own, separate from any god or sacral power. It is an I who can will the satisfaction of its needs and is wholly separate from an(y) other.

The world both offers itself and resists the efforts of this I. On the one hand, it offers the means for the self's possession, the fruit for one's picking, and the wheat for one's harvest. On the other hand, it also resists the self's efforts as in blight that lays the harvest bare or rains that rot the root. But even when it challenges and resists, it is precisely in overcoming resistance that the I makes the world its

DOI: 10.4324/9781003315612-6

own: it builds a silo for the drought, a dyke to ward off the seas, and a wing to fly the skies with. The world's very resistance is yoked to its overcoming. The world offers itself to me or it resists possession, but in either case, it concretizes an ego in the world. Is the human not the measure of all things – an ego which bends resistance to comprehension and possession, one who plucks a mango from the tree it turns into paper or plays in the same sand it turns into circuit boards for a cellular telephone?

## Enjoyment

We live "from" air, sleep, work, and "good soup" (Levinas, 2013, p. 110). This rather straightforward and intuitive truism provides an opening for one of the most fascinating and fruitful of Levinas's contributions. Enjoyment is either wholly neglected in large swathes of psychology (including many who are sensitive to Levinas in psychology) or is a crucial, almost identitary stock-and-trade concept for others, Lacanian psychoanalysis most particularly. Levinas's description of the egoic I, independent in enjoyment, offers important insights, both as challenge to (Lacanian) psychoanalysis as to the neglect thereof in other psychological quarters.

Without air, water, or sunshine, I cannot exist. I am, therefore, dependent on such contents of life but not as a relationship of cause and effect. The air I breathe and the water I drink becomes transmuted into me; it becomes me – as *my* energy or *my* strength. This nourishing transmutation of what is other than me into the same, into me, is the essence of enjoyment. "All enjoyment is in this sense alimentation" (p. 111), the provision of nourishment or necessities of life. It is, of course, so that I have to earn the bread I need to survive and that I have to work to exist, but I also enjoy the bread in my mouth and how it fills my stomach when I am hungry as I do the pleasures of working itself, which is not overwhelming drudgery all or always. Hence, while hunger, for example, is a need, a primal privation, it is also a feeding of life, a living of life: "What we live from does not enslave us; we enjoy it" (p. 114). What we live from are always more than the strictly necessary; "They make up the grace of life," Levinas notes in a poetic turn of phrase (p. 112).

If life is love of life and if to live is to enjoy life, then paradoxically, in my "living from," which is to say in my need and dependence, I am actually independent, sovereign, happy in my egoism. Inasmuch as what we live from, and enjoy, is more consummated than consumed, our dependency "turns into sovereignty, into happiness – essentially egoist" (p. 114). I can share an orange with you, to be sure, but the burst of flavor in my mouth, as I bite into it, the crunch of my teeth on its flesh, as I chew, and the satisfaction of a slaked enjoyment as I swallow with a contented sigh – those are all mine, only mine. "Independence through dependence! Mastery on the basis of needs. A *happy* dependence" (Peperzak, 1993, p. 152).

This egoism of life is not about a knowing in reflection; it is not a relation of knowledge. The mode of enjoyment, Levinas says, is *sensibility*, a "naïve and spontaneous feeling at home in a world that has not yet taken the form of an order of things, objects, instruments, and rational relationships" (Peperzak, 1993, p. 156).

Enjoyment is prereflective; it is not within, or a function of, theoretical self-consciousness. As such, it gestures to the beyond of ontology; it is "more than" Being, a "vital autarchy of the I" (p. 154) that cannot be explained in terms of Being alone. Indeed, one does not *know* sensible qualities, such as the green of the leaves, as much as we live them. "Beyond instinct, beneath reason" (Levinas, 2013, p. 138), we enjoy the world before we think it; we stroll on a moonlit beach, take in the smell of the earth after rain, or savor that first glass of orange juice in the morning in lived sensibility and corporeal affectivity. For Levinas, this is an affectivity within which the ego pulses, not as one psychological state among others (like sadness, for example) but the tonal background for other affects. Sensibility in enjoyment is the throbbing engine and "pulsation" – the very heartbeat – of the I.

One hears a muttering objection that sometimes life is despair and certainly not enjoyment. In fact, in previous chapters, we've already acknowledged existence as suffering, notably by one's enchainment to existence. Keep in mind, though, that the content of existence is not existence, even as it becomes part of existence; the food I eat is not life, but life is also the food I eat. The original pattern of egoic independence and autonomy is "living from" and enjoyment, of which the "'intention' is happiness" (Peperzak, 1993, p. 150). To despair of life is only because life is originally happiness. Suffering is a falling away from this vitality, a failing of happiness – somewhat like the Augustinian notion of evil as having no independent existence but only as a turning away from the good. To hate life means there must be a life to hate, one which is, in the first place, neither lack nor dependence but enjoyment. All experiences of pain or disgust are preceded by an originary gratification and pleasure, a "love of life," and "every opposition to life takes refuge in life and refers to its values" (Levinas, 2013, p. 145). It is because I want to be happy that I engage in my projects, not that I engage in my projects to be happy. Again, suicide provides an instructive example. The person contemplating suicide despairs over life and wants to escape suffering but also loves the life over which they despair inasmuch as it could be different, inasmuch as there is an implicit regret for, or about, that desire: I want to die, but I am sorry that I want to die. It is impossible to commit suicide without a sense of futility or defeat. Having heard that Lady Macbeth had just died, prompting the famous "out, out, brief candle" response, Macbeth fixes upon his own death – "gin to be aweary of the sun/ and wish th estate o th world were now undone" (5.5.51–52). He wishes futilely, he knows all too well, that the world will cease when he does so that he can die without regret, without the knowledge that there will be those left behind, whom he has hurt and whose lives he has so profoundly impacted. "Suffering at the same time despairs for being riveted to being – and loves the being to which it is riveted" (Levinas, 2013, p. 146).

It is so that that which we live from and enjoy does not always bend to our labor or does not always gift itself as easily; I bite into my orange to discover it has been overcome by worms and teeming fungi. There is an "insecurity at the heart of enjoyment," an independence "as precarious as a ship at sea" (Perpich, 2008, p. 108) which negotiates calm waters wholly aware of storms that may rise up the next day or the next week. We suffer our enjoyment because of the way things come to us, because of the elemental, the medium (mileu) in which we take hold of them.

## The Elemental

Though not absolutely (philosophically) precise, it is also not entirely incorrect to think the elemental in terms of an "extension" of the il y a. The things of our enjoyment form within a medium (milieu) in which we take hold of them; they are found in "space, in the air, on the earth" (Levinas, 2013, p. 130). This medium is non-possessable and has its own "density." It is the elemental. There is an intuitive question, and some intense scholarly debate, about whether Levinas is not merely inventing a word for "nature."[1] In our view, it both is and it isn't; put differently, whereas nature can be (part of) the elemental, the elemental is not nature, as such. The elemental retains the threatening, disquieting, enigmatic, anonymous, form-less, and indeterminate quality of the il y a, which conceptions of nature does not. Moreover, the elemental is of an enveloping, immersive surround, a sense which nature does not quite convey in our understanding of it as something "out there." The elemental is never a thing, and even by our seeming domination of it, we can never turn it into things. For example, the ship's captain may harness the sea and the wind to a human end or the pilot the wind and air to fly, but this domination does not turn the element into a possessable form or thing. Notwithstanding laws that we can discern and that can be known and taught (force equals mass times acceleration), the elemental is content without form, uncontained. "The sky, the earth, the sea, the wind – suffice to themselves" (p. 132). At best, we find an edge, a side, a foothold by which we can access this medium in which we are steeped.

Hence, our dependence on the things we enjoy cannot be guaranteed. There is disquietude. In enjoyment and happiness, we see the movement of the self as a sufficiency of the I at home with itself. Yet its sufficiency is still in the non-I, in "something else," never of itself, enrooted in what it is not. The world from which I live does not guarantee a tomorrow of plenitude. What I live from vanishes upon its nourishing surrender, and I cannot be guaranteed its future availability when I need it – "enjoyment is without security" (p. 142). It is thus that I seek or build a dwelling, within which I can store things for enjoyment, by the labor of the hand and the grasp of knowledge.

## The Dwelling, Labor, and Possession

Egoist being throbs and pulses in enjoyment. The elemental, however, renders it an insecure enjoyment. Thus, it becomes necessary to find an islet, a side, to the ele-mental, which might afford a place, a position, which will afford the existent some withdrawal from it, but also from which one can venture back out. The dwelling or home allows such a "street front" that both opens onto the elemental and functions as a kind of trench in it – an interior, a secrecy to which separated being may retreat and from which it may commence, having gathered itself. The dwelling becomes the condition for human action and reference.

Levinas's dwelling is not like the Heideggerian home; it is more than implement or tool, more than the instrumental "gear" of a life. Neither are the furnishings of the home and our food or clothing "mere" equipment (in the sense of Heidegger's *Zeug*); it is to adorn, shelter, and restore us. We enjoy them or suffer from them; they are ends. The Levinasian home is not lived as tool, but more radically, its particular privilege comes from it being the condition for human activity, for its commencement. I reach out of the home into the world, grabbing things I need and enjoy by the labor of the body, which I bring back to my home. Quite practically, I collect and recollect to the home. I withdraw from the elemental the fruits of the earth and the fish from the sea which I store in the home and which affords me the ability to delay enjoyment and fend off the threat of an insecure tomorrow. I withdraw from the immediacy of the elemental to marshal my forces, as it were – and to postpone the inevitable. In storing and retreating, the home "founds possession" (p. 157); it is a condition for the ability to say "me" and "mine."

The dwelling is not in the objective world, as Heidegger's hut and bridge is, but the objective world is situated in relation to my dwelling. This harkens to our repeated assertions about the body as our vantage point on the world, and if we now say something similar about the home, then the dwelling, indeed, is to be read in relation to the ego. It is the place of the I's retreat, of the I's recollection, of the I recollecting itself to itself. The home is the concretization of the ego in the world. Because I have stored and brought into the home, I've wrought a delay; I do not have to rush out to collect water from the creek, hunt down a deer, or brave the elements for a trip to the supermarket because I have water and a chicken in my refrigerator. As such, I can pause and collect myself; there is a distance from the elemental that allows a for-itself, an inner recollection, the possibility of reflection and indeed representation. Memory "is the essence of interiority," an assumption of "the passivity of the past" to master it. But the for-itself of the dwelling also allows a future. There is a relation with what is, but as though the presence of what is, is not entirely accomplished, has not entirely arrived yet, and only is in terms of a future, a postponement. In the "safety" of the dwelling, the distance from the elemental menace is the future, in the future. To be conscious is to have time.

Existence proceeds from the intimacy of the home, a first concretization. Other conceptions of the self – idealist conceptions, for example – fail to take concretization into account, as if the self is in some ether, reflecting and contemplating. Similarly, intellectualist views which holds the world to impassive contemplation *also* misses the importance of the dwelling. It is in the refuge of the dwelling that contemplation can occur – the domicile makes the inner life possible. Whereas the disquietude about the uncertain future of enjoyment can be addressed by the self through labor and possession, labor and possession are possible only on the basis of "recollection and representation . . . produced concretely as habitation in a dwelling or a home" (p. 150). The home provides a space for recollection and an inner life, a consciousness of an insecure future and death.

One can say that with dwelling, the world is produced. By its possessive grasp, labor suspends the element's independence, but labor and possession "would be impossible in a being that had no dwelling" (p. 159). The thing grasped and collected becomes a phenomenal possession, available for enjoyment in the future. But it is now also open to exchange; no longer the thing itself, it can be compared, quantified, and valued in money. The home allows for a world to be formed, a world-for-itself, for the self-reliant ego.

### Doors, Windows, and a Welcome Mat, the Feminine

The domicile makes the inner life possible. But it is also so that the existent is within what she possesses. One cannot escape the elemental altogether; night scratches at the window, doors rattle against the wind, and gutters buckle under the weight of heavy snowfall. The dwelling is both an enclosing comfort, a respite and interiority, as well as a passage to the exterior. It is a doorway to exit to, and enter from, laboring mastery, and windows look out as the elemental looks in, simultaneously removed and connected. The elemental is always close, as threat and as possibility.

But the home is also of an intimate and welcoming sort. Firstly, we adorn and embellish the home. The furnishings of our home, and the acquisitions of our forays from home, are welcoming to the proprietor. We sink into a favorite chair, drink from a favorite glass, or read in a comforting, sunny nook positioned just so to catch the warm afternoon glow. This dimension of interiority is about more than simply making life enjoyable but invokes a certain familiarity and intimacy, a closeness, that is produced as a "gentleness." There is, in recollection and representation, a familiarity which presupposes an intimacy with someone; recollection is reflection in a world already human, solitude is such in a world I already know to have others. "Recollection refers to a welcome" (p. 155), an intimacy with someone, albeit in absence. This is not the face that reveals itself in "majesty and height," the subject of the next section, but it is the welcome that makes welcome possible.[2] The home (or the psychotherapeutic consultation room, say) is not only a place I can retreat to and collect myself but also one that has to be welcoming to the other, where I can receive the other to share my space and my possessions with. Levinas calls this feature of the dwelling the *feminine*, or woman, a condition for interiority and inhabitation. This characterization has garnered much debate and criticism, Levinas's continued defense – that he is not referring to an actual woman as such – notwithstanding. We postpone discussion of this aspect of his thought till Chapter 8.

For now, suffice it to note that in a sense, we are on the threshold of the meeting with the other, of the doorbell ringing, with who knows who demanding our attention. Even as this section articulates much of the figures, tropes, and "characteristics" of the solitary and separate ego and I, it also sows the seeds for what will surpass that economy. In the freedom of recollection and in the solitude of the dwelling and possession, how is it that the existent does not solipsistically lose itself in its possessions and its enjoyment? Only by its being uprooted, by its possessions being questioned, by the knock on the door, the appearance of the other. The violence of egoistic economy, of a self-reliant construction of a world-for-me, is revealed by the appearance of the other.

## The Other and Infinity

Turning to the appearance of the other and the radical pronouncement of an ethical metaphysics, the shortest section in the book, we find that much of it has already been circled around, prepared for, and/or alluded to in one form or another. This is also true for the extensive elaboration of the ego in self-sufficient enjoyment. The twist in the tale will be that the freedom of the ego, in fact, is the gift and investiture of the other. The self, we learn, is only that by the appearance of the other and is not "first" or "primary" at all. In a way, what came before, in section I earlier, is now revealed as having been made possible by the other of section II! Almost like the flashback scene in a movie or novel, this "after" completely upends, realigns, or modifies what came before. Yet at the same time, the flashback scene (or the third *Star Wars* movie, which is "really" the "first") also only makes richer sense now by what came "before." The psychologist knows this sequence all too well – of the presenting problem or symptom, seemingly with its own life and dynamic, being wholly reoriented by the recognition of the "primal scene" that energized it. And in that recognition, that past that was never past is itself now seen anew and differently. The story of the same in the world, of a self-sufficient I with no apparent need for an other except inasmuch as they are needed for the project of existence, will be wholly upended by the appearance of the other. At the same time, however, it is only as an independent, self-aware I that the appearance of the other can make any claim on me and that transcendence and "the interval of separation" can evoke response and responsibility. We recall, from the previous chapter, our discourse on the "and" in *Totality and Infinity*, of the inseparable yoke between two asymmetrical, radically different entities.

## *The Face*

*Le visage d'Autrui*, the face of the other, is the term and figure by which Levinas will introduce the other and ethics ("The way in which the other presents himself, exceeding the idea of the other in me, we here name face" [Levinas, 2013, p. 50]). It is wholly understandable if our initial response to this common term – the face – is in the order of vision and the phenomenal, a sensible datum. In psychology, we go even further; we make a distinction between sense and perception. There is hardly an introductory psychology class that does not teach students how sensations are the stimuli picked up and registered by the sense organs, such as the cornea or the iris, the taste buds, the eardrum, or the nerve receptors of the fingers, but that perception is the interpretation of those electrical impulses by the brain. I have quite literally said to such a class that while we sense with our eyes, we see with our occipital lobes. In a way, and to the imagined surprise of some, such a neuropsychological argument aligns with Husserlian intentionality (*"interpretation makes up what we term appearance . . .* I hear a *barrel organ* – the sensed tones I interpret as *barrel organ tones"* [Husserl, 2001, p. 341, emphasis in original]). We've already seen that such an account misses something – the plane on which sensible life is led as embodied enjoyment. We've already seen that this enjoyment is different from perception in that it is endowed with a dynamism other than perception; the representational content dissolves into affective content, as when I eat an apple, my experience is not objectifying but affective. The face, it turns out, will upset the representational apple cart even more intensely and deliberately.

Admittedly, the notion of the face is well worn and explored, perhaps too much so, especially in psychology, where it is often reduced to some banal, technocratic empathy by which the other is supposedly "seen" and acknowledged by caring eye contact and an understanding "uh-huh." The Levinasian face thus presents a tension well worth revisiting. On the one hand, the face "concretizes" infinity and transcendence, but on the other and simultaneously, the face is not in the order of the seen. One could recast this dilemma in terms of the face as a perceptual object and the face as an "ethical modality" (Perpich, 2008, p. 55), of the face as given to consciousness (in the order of ontology) and the way it is experienced (as an order of ethics) (Perpich, 2005, 2008). What is ultimately "concretized," by way of preview, is not the face as object but the "concrete appearance of the idea of infinity that exists within me" (Hand, 2009, p. 42), of the face as an ethical responsibility (Bernasconi, 2005).

Things in the world offer themselves to me in vision, and I access those objects by exercising a power over it, by bringing it to enjoyment and comprehension – the wherewithal to know what ingredients to gather for good soup and a bowl and spoon to enjoy it with, for example. The face, however, refuses this economy; it cannot be comprehended and encompassed (circumscribed, enclosed, encircled, surrounded, contained). There is a difference in the way objects are given to consciousness and how human beings are encountered. We can see the face but can never quite exhaust its meaning; we cannot see it as we do a pen, a tree, a piece of bread, where the alterity of the seen turns into a content. Neither are the other senses of any totalizing help: I cannot come to a final knowledge of the face through touch or smell or taste – as I would prod and poke a bug, or smell milk to "see" if it is "bad," or taste a strange white powder to figure out "what it is." For Levinas, "the epiphany as a face determine[s] a relationship different from that which characterizes all our sensible experience" (p. 187). The face offers more than what can be seen; it exceeds the senses, sensibility, and perception. As such, it represents "the rupture of phenomenology," the face as enigma.

Again, let us be clear, I see a face which can be described in material and categorical presence – a brown face with hazel eyes, flattened lips, and an equine nose. But this is already only a description in relation to other faces, a comparison to other noses, lips, and skin tones. It is not of the face I face but a comparative and relative knowledge, as with dogs, for example, where the difference is precisely in terms of distinguishing characteristics of breed, or spots, or height, or eyes. The human face, however, contests such comparison. Even the racist, whose racism operates precisely on an attempt to flatten alterity such that "they all look alike," such that "they are all the same," cannot sustain such a delusion – hence, his recourse to murderous and genocidal attempts to turn the Black and the Jew into something non human, an animal or parasite of a different genus and specie. As we will see shortly, such attempts at total negation of the other will fail before the ethical resistance of the face. The human face cannot be exhausted in a genus and a system of spatial and temporal characteristics; there is always more, a singular excess. "The infinite in the face does not appear as a representation" (Levinas, 1978, p. 185); there is a radical alterity, forever and wholly outside of my knowing or totalizing grasp. The relation with the face is, therefore, not, in the first place, a spatial or visual relationship but an ethical one.

The face comes to vision with a certain address; its look addresses me. In the therapy room with the patient, at my front door accepting a package from the mail carrier, or at the traffic stop where the panhandler jangles her change cup in my direction, they all look at me and address me – just me, individually. In this address, there is "something primary and fundamental" (Morgan, 2011), something primordial, anarchic (outside of history and time), transcendent, and infinite – a sense of vulnerability and destitution and a plea not to hurt, violate, or kill. Late-night television commercials seeking donations for all kinds of charities and relief organizations – from rescue projects for dogs or cats to refugee relief or "saving children" from all kinds of traumas – capitalize on this plea; they present the face just so, eyes piercingly and vulnerably looking at us from the television screen, or with the head cocked just so over the shoulder, defenselessly, to some excessively sentimental background soundtrack. (We revisit, in Chapter 8, the question of whether the non human animal has a face. One can already glimpse some of that difficulty with the observation that these commercials may work with the "pleading" faces of "sad" dogs or cats but would probably fall flat with the "faces" of snakes, bees, or endangered bats.) The point is that what these commercials exploit in their pleas for help is in fact a feature of the face's appearance always and everywhere. The face "reveals" and "issues" a primordial moral summons.

The tension between the concrete face and the nonphenomenal face figures in an imagined objection: Surely, the assailant rushing at me with a knife, or the person screaming at me that I am an idiot because I made her coffee with two shots of espresso instead of three, hardly conveys destitution. Even so, and even in those circumstances, the specific face nonetheless carries the traces of the transcendent face, which is always to single me out with the burden of a response and a responsibility. "To face someone is both to perceive him and to answer to him" (Lingis, 1987, p. xxx). If one notices the eyes, or the shape of a specific face, one has already "missed" the Levinasian face; vision has moved into grasp, and we are in the arena of the comprehending spatial, the comparative, and the ontological. But at the same time, the transcendent face and ethical summons can only be announced by the concrete face which both "calls forth" and "tears itself away" from presence (for the moment, we both wish to signal to the reader, but also keep in abeyance until a little later, the importance of language and discourse as a way in which the face "speaks"). The face appeals to me, addresses me, calls me to respond, and challenges my egoic self-sufficiency.

### Freedom and Responsibility

I have deliberately titled this section in a way that is reminiscent of an existential and humanistic psychological bedrock, even a cognitive behavioral one, albeit less ontologically explicitly so. From it issues a psychology of personality and a clinical practice that privileges an egoic responsibility to an authentic life and self in free, aware, and actualizing choices. A rather simple, introductory example will lead us into Levinas's radical challenge to such conceptions. Imagine sitting comfortably in one's home, with a glass of wine and a bowl of olives perhaps, listening to music and reading a book. Ensconced in solitary enjoyment, in single thought and reminiscence, the doorbell rings to interrupt my independent pleasure. The person at my door not only disturbs the comfort of my (being at) home, in a material sense, she also poses a challenge to my psychological and ontological sense of self, my "me-ity." For Levinas, the egoic economy and world for itself is not freedom at all. In fact, in a creative and seemingly illogical twist, it is much rather in my obligation and responsibility towards the other, arising as it does from that disturbance of my self-sufficiency, that freedom is realized! Put somewhat simplistically, but not altogether in error, I am more "me," more "myself," in the encounter with the stranger at the door than I am sitting in my chair, sipping my wine.

We've already seen a glimpse of this insight in *Existence and Existents*; recall Levinas stating there, with respect to responsibility for our bodies and life, that "A free being alone is responsible, that is, already not free" (Levinas, 2001a, p. 79). The self cannot be self-ruling if it does not have some obligation to be so; we can discover our freedom for ourselves only if responsibilities demand it of us and provide opportunities to be so. Hence, "I understand responsibility as responsibility for the Other" (Levinas, 1985), and in that recognition, I become free, liberated to respond. In a very real sense, the presence of the other enables me to be myself and to recognize myself for the first time in the response to my responsibility. "To be an I then signifies not to be able to escape responsibility" (Levinas, 1996a, p. 55).

At first glance, it is true, freedom as obligation seems like a contradiction in terms (even the etymology of the word suggests so [*ob*-towards + *ligare* – to bind, as in *liga*ment]). In Levinas's hands, however, that the self finds itself called to responsibility is not a deprivation of freedom, as it affords the opportunity to respond in uniqueness and by the signature of my singularity. It is the relation to the other in time, and in all of the instants of time, in responsibility and obligation, that inaugurates the self, that allows "me" to stand up and stand out (to ex-ist, that is), to say *Hineini* (a favored characterization of Levinas's, from Hebrew, meaning "here I am"), as Abraham did, without question or hesitation, when God called on him.

Inasmuch as "freedom itself would be impossible without responsibility" (Hutchens, 2004, p. 18), the investiture of the other's demand is my freedom, my separateness. Thus, we've come to the "flashback scene," to the unravelling of the I as self-sufficiency. It turns out that the moments of solitary enjoyment have, in effect, been granted to me by a prior moment, the meeting with the other. Subjectivity is "welcoming the Other, as hospitality; in it the idea of infinity is consummated" (Levinas, 2013, p. 27). Pulling the I out of its egocentrism, now, my egological enjoyments – my home, my bread and water, my labor, my possessions – receive their definitive meaning inasmuch as I put it into the service of another, to whom and before whom I am responsible. Truth be told, the other has always been there, in the shadows of Levinas's description of the I in seeming self-satisfied sufficiency. The "possession of things issues in a discourse" (Levinas, 2013, p. 162), "work involves tools that I borrow, inherit, or share with others" (Capili, 2011, p. 681), and the adornment of a welcome mat and the necessity of a doorbell all invoke an other already "there" and/or to come. As with the home, so, too, with our therapy rooms or the preparations for our research subjects – arranged for the arrival of the other and in service to the other. By further analogy, for our professional identities, we can only be therapists if we have patients. That we can call ourselves therapists or researchers or professors is bestowed upon us by the patient, participant, and student who shows up and whom we serve, such that our training (by other others who serve us) is a preparation for their arrival. They give us our professional selves; we become ourselves in responsibility to them.

We should nip a sometime objection in the bud: the self for another is not to annihilate the oneself. Levinas is clear on this score: the self-aware agency of the individual subject is crucial to the encounter between two freedoms. It is only as an I that the other can be met – an I that is separate and possesses the ability to be self-sufficient, self-satisfied, and "sovereign within its self-established economy" (Capili, 2011, p. 680). In an almost circular or intertwined manner of a helix, the I is granted the ability to be most itself by the other, and to be most itself for the other, it needs to be an I for itself. In an undergraduate class on Erik Erikson and Freud, recently, I tried to explain the developmental task of the ego during adolescence – that it has to come to a secure sense of itself in order, paradoxically, to make itself vulnerable in the intimacy of early adulthood. "How can you give of yourself to another in love," I said, "if you do not have a sense of what there is to give?" It is only the strong and observing ego, I continued, that can allow itself to be weak in the face of love. The Levinasian modification to the preceding example, of course, is in the priority of the other for subjectivity, but it highlights the importance of the response(ability) of a separate I.

Levinas's responsibility is extreme, hyperbolic even. It is *indeclinable and passive* (in the etymological sense of passive as a suffering, as something one is exposed to or which befalls one without having a say in the matter). One does not choose responsibility as much as it chooses us and imposes itself on us. We cannot say no to it; it has already singled us out for response (echoing Sartre's existential dictum that not choosing is a choice, not responding likewise is a response). Levinas's responsibility is also *individual* and *untransferable*. The ethical relationship is incumbent on me alone. "I can substitute myself for everyone, but no one can substitute himself for me" (Levinas, 1985, p. 101). It is as if I am the last human, in every instance, who can respond ethically; I am selected and elected, singled out, as the ghost does Hamlet – beckoning him as if, Horatio says, "it some impartment did desire to you alone" (Shakespeare, Act I, Scene 5, ln 58–59). Hamlet can but say, "I'll follow thee" (ln 86), which is also to say *Hineini*, here I am. As responsibility is individual, it is also *non reciprocable*. I do not hold the other to my standard nor expect any reciprocality. Do unto others as they would unto me is not the standard here. "I am responsible for the other without waiting for reciprocity, were I to die for it" (Levinas, 1985, p. 98). Responsibility is thus *assymetrical*. In its expression, the face appeals to me, by its destitution and defenselessness, "from on high." (As we will see in the next section, on ethical resistance, this dimension of height does not imply the power of an authoritarian master as much as the power of a penury, of the "glorious abasement . . . of the poor, the stranger, the widow, and the orphan" [Levinas, 2013, p. 251].) Responsibility is also *unlimited*; my obligations to the other always demands more and always *exceeds my ability to fulfill them*. I am persecuted by the ethical demand, in a sense, and I am always found wanting because ethics is not just a part of my existence, not simply one of the things I do amongst others; it defines the entire domain that I inhabit. "The I always has one responsibility *more* than all the others" (Levinas, 1985, p. 99, emphasis in original). I cannot be indifferent; I cannot say this or that is not my affair. Whenever and wherever someone is persecuted, violated, or goes hungry, it is my concern. It is true that we cannot humanly do all for all; whereas there must realistically be some kind of betrayal, what is important here is the impossibility of saying it is not my watch – "not to achieve moral certainty, but never to let go of the demand for it" (Perpich, 2008, p. 81).

### Ethical Resistance

If the face opens a "primordial discourse" (Levinas, 2013, p. 201), it is fundamentally an ethical injunction not to kill, not to do violence; "The first word of the face is the 'Thou shalt not kill.' It is an order" (Levinas, 1985). But we do kill, we do commit violence against the other. What are we to make of this seeming contradiction, or indeed, of Levinas's assertion that the face of the other *cannot* be killed?

We've mentioned that the face resists my powers of comprehension, possession, and labor. In the case of the things in the world, I appropriate and dominate them to my use. The pipe, the bookshelf from Ikea I put together, the flowers I pluck from my garden to beautify my home – all these are grasped in labor and comprehension and preserved "for me." The other, however, is not available to me in such a way – they resist my egoic powers and challenge it. We may try, and we are seduced to do just that – to bend the other to our wills and desires, to knowledge and understanding of who they are, their motives, their being. Because it comes to us in sensible form, the other provokes the self, the same, to power, to the will, possession, and representation. The face arouses those powers by its appearance in sensible form; thus, it becomes gendered or raced, calling up all kinds of images, ideas, impressions, means of description. As countenance, as what is seen in sensibility and given to representation, the face tempts the same to reduce the seen to a theme, a knowledge of the seen, to the I's will to possession and self-interested projects, needs, or enjoyment. Whether by the other as a means to sexual satisfaction, for example, or by stripping her alterity by concept, category, or diagnosis, we attempt to totalize the other away from the this-here-now to a generality of type, or an essence. The status is of "a determination of the other by the same, without the same being determined by the other" (Levinas, 2013, p. 45), to absorb the alterity of the other into the habitual economy of the same.

Murder goes further. It lays claim to a total negation. It is not to appropriate in knowledge, as in a diagnosis from the DSM, or from need, as in slaughtering a chicken to eat, but in fact to renounce comprehension altogether. To kill is not to dominate but to annihilate. The face appears as a sensible datum, as a material presence, and is thus exposed to my powers.

> The Other who can sovereignly say no to me is exposed to the point of the sword or the revolver's bullet . . . and is obliterated because the sword or the bullet has touched the ventricles or the auricles of his heart.
>
> (Levinas, 2013, p. 199)

However, what the face conveys is not (only) sensibility; the modalities of power – of possession and representation – is undone as the face immediately expresses the ethical depth of an ungraspable beyond. It undoes and dismantles the sensible domain in which it initially appears such that "the relation with the face can surely be dominated by perception, but what is specifically the face is what cannot be reduced to that" (Levinas, 1985, p. 86). It presents an *ethical resistance* inasmuch as killing the person does not eliminate the responsibility not to kill (Gutting, 2001), does not destroy the transcendent ethical command, which is "stronger than murder" (Levinas, 2013, p. 199). Indeed, the other is the only being I can wish to kill because it is, as an independent existent, the very being that exceeds my power. In a remarkable reversal, the face introduces my capacity for power; the face "does not defy the feebleness of my powers, but my ability for power" (p. 198).

We should be careful, though, to think this ethical resistance as a counter-power, as two forces in opposition, battling it out, or of a resistance so vast and powerful – like "the remoteness of a star" (p. 198) – that my powers cannot overcome. Nothing could be further from Levinas's truth; the ethical resistance is disarmed, a resistance that has no resistance. The order is not to kill, but it has no means of persuading me to obey. It is, simultaneously, a power that is as majestic as it is miserable, magisterial as it is destitute, a poverty from on high. It is a power which, in its powerlessness, exceeds the language of power, instituting in its place something other than relations of competition, power, or strife – that of ethics, goodness, and peace. The face transcends the register of power altogether. One cannot encounter another without experiencing the moral status of the other, the fundamental moral ground and claim of an ethical responsibility. The face appears in my world but does not belong to it, and as such, I cannot harm it. Whereas one can kill, the other cannot be killed. The otherness of the other cannot be eradicated, and having killed, the injunction not to do so is not absolved – killing becomes "impotent." "I can never divest myself of my ethical obligation" (Williams & Gantt, 1998, p. 261). That is, while I can kill an other, the other is inviolable; the face appears in my world but does not belong to it, and as such, I cannot harm it.[3]

In the testimonies of survivors of the Shoah or of victims appearing before the Truth and Reconciliation Commissions (TRC) of South Africa and the Gaja commissions of Rwanda, one finds time and time again this refrain put to the perpetrators: "How could you not see a person, a human being?" "How is it that the face of this man, this father and husband, this kind man, evoked no sense of humanity in you?" In one memorable exchange from the South African TRC, Tony Yengeni asked the notorious South African torturer, Jefffrey Benzien, how is it that his moans and cries, as Benzien tortured him, had no effect on the torturer. To which Benzien replied in a whisper, "Not only you have asked me that question – I, I, Jeff Benzien, have asked myself that question . . . what type of person am I?" (TRC Hearing, July 14, 1997). Studies with Rwandan killers relate a similar pattern:

> They [meaning the Tutsi] no longer were what they had been, and neither were we . . . I had taken the life of a neighbor . . . I mean, at the fatal instant I did not see in him what he had been . . . his features were similar to those of the person I knew but it was not the same . . . Still, I do remember the first person who looked at me at the moment of the deadly blow. Now that was something. The eyes of someone you kill are immortal, if they face you at the fatal instant. They have a terrible black color. They shake you more than the streams of blood and the death rattles . . . the eyes are the blame of the person one kills.
>
> (Hatzfeld et al., 2006, pp. 18–19).

The prohibition against killing paradoxically only makes sense to the extent that the transcendence of the other opens up the possibility of murder as it prohibits it.[4] The face invokes my powers of nihilation at the same time that it indicts them. The face of the stranger is not only an occasion for hospitality but also for hostility. Both these words, after all, share the same etymological root – lord, master, host [*hospes*], who can welcome in hospitality and who can kill in hostility. (The *hospes* of host will also, in *Otherwise than Being*, give us the knotted conflation of host and hostage at the same time. We'll have to wait for that development in the next chapter.)

Given the formal structure of infinity – "an ideatum that surpasses its idea" (Levinas, 2013, p. 49), a thought that thinks more than it can contain – the face is precisely that. It is, however, an infinity not of reason nor of representation but a revelation in the ethical ordeal. It is *not* an infinity of the mystical, the supernatural, or the ecstatic divine; it is infinity in the finite and material. It is also an infinity that is *not* constituted by the self or the same, which can neither give the infinite to itself nor refuse it.

## Language and Discourse

Language occupies a central place in the meeting with the other. If the other is of an absolute alterity, language is the manner by which the autochthonous I leaves itself. Language is not merely a system of signs or a means of communication but a way of reaching (a bridge of sorts) to the other, across a distance without distance, from and to a non-sited site. The face of the other is a speaking face: by the "message" of infinity in its appearance but *also* because it actually speaks. We can even put it stronger: the face of the other is the origin of language and meaning. Speech emerges; the desire to communicate emerges because we find ourselves addressed by the other. We are called to speak; we speak because we are addressed. This addressing to us from the other is the condition of possibility for language. Language is one's response to the command of the other. In responding to the demand, language comes to the fore in an upsurge of consciousness, of rationality that seeks to put into words oneself and one's freedom in response. The discovery of one's freedom takes the form of speaking[5] as "the essence of language is the relation with the Other" (p. 207). "Language is the door through which the other comes in" (Llewelyn, 1995, p. 93) and already a response to the encounter. Is not, for example, "the first word *bonjour*? . . . *Bonjour* as benediction and my being available for the other man. It doesn't mean: what a beautiful day. Rather: I wish you peace" (Levinas, 2001b, p. 47). As in French, so, too, in other languages: the blessing and welcome of Levinas's bonjour is also that of *goeiedag, guten tag, buenos dias*; in isiZulu, we say, "*Sawubona*," which means, "We see you" (not only I see you, but *we* see you because my eyes are connected to my ancestor's eyes, who also sees you), to which you respond, "*Yabo, Sawubona*" ("Yes, we see you too"); in Italian, *ciao* comes from *s-ciao su*, literally, "I am your slave," or "I am at your service"; *shalom* in Hebrew and *salaam alaikum* in Arabic are both wishes of peace (as is *aloha* in Polynesian languages but also love and compassion); *namaste* in India, from the Sanskrit root, is literally "I bow to you."

In speaking to the other, in conversation (*conversare* – taking turns), the other exceeds my intentions. I cannot know the other's response in advance as I cannot know my own; I suspend my own understanding to wait, respond, to wait. While it cannot renounce egoism, discourse allows the I and the other to relate: "the I at the same time asserts itself and inclines before the transcendent" (p. 40). The tension – one which will return in *Otherwise than Being* as the saying versus the said – is that language involves thematization, universality, ontology, and a certain totalization. There is no such thing as a private or individual language, at least not outside of psychosis or hermetic solitude. The act of speaking, however, and the surprise of the other's speech, even as simply as what they will say or how what they say challenges me and calls me to response, can never be captured or represented by totalizing knowledge (Moran, 2000). As such, language and speech recognize a right over egoism, and the formal work of language is to attempt a presentation of the transcendent. As a relation between separated terms, language presents the transcendent. Even as the other may be presented as a theme, their presence is not reabsorbed in their status as theme. We may thematize the other, but "already it is said to another who, as interlocutor, has quit the theme that encompasses him" (p. 195) and who rises up "behind the said." It is in language that the other is able to address me and through which the enigma of the other is maintained.

The other does not give her interiority in speech; she is always able to lie. Deceit and veracity, however, presuppose the authenticity of the face, a "primordial word of honor" (p. 202). This language is not mystical or supernatural – where "discourse become incantation, as prayer becomes rite and liturgy," and the "interlocutors find themselves playing a role in a drama that has begun outside of them" (p. 202). Neither is it rhetoric or the beguiling rhythm of poetry. Instead, it is a breaking of rhythm; it is of rupture and commencement, of interlocution and response. It is terrestrial, commensurate with her who welcomes, and instead of offending my freedom, it calls it to responsibility and founds it. "It is peace" (p. 203).

### Justice and the Third

If our emphasis has been on the face-to-face encounter, on two, it is simultaneously true that there are other others. There is another, a third, who is not directly involved in the face-to-face encounter of the two. I am also obligated to them. The "epiphany of the face . . . attests the presence of . . . the whole of humanity, in the eyes that look at me."[6] (p. 213), and knowledge of the third party not only introduces the "inevitable question of justice" (Levinas, 2001b, p. 115) but also widens my responsibility in "the birth of the question: What do I have to do with justice?" (Levinas, 2004b, p. 157).

However, in the consideration of the third, and our obligation towards those other others, we enter into the realm of reason and rights. We move from singularity to mutuality, homogeneity, and reciprocity. For it to apply "equally," "impartially," and "fairly," the political law has to be blind to the particular individual, which, by the assumption of reciprocity, "no longer involves generosity" (Levinas, 1999, p. 101) as much as it does calculation and exchange. The response, as serious and committed as it is, or needs to be, is in the orbit of an ontology and within a temporal and contextual presence – one in which the third, the neighbor of my neighbor, is of a distance that does not quite have the power to eviscerate me in the responsibility of the ethical infinite (Eisenstadt, 2012) incumbent on the face-to-face of the two. "To the extravagant generosity of the for-the-other is superimposed a reasonable order . . . of justice through knowledge" (Levinas, 1996a, p. 169). As such, for it to nonetheless gesture towards the ethical good, for it to retain some measure of the infinite saying, justice must be premised on the "firstness" of the ethical; justice, "exercised through institutions, which are inevitable, must always be held in check by the initial interpersonal relation" (Levinas, 1985, p. 90).

It is common to think of justice as the pursuit of rights, as a question of fair and equitable distribution of privileges, and as a mirror to the state or institution's moral character. But by linking justice to ethics and responsibility, Levinas shows how justice is incumbent on each of us and pulls the rug out from under us when we shirk or otherwise give to others the responsibility which is each of ours, singularly

(Laubscher, 2022). Responsibility in justice particularizes me, accuses me, at every instant: "It is not the last judgment that is decisive, but the judgment of all the instants in time, when the living are judged" (Levinas, 2013, p. 23). In this sense, his is an activist position, one in which "I am called to act as a prophet in order to call the State to greater justice, to respond to the other beyond the call of law" (Wolff, 2011, p. 26).

Beyond the comments interspersed throughout the chapter and referring the reader to existing appropriations of Levinas into psychology (recall the comment that *Totality and Infinity* is the text of choice for such translations), we return to *Totality and Infinity* (as well as *Otherwise than Being*) for additional thoughts and questions for (and from) psychology in the final chapter.

## Notes

1 Sallis (1998) provides a good introduction and exposition of the issues attendant upon this debate.
2 Levinas likens the familiarity of the home to the thou [*tu*] of familiarity as opposed to the you [*vous*] of the face that appears from "on high." The reader will be correct to assume a reference to Martin Buber's I-thou relationship, which Levinas wishes to distinguish his views from, mainly inasmuch as Levinas believes there is an equivalence, an interchangeability to the I-thou relationship as opposed to the asymmetry of his I-other.
3 Levinas does not denounce violence in an absolutist pacifist sense; he recognizes and agrees with the right of nations to have armies. He attempts to show, though, that violence can never succeed in its aims. In its extension to the national political, the challenge to my egological paradise of safety and security, to my identitary recognition with the nation or state as home, the notion of the stranger that may wish me harm, the upsetting realization of others that do not see things my way, cannot be eradicated with a bullet or missile no matter how many actual insurgents or terrorists are killed. The encounter with the other is primarily peace; violence can only be a second or secondary response. And even if justice for others demand the violence of war.
4 As an aside, whereas murder renounces all comprehension, and is of negation, hate and torture is paradoxical, for one wants to radically negate the other, but one also wants the other to suffer, to retain subjectivity, such as it is, on the edge of murder. Hate is not simply to reduce the other to an object but to forcefully enclose them in subjectivity. Put differently, the other must realize their objectification and, for this reason, needs to remain a suffering subject. Hate wants the death of the other but without killing her, leaving her living on the verge of destruction as a testimony to the triumph of hate
5 The address that begs a response is true even when one refuses to speak. Just this morning, I listened to an interview with a representative of the Israeli government who stated, adamantly, that there will be no meetings, no conversations, with Hamas or the Palestinian Authority. Clearly, even this refusal to speak, to face the other that is Hamas, concedes already the presence and call of the other; even though I can refuse to speak to the other, a response is demanded. To say I will not respond is to respond.
6 The reference here is to a famous section of the Talmud that whoever saves a life saves a whole world. The Talmud continues that whereas "a man strikes many coins from one mold, they all resemble one another . . . [God] . . . fashioned every man in the stamp of the first man, and yet not one of them resembles his fellows. Therefore every single person is obliged to say: the world was created for my sake" (Talmud, n.d., pp. 41–42). The close alignment of the Judaic teaching and the philosophical insight is clear.

# Chapter 7

# Otherwise than Being

In 1974, Levinas published *Otherwise than Being, or Beyond Essence*. Inasmuch as we've argued for *Totality and Infinity* as a groundbreaking scholarly achievement, *Otherwise than Being* is no less so – and in the opinion of many, even more so. Indeed, it is a commonplace to think of those two texts as defining bookends to Levinas's oeuvre,[1] the two great pillars or struts by which everything else is supported and given shape. Setting aside some obvious problems and omissions with the image (such as the assumptions of equivalence and symmetry between pillars, or of "the rest" as "mere ornamentation" upon the pillared fundamentals, or the neglect of the soil [Judaism? Europe? The Shoah?] upon which the pillars itself rests), what it does is impress upon us the incontrovertible high regard for OB.

Maybe, though, we should not be quite as quick to dismiss images and metaphors. We know this as psychologists, Jungian depth psychologists especially, where we often invite the image or metaphor as an opening for therapeutic thought and conversation. Hence, as I wrote the preceding paragraph, about images and Levinas's oeuvre, my mind conjured up – or more appropriately, was visited by – a memory of the wrenchingly beautiful Dohany Street Synagogue in Budapest, Hungary. Could I think, and describe to readers, the pathway to the synagogue, with flowers and smaller, but no less meaningful, artifacts along the way in terms of the early work, opening up into the interior of *Totality and Infinity*, as well as the altar of *Otherwise than Being*, and all around, the texts of the Talmudic and Jewish writings on the walls, the interviews and essays the commentary of the ambience and furnishings, all one whole, the perfection of its desire nonetheless scarred as it may be by the imperfections of the builder, the congregants it shelters and prohibits, the times and the climes, the climes of the times?[2] There is, certainly, some kind of strange "unity" to such an image, one that would be consistent with the notion of the one great idea, of the hedgehog that is Levinas. But then there are so many ways to interpret the adornments and the architecture of the edifice – the heteronomy of alterity, which, as we already saw, is also to say freedom. Moreover, in a courtyard to the rear of the Great Synagogue, there is a haunting memorial in the shape of a metal weeping willow tree, the leaves of which are all inscribed with a name; it is called the Tree of Life Memorial,[3] also because it is a tree of death, of the dead of the Holocaust, to be faced in life, in our lives. As I write here, in Pittsburgh, a mere

DOI: 10.4324/9781003315612-7

mile from the similarly named Tree of Life synagogue which suffered the deadliest anti-Semitic attack on the US Jewish community, in 2018, I must think this memorial in the present, a reminder, in the words of Primo Levi, that "it happened, therefore it can happen again . . . it can happen, and it can happen everywhere" (Levi, 1989, p. 199). It also reminds us, as Levinas does, that neither the other nor a place, especially that of a great synagogue, that neither an image, a text, language, or an oeuvre can exhaust meaning and always holds in reserve an excess of what it gives. "(C)ontrary to what our desire cannot fail to be tempted into believing," Jacques Derrida echoes, "the thing itself always escapes" (Derrida, 1973, p. 104). As with Derrida, so, too, with Levinas; as with *Totality and Infinity*, so, too, with *Otherwise than Being*.

We've organized this chapter in two broad sections. First, as has been the case in previous chapters, we introduce the text broadly – a docent's brief contextualizing guide to the bimah, as it were, in keeping with our image earlier. To do so, we also introduce some of the key points of departure (and/or intensification) from *Totality and Infinity*. We then proceed to examine some of the central (non)concepts and insights from the text. We also intersperse some challenges and questions for an otherwise psychology.

## Approaching the Text

A few weeks ago, I reread a section of *Otherwise than Being* when my wife walked into the room, asking me what I was reading. Spontaneously and without thinking, presumably from a background as an amateur musician of sorts, I quipped, "Sibelius, Violin Concerto in D minor." Some readers may know this concerto, one of the most beautiful and one of the most difficult violin concerti in the repertoire. Whereas Freud would say that the quip hides as much, and more, of what it reveals, the conscious link with *Otherwise than Being* as "most beautiful and most difficult" bears easy acknowledgment. Admittedly, "difficult" is a descriptive often associated with a philosophical text; "beautiful" much less so. Scholarly prudence and socialization pressure my finding alternatives for "beautiful" – like brilliant or ingenious, even dazzling; beauty is reserved for poetry or works of art, not a scholarly treatise. But if art is about an experience that precedes explanation, the "setting-into-work of truth" (Heidegger, 2002, p. 55); if the beautiful is Kant's singular presentation of what does not allow representation (Kant, 2007a); or if philosophy – the love of wisdom – is also, and at the same time, Jean Luc Marion's (Marion, 2018) philocalia, the love of beauty, we may well have an argument for the use of the word. I suspect that Levinas might object some – his interest is in the good, more so and well before the beautiful. His hesitant and uneasy relationship to aesthetics and art is (well) known. Like the work of art, though, the text escapes its author and becomes ours to receive also in our own singular ways. As such, my first characterization of the text, in the way we convey first impressions to someone else, is indeed of most difficult, even exceedingly difficult, and most beautiful, even poetically beautiful. Simon Critchley seems to have a sense of these conjoining terms: OB is "beautiful to dance to," he says but also quite "frustrating when you can't hear the music or have no sense of rhythm" (Critchley, 2015, p. 69). What underlies both the beauty of the dance and the maddening frustration of its strange rhythm is the way Levinas (has to) use(s) language to an impossible end: to describe something indescribable. He has to account, *in being*, for that which is outside of being, that which is otherwise than being.

Three years after the publication of *Totality and Infinity*, Jacques Derrida published *Violence and Metaphysics* (Derrida, 1978), a by now rather famous commentary and, I daresay, nearly 60 years later, still the most incisive and original. The article's tone strikes one; it is modest and humble, with Derrida saying it's not as if he is posing objections to Levinas's work as much as he is struggling with questions that Levinas poses to us. Even so, some people have described this article as a critique and Derrida's praise as damning; others see it as less critique than a deconstructive reading. Whatever one's characterization, it is pivotal in several respects. The most substantial challenge derives from "lodging oneself in traditional conceptuality in order to destroy it" (Derrida, 1978, p. 111). Derrida's most trenchant observation is that *Totality and Infinity*, for all its criticism of ontology, still utilizes the language of ontology, still relies on concepts, metaphors, and habits of thinking which Levinas decries. Talk of same and other, notions of origin, light and darkness, inside and outside, and so forth are all still in the ontological orbit and in fact presupposes what it seeks to transgress. Moreover, or as such, "in the course of articulating his claim that ethics is beyond being and so unthematizable, he makes a theme of the unthematizable" (Bernasconi, 1991, p. 149). The presentation of the other and transcendence poses problems because it needs language, which is a totalization, to be understood. This problem is exacerbated in writing, where the present other is not available to engage in questioning conversation. Additionally, if one posits an ego, it is unclear how the other can be envisioned anyway other than a phenomenon. It is thus conceivable that in the final analysis, Levinas is as "incapable of talking about transcendence" (Peperzak, 1993, p. 211) as he accuses an ontological Western philosophy in general. With *Otherwise than Being*, Levinas responds spectacularly, his understated characterization notwithstanding:

> *Totality and Infinity* was my first book. I find it very difficult to tell you, in a few words, in what way it is different from what I've said afterwards. There is the ontological terminology. I have since tried to get away from that language.
>
> (Levinas, 1988, p. 171)

Interest in transcendence remains. One glimpses this continuing interest from the title already, a rather uncommon phrasing for English speakers. What can be otherwise than being, which is to say outside and/or beyond being? Put differently, what is beyond or outside of life and death but not in the sense of some religious supernatural, or as an afterlife that has left being, or a karmic reincarnation into being as something completely other?[4] The question is, What transcends being, here below? That is, a transcendence *in being* so indefinably elsewhere but at the same time rooted in material and everyday existence. Levinas actually tells us what *Otherwise than Being* is about in a way that is both uncharacteristically structured as it is characteristically dense and enigmatic. It is the following:

i.   "to see in subjectivity an exception" (Levinas, 2004b, p. xlvii) to the connection or conjunction of being and beings in the ontological difference. That is, there is something about human subjectivity, its sense of self, which defies the (traditional) ontological distinctions of a self-contained, ego-centered individual living life.

ii.  To glimpse or "catch sight" of this "something," which is nonetheless located "in the substantiality of the subject, in the hard core of the 'unique' in me, in my unparalleled identity" (pp. xlvii-xlviii). Thus, there is no deep and hidden proprietary "me," or if there is a deep and hidden "me," it is in fact *not* "me" but other, a substitute.

iii. To find that this substitution is "prior to the will," prior to my agency, the result of an "exposure to the trauma of transcendence" (p. xlviii) and a susception which is not of my choosing.

iv.  "to derive praxis and knowledge in the world from this nonassumable susceptibility" (p. xlviii).

We see already an early difference in emphasis from *Totality and Infinity*. If the focus there was on the relationship of the egoic self to itself and the ethical demand of the other, the emphasis now shifts to the self itself, for its very constitution, and for its consequent response to the other. "The ethical relationship with alterity is now described with concepts opposed to those of presence, the present, aim or intentionality" (Lingis, 2004, p. xxi). There are other differences as well, or rather, different implications for the different "existential structure of being-for-the-other" (p. xxi): *Otherwise than Being* presents a more radical conception of ethics (inclusive of more "extreme" language to do so); a more radical and complex view of justice; a more pronounced conception of diachronic time (the self is obsessed by the other from a past that has never been present); the introduction of new terms and concepts to mark just this radicality (e.g. proximity, substitution, kenosis, obsession, the neighbor); a change in the idea of originary solitude – from the solitude of the existent emerging from the il y a (as in *Existence and Existents* and *Time and the Other*) to the solitude of the atheistic ego (as in *Totality and Infinity*), to the solitude of obsession, a pre-originary anarchy of subjectivity (Maldonado-Torres, 2002).

   At the risk of a too simplistic and banal comparison, a rough, ready, and introductory summary table might list the progression and difference from *Totality and Infinity* as follows. Some of these will not make understanding sense yet, but it may help to orient and organize the journey in terms of the sights and sounds that await us.

| Totality and Infinity | Otherwise than Being |
|---|---|
| Focuses on ethical alterity, that is, on the other and the visage (face). | Focuses on ethical subjectivity, that is, on the "me-ity" of the self who meets the other. |
| Discourse and conversation involve language as the relation with the other; it is an expression of infinity, a "letting be" which "solicits the other." | Discourse and conversation involve the saying and the said. Saying is the ethical, which is exposure to the other, which comes before the said, the ontological of content and theme. |
| Justice is derived from the conception of the third, arising from the obligation to the face of the other. | Justice is based now on the conception of the neighbor, arising from substitution and a responsibility prior to the ego. |
| Emphasizes the epiphany of the face and speaking. | Emphasizes the selfhood of the subject as already subjected to responsibility. |
| Welcoming of the other to the same arises from the other upsetting the enjoyment and self-sufficiency of the same. | The other is already in the same, to constitute the same "from the beginning." |
| Stresses desire. The other is spatially "over there," beyond all categories and categorization. | Stresses responsibility. Focus is on the self, scooped out, denucleated, possessed, and haunted by the other within. |
| The other is overflowing, surplus. | The other is shock, trauma, persecution. |
| Key descriptive terms include totality, exteriority, height, separation, face. | Key descriptive terms include proximity, kenosis, substitution, persecution, illeity, enigma, obsession. |
| Subjectivity is investiture. | Subjectivity is radical passivity. |
| Relation to the other as exteriority, the meeting of two freedoms. | Relation to the other as obsession, the other in me. |
| Time as anachrony. | Time as diachrony. |

## Key Ideas

### Transcendence

We keep coming back to transcendence. It is key. The book starts with it and by way of a rather pregnant sentence: "If transcendence has meaning, it can only signify that the event of being . . . passes over to what is other than being" (Levinas, 2004b, p. 3). The descriptor for the sentence as a "pregnant" one may prove instructive: consider that if "my" pregnancy has any meaning, it can only signify that the event of birth passes over to what is other than me. It is not just that transcendence matters, but it matters at the heart of it all – the event of being or what it is to be. And what it is to be is to recognize, catch sight of, or otherwise glimpse being given by transcendence, an otherwise than being. Transcendence matters to the very notion of a subjectivity; it signifies that the ability to say "I" or "me" "passes over" to what is other than me or myself.

This transcendent passing over is not of the moment and is not in the present but is *diachronous*. Ferdinand de Saussure, we remind ourselves, is the linguist who introduced the terms synchrony and diachrony. A synchronic (*syn*, together + *chronos*, time) linguistic analysis is the study of language at a specific time, the present usually. But then there is also diachronic linguistic analysis, which looks at the evolution and a historical analysis of language over time, acknowledging in doing so that present usage is marked by the past in unseen ways and by processes and dynamics of which there are only traces and remnants. Hence, returning to Levinas, transcendence is not synchrony. It is, instead, diachrony, which is an outside of time, in time. It is outside the time of the present, even as it is in it. It runs through (*dia*) time rather than being settled in it. The present is marked by that past in ways we may not be aware of and that does not show itself, even as it is there, even as it is marked, even as it still carries the trace. Thus, we can preserve a relationship, a present, which breaks with synchrony in the acknowledgment of the challenge of a diachronic trace, of something from a distant past passing over. But this is not a past as we might be wont to think it – as a linear, regressive movement that can be traced to an origin, like a Freudian past. Instead, and in keeping with an analogy from psychology, this is more like a Jungian past, from a collective unconscious. It is a past that is "immemorable" and irrecuperable. I recently saw a bumper sticker that said something like "Thank the labor movement for your weekend," or the eight-hour workday. But whom do we thank, were we to do so actually? There is no first, no origin, no individual, no *one* to thank really. Or in another reference, Levinas's transcendence hearkens to a Biblical beginning: "In the beginning was the word, and the Word was with God, and the Word was God" (the Bible, John 1:1). In this beginning, there is no beginning, only an origin without origin. In a religious reading of Levinas, one might be tempted to say the Word of God, the first word of God, is but of ethical transcendence – Levinas's word.

### The Saying and the Said

As in *Totality and Infinity*, language is a central and abiding concern. In *Otherwise than Being*, however, it receives a remarkable deepening and complexity around the distinction between the said (*le Dire*) and the saying (*le Dit*). The tension and paradox remain: how to convey transcendence without thematizing it, how to say what cannot be said (Brody, 1995). The accusation of philosophy, and by extension psychology as well, is that it incessantly thematizes transcendence, turns it into a topic, a thesis, or an argument. By Levinas's terms, they have turned transcendence into a said. Hence, the said is the textuality of literature, or the works of civilization, statements and propositions about the world, truth, personal identity; put simply, it is the message or text, the work of an ego which emphasizes content. We recognize that content is crucial; one could say that communication as such hinges on content.

The saying, however, is "pre-original" and the "condition" for the said: "Saying is communication, to be sure, but as a condition for all communication, as exposure" (Levinas, 2004b, p. 48). Levinas actually lists the "characteristics" of the saying: it is "antecedent to the verbal signs it conjugates," antecedent to "linguistic systems and . . . semantic glimmerings," the "very signifyingness of signification," "the commitment of an approach," "the one for the other," and "the proximity of one to the other" (p. 5). To this initial list will be added even more, most notably a pre-original, transcendent "intrigue of responsibility" (p. 6), but the important point is clear – that the saying is prior to language, in fact makes language possible, and is ethical responsibility as such. Why would I speak but to address it to someone, to someone that appears or is proximal to me? This addressee is ultimately the reason for my language in the first place such that the saying speaks to that underlying situation or event that involves exposure to the other as a speaker or receiver of discourse:

> is exposed to the other as a skin is exposed to what wounds it, as a cheek is offered to the smiter . . . prior to the said, saying uncovers the one that speaks . . . in the sense that one discloses oneself by neglecting one's defenses, leaving a shelter, exposing oneself to outrage, to insults and wounding.
>
> (p. 49)

It is difficult to maintain this distinction between the saying and the said. The saying "moves into a language" (p. 6) and becomes a theme (a said) within it. Indeed, as soon as we speak about the saying, it turns into a said. The saying is never fully present in the said, yet the said is the only access we have to the saying. But by its movement into the said, and even as it is subordinated therein, the saying leaves a *trace* in the said (Davis, 1996). It is this trace that interrupts the said and remains beyond the content of the said (Strhan, 2012). "The plot of saying that is absorbed in the said . . . imprints its trace on the thematization itself" (Levinas, 2004b, p. 46). Thus, the movement of the saying into language comes at a cost and with a betrayal.[5] No said goes without a saying, and no saying is possible without a said, the consequence of which is that language betrays transcendence by the thematizing signification of its operation. A necessary support and indispensable ancillary to the saying, language is like a messenger who speaks about the sender without being able to speak the sender's own language, or like a God who never appears as itself but as angels, burning bushes, or ventriloquizing prophets. Even in the signifying said of the Judaic tradition, God holds its distance as G_d or in the many names of G_d, all of which belong but none which are exhaustively proper to it. However "sublime" and "apophantic," the angelic or ancillary is only mediation.

This methodological problem of saying that which cannot be a part of the said is not, however, to be descried as failure. Even if philosophy, and psychology, seem destined to betray the saying and responsibility, the knowledge of its motivating marching orders, of the original vocation of the saying as responsibility itself, prompts an "unsaying." The language of being and beings can serve as an ancillary or angelic mediation on the condition that they are accompanied by a critique of sorts, an "unsaying" of their betrayal. This is crucial: it is by unsaying that the otherwise than being can be extracted, incompletely as it may be. Even as every denial will be a new betrayal, insofar as the denial turns into a new said, herein is the notion that the way transcendence speaks is in a successive, nonsimultaneous, and diachronic manner – in a nonsynchronizable time of surprise that resists a gathering philosophy. The object, inasmuch as one can speak in those terms, is not for the "Saying saying saying itself" (p. 143) to come to a destination but in the movement to "expose the exposure instead of remaining in it as an act of exposing" (p. 143). Put more directly, it is unfurling, critical thought and a resistance to collapsing into settled expression. This notion of the unfurling and continuing unsaying is crucial to a perpetual responsibility, infinitely renewed in every instant.

### Substitution, Subjectivity, Proximity

The chapter on substitution forms the centerpiece of *Otherwise than Being* – also by Levinas's own admission. Arguably, it is the most radical and innovative contribution of the text. As in *Totality and Infinity*, subjectivity is structured as responsibility for the other. The separated egoist being of *Totality and Infinity* is gone, however, "replaced" now with substitution and proximity with which to convey this "process" (Critchley, 2015; Strhan, 2012). The chapter on substitution, even more so than the text as a whole, is a painful one to read, obsessive, torturously folding and unfolding, wrapping and unwrapping terms, approaching it from several angles, seemingly repetitive at times but always with a twist, a slight or markedly different view, angle, or refraction. At times, it may seem like the exact same sentence is repeated, until one looks closer to find one word altered or the word order of the sentence somewhat different. It is like "a modernist poem, fragmentary, imagistic, episodic, and non linear" (Critchley, 2015). But this is all quite deliberate. One might argue that Levinas is performing "unsaying" for us.

Another disturbing and disorienting feature of the chapter, however, is the language Levinas now employs with which to characterize the ethical. In the everyday, one is wont to use descriptives such as obligation and duty, right and moral action, virtue or goodness, the latter which Levinas himself used freely in *Totality and Infinity*. Here, however, ethical language is of obsession, persecution, trauma, expiation, and hostage – not exactly terms one would intuitively expect to be associated with ethics. Subjectivity, now, is given by an atemporal, ahistoric, primordial responsibility for the other. There is a *recurrence*: "The ego is in itself like a sound that would resound in its own echo" (p. 103). As an echo, the ego of the present resounds and relates to what came before it; it is as if there is another within me, an alien presence (where alien refers etymologically to "another"). Like a pronomial or reflexive verb, as in "I wash myself," or "I stopped myself from eating another donut," where the subject is the same as its object, there is another with me; I am never at home with myself, alone.

We have met the "for-itself" of the ego, the commonplace and Western understanding of the ego which reduces subjectivity to consciousness and self-consciousness in particular. We have also seen the challenge in Levinas's ego "for-the-other," in *Totality and Infinity*. What *Otherwise than Being* now proposes is a movement from the ego to the self as the "one-for-the-other" or the "other-in-the-same," the self "hunted down" in itself. "It is no longer a question of the ego, but of me . . . the identity of the subject comes from the impossibility of escaping responsibility" (pp. 13–14) because I have already been exposed to the other for my very subjectivity. It is like maternity, the metaphor Levinas uses to indicate an other in me. Like pregnancy, I am simultaneously host and hostage to the other. Like maternity, I am vulnerable before the other, singularly responsible for the other who is under my skin and whose close, proximal presence I suffer in respon-sibility to it. Or in another image, the "irremissible guilt" of my responsibility for the other is suffered like a "Nessus tunic"[6] which I cannot decline nor take off. As with maternity, so, too, with the Nessus tunic – I am accused from within, in and under my skin. Hypostasis is no longer of an I emerging from the il y a as I but of an I already assigned and tied in a knot of responsibility. The I of consciousness (an ego) is already a "borrowed mask," already an exile, already answerable to an older, prior assignation "older than the time of consciousness" (p. 106), from a time "before the present" (p. 106). The "ego . . . is in itself like one is in one's skin, that is, already tight, ill at ease" (p. 108). The extreme language continues, of a self being *persecuted* (from Latin, to follow completely/utterly *per-* + *sequi), obsessed* (from Latin, to be besieged), *traumatized* (from Greek, literally to wound), *inspired* (from *in* "into" + *spirare* "breathe"), *accused* (a calling to account), and called to *expiation* (to atone, to appease by sacrifice, from Latin *expiat*). The other in me is of a pure anteriority that is immemorial and that binds me, that orders me, that lacerates me and takes me hostage outside of my will.

This diachrony of responsibility is such that it cannot be chosen; it does not leave us free to assent or refuse a relation with it. It has chosen us before we even have any idea of it. Our freedom is preceded by a pre-originary exception, a nonfree obsession, the captivity of a hostage, as it were. We could use this language of Levinas's to an example. I teach an undergraduate course called *Science, Psychology, and the Holocaust*, which has a mandatory travel component attached to it. One of the places I travel to with students is Auschwitz; I have now been there seven or eight times. In the Birkenau section of the death camp, specifically *Camp Canada*, where the belongings of those destined for the gas chambers were sorted and valuables expropriated, there is a display of photographs – images of people who have never been identified in the years since. One, a young woman with a sad and attractive half smile, looked directly at me. Cradled in her arms is a sleep-ing child. There are no words I can type here to explain, illustrate, or convey the effect she had, and has, on me. But it is as if she was waiting for me, just for me, for all these years. She calls out to me, seizes me, accuses me, and reminds me of a responsibility I did not ask for, and would not want by my will, but cannot ignore, even if I do. It is as if I had no choice in the matter of meeting up with her, and every time I see her, it is only us and only my response that matter to her. She does not look at a camera; she looks at me. Sometimes, in the midst of frustrating travel hiccups and the demands of chaperoning 25 students all over Europe, I complain to my wife about why I keep teaching this course. She says it's a mitzvah; you do it for your students, not for you. I also know, though, that I do it for her, this nameless young mother and child, from a boundless and bottomless expiation, from an obligation that can never be satisfied or exhausted. She obsesses me. She haunts me. She persecutes me. I feel her in my skin, in my body, in the tears that sting every time I see her. She has laid siege to me, ordered and ordained me, by an obligation prior to commitment, an anteriority older than the a priori. It is a persecutory obsession that is not consciousness and cannot be reduced to it; it is without content, "an ego . . . unable to conceive what is 'touching' it, the ascendancy of the other is exercised upon the same to the point of interrupting it, leaving it speechless" (p. 101). I continue to find myself in that assignation, in my suffering response which is my responsibility – a responsibility without prior commitment, "called into question prior to questioning" (p. 102), commanded beyond and before the calculation of response.

In the summoning of myself by the other incommensurable with the conscious ego, one stands accused for what was never willed or chosen, of what others do without our knowing. Responsibilities do not result from decisions taken by a contemplative subject but from an accusation prior to any self-reflexive or conscious I. The self is condemned as it were from the start – condemned to a response, condemned to responsibility. These responsibilities haunt one, one is obsessed by them, and they do not result from decisions taken by a freely contemplating subject. It is as an anarchic obligation which is "prior to the will" (p. xlviii), "prior to every memory" (p. 10), "prior to essence" (p. 14), "prior to language" (p. 16), "prior to all objectification" (p. 48), "prior to any intention" (p. 49), "prior to consciousness" (p. 82), "prior to all mediation" (p. 84), "prior to all memory and all recall" (p. 104), and "prior to the act that would effect it" (p. 101). We could list even more, but the point is clear: "responsibility as the essential, primary and fundamental structure of subjectivity" (Levinas, 1985, p. 95) is a haunted subjectivity "answerable for everything and for everyone" (Levinas, 1996a, p. 90). The I stands accused and is found guilty without having had a say in the matter. I stand accused and my responsibility grows to the measure in which I fulfill it. I can never pay off the burden of my guilt; there is always more demanded of me than I can accomplish. "Responsibility for the other is the good. It's not pleasant, it is good" (Levinas, 2001b, p. 47).

But at the same time, "if no one is good voluntarily, no one is enslaved to the Good" (p. 10). For all the talk about obsession, of hostage taking, of being ordered and commanded, of a hollowing out of self, I am not repressed and I am not enslaved – because it is a responsibility to the good. Like love, it cannot be chosen but only welcomed. The good invests me with freedom, with powers, with the power of the good; like the investiture of a knight, the order is simultaneously an ordination, a conferring of holy orders. It is a finding of self at the very rupture of losing self. This loss of self is not like an enslavement, where selfhood is repressed and denied. Losing oneself in responsibility for the other is to find oneself in the truth of the good. There is thus a positivity in the response of responsibility, by the *proximity* of the other-in-me. As proximity it is not a knowledge but a sensibility. Proximity is not based on any existing relationship or identity, is not a concept or rational calculation, but like the saying and substitution is of the vulnerable recurrence of ethical responsibility. Since that which provokes me in the face of the other is absolutely absent, a past that was never present, cannot be presented or represented, cannot be unveiled or uncovered like a secret or a hidden message, what is responded to is the trace of that past – a trace that signifies without manifestation. It is a special kind of sign – not one a hunter can track down, or a historian can uncover, or a Freudian archaeologist can assemble. Such is my own responsibility without beginning, coming from nowhere, a past before all past presents – already gone, leaving the enigma, the intrigue, of responsibility, leaving a tear and a binding, a breaking point and a binding place. *Illeity*.

From the pronoun il (him), illeity would be "himness" or "itness." The term might best be described some with reference to religion. We do not enter into a direct relation with God, but we are able to sense, to feel the itness of God by the traces of its/his/her/their presence in the world. Let's say, for example, by the splendor of nature or a visitation by the angelic, the spirit. God is glimpsed in the third person and as a trace – never directly and always by the remove of a thirdness. This is not the I-thou of Buber because the thou is still too direct, too present, too thematized, too available to concept and grasp, too much of a sign. The trace of transcendence in responsibility, as illeity, is not present even as it inspires, even as it obsesses, even as it commands. It affords a relation, albeit then a meaning that is pre-eminent, before my meaning, before the ego seizing it in meaning. "I am obliged without this obligation having begun in me, as though an order slipped into my consciousness like a thief" (p. 13).

The kenotic self, an ego hollowed out, is to give uniquely and singularly.

> To be oneself, otherwise than being, to be dis-interested, is to bear the wretchedness and bankruptcy of the other . . . a hostage, always to have one degree of responsibility more, the responsibility for the responsibility of the other.
>
> (p. 117)

It is by this kenotic substitution that I can weep for Hecuba: "it is through the condition of being hostage that there can be in the world pity, compassion, pardon and proximity – even the little there is, even the simple 'After you, sir'" (p. 117). This is where the psychism (the way we experience our experiences as individuals) comes in; the inspiration of the other-in-the-same constitutes the human psychism of respiration and the acts of responsibility. As such, the other in me does not estrange me from my freedom but conditions it. And not simply or purely in the sense of the spiritual or the compassion or pity of the heart but corporeally. In fact, this is what Levinas starts from – to work with one's own hands for the other, to take the very bread from one's lips to still the other's hunger:

> how is responsibility for the other translated? . . . It is a matter, eventually, of nourishing him, of clothing him. It is exactly the biblical assertion: feed the hungry, clothe the naked, give drink to the thirsty, give shelter to the shelterless. The material side of man, the material life of the other, concerns me and, in the other, takes on for me an elevated signification and concerns my holiness.
>
> (Levinas, 2001b, p. 52)

In the end, it is also the most practical to do – the gift not "of the heart, but of the bread from one's mouth, of one's own mouthful of bread," the openness "not only of one's pocketbook, but of the doors of one's home" (2004, p. 74). Levinas sometimes cites a Jewish proverb in support, "The other's material needs are my spiritual needs."

"Having-the-other-in-one's-skin" is to effect the freedom of a singular response. The inspiration, the breathing into, of the "other-in-me" is not only of accusation but also respiration; by the breath of the other in(to) me, my breathing is occasioned. Bernasconi, in a remarkable article titled "What is the question to which 'substitution' is the answer?" (Bernasconi, 2002), argues that the answer is the possibility of sacrifice. As such, it is not simply expiation, even as it is that too; it is also – in sacrifice – a gift to the other from the gift that comes from the other. Substitution, as the passage of the other's calling into my own voice, the one-for-the-other as the basis of the ethical and of sacrifice, cannot be accounted for in the Western philosophical tradition. Its preoccupation with consciousness and its egological notions of self prevents it, and psychology, from seeing that "substitution is not the psychological event of pity or compassion . . . but taking responsibility for their responsibilities" (Bernasconi, 2002, p. 239). Hence, we are not talking about empathy – at least not the empathy as we have been occasioned to think it, as a movement from the self with which to "understand" the other. One would have to rethink empathy as the call of the other-in-me.

Keep in mind that this is not an empirical ego – that this "inspiration" which "arouses respiration," this "pneuma of the psyche" precedes the "empirical order, which is . . . already conditioned in a system" (p. 116). Inasmuch as there is unity, inasmuch as there is universality, it is not "what my gaze embraces in . . . apperception, but in the self as sub-jectum," "under the weight of the universe, responsible for everything . . . for what is incumbent on me from all sides" (p. 116). It regards me, in both senses of the term – as what accuses me, as what looks at me, and as my affair – as my regard. Substitutability, a taking place for the other, is a "taking responsibility for their responsibilities" – and for the persecutor as well as the persecuted. In an interview with Levinas, Phillipe Nemo exclaims, "You go that far!" (Levinas, 1985, p. 99). To the earlier story of the woman at Auschwitz, I now have to add the responsibility of her tormentors and killers; I now stand accused and answerable to her for her Nazi murderer. She looks at my expiation, my living justification, as her killer; I bear the responsibility in proximity for those who gassed her and her child and am bound to an accounting before her. Her why and her plea and her suffering is not why did they do it, but why did you do it, why did you do it because you carry the responsibility of their responsibility. He stands by this extreme formulation; Levinas responds to Nemo, *"But only for me."* I cannot expect my students, or you, to carry this responsibility; my responsibility for the other cannot be universalized. For you, for them, for my wife, I demand justice and the law.

## Justice and the Neighbor

The initial for-the-other "is contested by the appearing of a third, fourth, fifth human being – all of whom are my 'others'" (Levinas, 2001b, p. 51). The proximity of the neighbor and the neighbor of the neighbor are all alongside the one approaching me, and to them I cannot be indifferent – to them I am no less responsible, to them are due a justice which cannot do without a calculation, a synopsis, a theme, a law, an equality of rights. The neighbor is the term for that always already proximity of the other. For them, the equality of unequals is demanded, and as they rise up behind every face, my "for another" is also "with another" in justice. The neighbor is one *"before whom,"* *"to whom,"* and *"for whom"* I must answer (Levinas, 2004b, p. 12, emphases in original). The modification of *Otherwise than Being* is in yoking justice to proximity, which is not a term, condition, or concept of consciousness; it is not that we achieve consciousness by which we realize that there are other people with whom we then enter into relation with. Proximity is there before us, before we entered on the scene as consciousness. Because the other facing is always other to some other, a neighbor, the face of the other is always also a confrontation, an accusation, of a third. The ego can no longer prioritize the proximally close only but must give attention to all. The infinite obligation becomes the duty of justice. The one-for-the-other now also obligates the organization of society in which justice is exercised. The radical inequality of infinite responsibility does, therefore, not exclude reciprocity on the level of justice but "founds" it.

But because those other others are not present to me in the face-to-face, what is required is an abstraction, a theory, a said, a thematization – a statement of rights and an ethical code. Others must be compared, judgments must be made, one must weigh and think and compare the incomparable. A terrible conundrum this, for those of us who must act, for those of us caught between Martin Luther King Jr.'s promise that the arc of the moral universe might be long but bends towards justice, on the one hand, and the demand, here below, that "justice doesn't wait. It is that which must not wait" (Derrida, 1992, p. 26). It is a responsibility lodged between the saying and the said, in the incalculable calculus of the other's demand. "Justice is awakened by charity, but the charity which is before justice is also after" (Levinas, 2001b, p. 52)

## An Exorbitant and Everyday Psychism

Levinas's descriptions of substitution and ethical responsibility run the risk of dismissal as utopian or simply just too excessive and exorbitant to have any practical meaning. Nothing is clear, and everything is torturously ambiguous; the saying never shows itself, must inevitably be betrayed, and I am responsible for everyone, everywhere! At the same time, however, Levinas points to the simple act of holding a door open for someone, saying, "After you," as bearing witness to the ethical. "Its being utopian does not prevent it from investing our everyday actions of generosity or goodwill towards the other" (Cohen, 1986). Moreover, as the saying calls for the said, responsibility requires justice, which is in the world and where one can work to a concretized ethics of respiration by inspiration. There is always betrayal, to be sure, but there is always as well the possibility of the reduction of betrayal (Chanter, 1999). For ourselves, as well as for psychology, the temptation is to land somewhere, to have some certainty about an action or a meaning, but the lesson here is of an incessant and recurring beginning and wandering – indeed by the figure of Abraham and not Odysseus. Truth be told, as psychologists, we are already attuned to a way of listening, to a way of being with an other, which philosophers have not quite gotten to. It is a rather strange thing to say, but we may be more ready, more able, more receptive than philosophy for Levinas's message when it is not a theory but an action, a response in being-with. Psychoanalysts, for example, routinely listen for what is unsaid, for what is "beneath" what is said, or what is betrayed by the said in ways that are not direct or phenomenal. Humanistic psychologists, similarly, listen deeply for an affect and experience beneath, behind, or otherwise hidden from the patient. They conceive of deep empathy as that movement into the world of the other, respectfully to dwell there. Psychologists of all stripes are attuned to the sensible, even as they've banalized it to nonverbal behaviors and even though they are not sensitive enough, or sensible enough (and even as training programs woefully diminish the corporeal or banalize it as attentiveness to nonverbal behaviors). The point is that we are already oriented to the other in pain. Our fault is the egoic ends to which we ply such attentiveness. We do not start from the ethical or from ethical demand. We do not recognize the haunting obsession of the other in the same in order for our response to be all of apology, expiation, and witness. That is the challenge by which to reorient our attentiveness and presence for the other.

## Notes

1  Peperzak (1993, p. 209) describes OB as "the second opus magnum."
2  A synagogue might be the most apt such image for Levinas, but the reader could well substitute a mosque or a church – the Taj Mahal or St. Peter's, say – for the image's sentiment.
3  Formally, it is called the Memorial of the Hungarian Jewish Martyrs.
4  It is true, Levinas says, that "the ancients" (which may include religious leaders) have already caught sight of a beyond, but whereas Levinas's journey parallels the difficulties

of their climb, "as well as its failures and renewed attempts" (2004, p. xlviii), his is not to replace philosophy with prophetism but to translate some insights of a prophetic tradition into the language of philosophy.

5  There is more than one kind of betrayal. In disclosing a secret or in reneging on a promise, there is betrayal; I can also betray by dissimulation or subterfuge – what I disclose is not true (I can spread a rumor that you're gay when you're not). But I can also betray through the truth or knowledge (by my telling that you are gay, I can make you into a theme, "a gay"; by the reduction of all you have told me, I betray the saying by turning you into a principle or a diagnosis – anorexia nervosa, purging type).

6  From Greek mythology, the Nessus cloak or shirt was the poisoned means by which Heracles was killed. Wearing the cloak, its poison infected all of his body, leaving him in excruciating and inescapable pain, until he threw himself on a fiery pyre.

# Chapter 8

# Challenge and Critique

As with any thinker, there are those who will disagree with this or that insight, interpretation, or concept; and as with any theory, changing demands of culture, history, and context will pose similarly critical challenges. Rather than specific conceptual challenges, such as Freud's penis envy, for example, we focus here on broader, more thematic questions pertinent to the thinker's philosophy and/or psychological anthropology; for example, if, or how, Jung's racism shelters in the theory. To be sure, specific theoretical concepts may feed into such a broader critique; hence, penis envy may be an evidentiary exhibit for the larger argument on Freud/psychoanalysis and women/patriarchy. Levinas has been challenged on several scores and from several quarters, including with respect to issues of sexism and ethnocentrism, as in the examples of Freud and Jung's. We make no pretension to an exhaustive examination of such critiques and have elected to examine only a select few broad issues we consider particularly salient to our social and political present, as they are to contemporary psychology.

## Levinas and Nature/Non Human Animals

It is no longer controversial, at least within sane quarters, to recognize a natural world in peril. Human presence is directly related to a biodiversity crisis where animal species go extinct at between 1,000 and 10,000 times the natural extinction rate and a climate crisis where the very ecological balance of the planet, our dwelling, tilts towards cataclysmic possibility. There is a long record of thought, from preliterate cosmologies and religion all the way to contemporary ecological and environmental sciences, about the nature of human being's relation to the natural world and indeed their responsibility towards nature and other animal species in care, companionship, and/or patronage. All of which seem to swirl into the funnel of the present and the sense of a crisis demanding a new thought and action. In psychology, the field of ecopsychology has been particularly attentive to the bond between humans and the "more than human world."[1] (Whereas clinical and counseling psychology have explored non human animal companionship in relation to therapy and mental health, we've omitted a review of such scholarship given the

DOI: 10.4324/9781003315612-8

broader focus here on an environmental ethics, as opposed to a clinical therapeutics.) It follows rather intuitively to plumb the thought of the pre-eminent thinker of alterity and ethics for insight, if not guidance, as to an ethical response to an environmental suffering.

As it is, Levinas does not provide us with an easy environmental ethics. In fact, translation and appropriation of his radical and inspiring ethics to the more than human world is riven with controversy and challenge. At first glance, Levinas seems quite "uninterested in the alterity of animals and the possibility of ethical claims coming from the natural environment" (Perpich, 2008, p. 150) and his work reflective of a worrying anthropocentrism and/or a repackaged (at best) enlightenment liberalism of environmental stewardship. Even so, several authors and commentators have attempted to find resources, if not evidence, in his work for an environmental ethics and responsibility.[2] As Larios (2019, p. 2) puts it, "Levinas himself was anthropocentric, his philosophy need not be so."

In the early work, an argument can be made: nature serves as the elemental backdrop for the existent's egoic emergence – "finding oneself in warmth, in air, in light . . . sensibility awakens, arises" (Lingis, 2010, p. 68). As we've already seen, a crucial mode of relating to the world is through labor and in enjoyment. And while the creative contribution of enjoyment provides a tempered sense of a "joyous and impatient appetite for the world . . . an intrinsic tonality of joy" (p. 70) and an "essential sincerity of our attachment to the things of the world" (p. 72), it is eminently reasonable to conclude, from the early work, that the environmental surround is primarily to serve human ends, indeed as means to human ends. Working over the land and hunting and slaughtering for food are not aimed at a face; "They still belong to labor, have a finality, and answer to a need" (Levinas, 2013, p. 198).

But what of the conception of the face? Can one extend the obligation of the face to non human animals? Put differently, does a snake have a face, even if a plant does not? Levinas himself hesitantly references this very example, upon being directly questioned whether the animal has a face: "it may be, to the dog perhaps, but to the snake . . . I don't know if a snake has a face. I can't answer that question" (Levinas, 1988, pp. 171–172). One could complicate matters further by asking about the eyes as that by which the face is rendered; it is, by Levinas's own admission, after all, that justice is demanded by the third party which "looks at me in the eyes of the other." By the religious command of Ahimsa (in Hinduism and Jainism, for example), as well as a secular vegetarianism that does "not eat anything with eyes," the clear assumption is of a face that poses an ethical command not to kill. Some authors have consequently "extended" the demand of the Levinasian face to include the non human animal (e.g. Davy, 2007; Diehm, 2000). In a way, they seek to extend Levinas's thought beyond his own understanding thereof. One might argue that since the face is not to be reduced to *a* face, something to be comprehended and thematized – it is not, in the first instance, a matter of perception – it is entirely possible for me to be called to ethical responsibility by a suffering appeal prior to thematization. If alterity is not simple difference:

> then how on earth do the differences between (human) faces and the faces of others whose differences mark them as nonhuman drown out the call that emanates from their faces? What does biological 'nonhumanity' have to do with one's status as *other-than*-human?
>
> (Diehm, 2003, p. 173)

The face "has a meaning prior to my conferral of meaning . . . independent of my initiative and power" (Burgat, 2015, p. 184); hence, if the face is not a face, as such, and if a neck can also reveal the weakness of the face (as in Levinas's own admission), why can the non human animal's vulnerability, suffering, and plight not appeal to us and obligate us?

Moreover, even if one were to concede nature and non human animals in terms of the elemental and the human relationship to it marked by labor and enjoyment, it is also true that Levinas's view is creatively new, perhaps even that his anthropocentrism is not "usual" or common. Inasmuch as the I "bathes" in the elemental and is "nourished" by it and inasmuch as the environment is a "sensuous medium," the light by which sensibility arises (Lingis, 2010), an ambient sonority within, and by which the I vibrates, our attachments to the things of/in the world cannot be thought in terms of greed, exploitation, or selfish narcissism. Instead, it is marked by sincerity and the possibility of an eco-posthumanism marked by an "ecology of existents" (Boothroyd, 2019, p. 776) as opposed to a humanism of goodly care and stewardship. Here, again, we find an unfolding deepening of the oeuvre and a reminder of that Derridean image we've referenced so often already – of the same and different wave crashing on the shore. If, as we've already argued, the early work seems to suggest an elemental surround of means to egoic ends, Levinas's return to the il y a and sensibility in *Otherwise than Being* allows for a reappraisal of enjoyment and labor. It becomes clearer that there is no ego prior to enjoyment but that the ego materializes in and through enjoyment (Guenther, 2007). Enjoyment is both egoistic and ethical such that the self "who devours its bread in blissful ignorance of the Other's hunger" is also the self who "tears this bread from its own mouth, in the midst of enjoyment, to feed someone else" (p. 220). There is, in the midst of enjoyment, a command to responsibility, an ambiguity of the body as "enjoyment and suffering" such that the opposition between human and animal becomes more and more tenuous (Guenther, 2007).

Such readings, however, have to struggle with some thorny complications. Language, for example, is crucial to the appeal and demand of the face, and because the non human animal does not have language, on Llewelyn's (1991) reading of Levinas, they cannot make an ethical demand on us as fellow humans do. "The beginning of language is in the face . . . it calls you" (Levinas, 1988, p. 169) as the *revelation* of the other and, above all, "the fact of being addressed" (p. 169). Derrida, particularly, has taken Levinas to task here (Derrida, 2003a, p. 121), with respect to a "Cartesian" assumption of the "animal-machine that exists without language and the ability to respond." The lesson of Derrida's for psychology is also appropriate to Levinas: whereas we privilege language in the therapy room, perhaps more than we ought to, we are also nonetheless attuned to the sigh, the moan, the tears of the patient. Indeed, we are called to a response by those tears, by what they mean to say, in silence. Could one not, in the end, say that the animal's vulnerability is all the more pressing precisely because the silence of its plight speaks? Suffering does not have to be expressed in words for me to recognize an appeal and a demand. Is there not, then, room to ask whether other species and "also the trees and the rivers, the sun and the stars put demands on us?" (Lingis, 2010, p. 80).

One invariably has to reference "Bobby the dog" from Levinas's recounting of a stray dog who "befriended" concentration camp inmates and enthusiastically greeted them on their return to the camp from the brutal workday: "For him – it was incontestable – we were men" (Levinas, 1997, p. 151). This dog, whom the inmates had named "Bobby," Levinas famously characterized as "the last Kantian in Nazi Germany," more attuned to the moral and ethical imperative than the Nazi guards to whom the prisoners were nothing but "a gang of apes" (153). Bobby was more "human" than the humans. It transpires, though, that Bobby is only "apparently" Kantian (Boothroyd, 2019); Levinas continues to qualify the dog as the last Kantian by adding that he is so even as he lacks a "brain needed to universalize maxims and drives" (Levinas, 1997, p. 153). The dog lacks reason, language, and consciousness by which to discern the singularity of (his/its) responsibility. Even if Bobby is a "descendant of the dogs of Egypt" (by which Levinas references his Talmudic exegesis of those dogs whose howls and happy yips signify a "knowledge" of the angel of death and the arrival of the messianic Elijah), even if they have a moment one could consider transcendent or ethical, such moments stem from an "unnatural nature" and a denial of their "vital nature" (Herzog, 2013).

> You ask at what moment one becomes a face. I do not know at what moment the human appears, but what I want to emphasize is that the human breaks with pure being, which is always a persistence in being. That is Darwin's idea. The being of animals is a struggle for life. A struggle of life without ethics. It is a question of might.[3]
>
> (Levinas, 1988, p. 169)

As such, nature is driven by conatus; it perseveres in being, which stands in contrast to the alterity and transcendence of the human, where "the *event of being*, the *esse*, the *essence*, passes over to what is other than being" (Levinas, 2004b, p. 3). Human beings are such precisely "because they can escape their being rooted into being" (Herzog, 2013, p. 362). Whereas nature is a Darwinian battle for survival, blind to otherness, the human is transcendentally turned to the other, kenotically given by the other, able as such to break the bonds of being. To be ethical is to prioritize the other before the self, a uniquely human capacity which recognizes that "there is something more important than my life, and that is the life of the other" (Levinas, 1988, p. 169).

One may ask, What of those countless examples of dogs, whales, dolphins, chimpanzees (I recognize that these are all mammals, which adds another wrinkle) who have sacrificed themselves for others and did so outside of their own species, thus challenging the possible charge of instinctual and speciecist preservation? If Levinas equates the human with the ability to break with being in the singularizing recognition of responsibility, the fact of the matter is also that to be human, this kind of human, is not a fact of biology. In a way, inasmuch as there are non human animals who break with the law of self-preservation, responding as they do to the other without concern for themselves, first, would they not qualify as "human"? And as for the rejoinder that non human animals cannot recognize their mortality or that of another (and ipso facto, the ethical imperative, written as it is in the face, not to kill), we have, again, examples of elephants who seem to do just that and even mourn, or dogs who seem uncommonly attuned to the danger and even pending deaths of human companions. Moreover, even if "one cannot entirely refuse the face of an animal" inasmuch as it is "via the face that one understands, for example, a dog" (p. 169), it is ultimately the human face that allows, through transposition, a recognition of the animal face. The "world becomes intelligible before a human face . . . Man, after all, is not a tree, and humanity is not a forest" (Levinas, 1997, pp. 22–23) such that "the priority here is not found in the animal, but in the human face" (Levinas, 1988, p. 169).

If a direct and first-order ethics is difficult to derive from Levinas's thought, the close and entangled relationship between the ethical and the political might provide resources for an ecopsychology and/or ecopolitics. The other not only demands my responsibility but also judges my irresponsibility, inclusive of my actions that cause harm to his or her dwelling, livelihood, and well-being. The hamburger patty I eat from cows raised on land cleared in the rainforest and from indigenous people having been forcefully displaced or the consumer desires I embrace and desire for which children labor in oppression are but a few of the many examples where the ethical entanglement with politics opens a space for an ecological and environmental justice. When the human face obligates us by his or her hunger, is he or she not also demanding from us a response "for the herds and flocks in his or her care, and the deer and quetzals in the forest he or she cares about" (Lingis, 2010, p. 81)? "It may be true that Bobby fails to teach us the infinity of ethical transcendence; but perhaps there are other lessons to be learned from barking dogs" (Guenther, 235).

## Women

Levinas's view of women and/or the feminine has also generated much debate, controversy, and interpretative positions.[4] There are those who, without equivocation or doubt, brand him as sexist, while there are those who argue that there *is* a difference between the sexes, and Levinas calling it out is actually to combat a more pernicious universalism, akin to the racist who denies the lived experience and history of Black people in the argument that "we are all the same" or as a goodness "that does not see race." Still others ("too numerous to name . . . most of Levinas scholarship" [Katz, 2004, p. 172]) would simply ignore Levinas's "feminine" as an unfortunate but insignificant trope that pales against the thrust of his broader message (Chanter, 2001a; Katz, 2004). There are, however, also those who take Levinas at his own word and who caution against thinking the feminine in terms of empirical gender, as it supposedly does not refer to biology at all. And then there are questions of a perhaps unacknowledged influence of Levinas's Judaism, a religion which is matrilineal, where the very fact of being a Jew is conferred by woman but also where orthodox and conservative Jewish women experience extensive patriarchal restrictions to their freedom. Of course, this last statement resurrects the question as to the extent one should bring Levinas's Talmudic writings to bear on his philosophy, all his assurances that they are "separate" notwithstanding. Is such "separation" even possible or believable?

To complicate matters, Levinas's use of terms and notions related to sexual and gendered difference vary across his oeuvre. In the early work, for example, the feminine is associated with Eros and the caress of the erotic. In *Totality and Infinity*, it is the dwelling, marked by the feminine as the other which renders it welcoming, familiar, and hospitable. Finally, in *Otherwise than Being*, the image of maternity becomes the most haunting one for the other in me. Is it possible to charge Levinas with dangerous stereotyping and/or sexism across all these instances? And if not, what would a more nuanced critique entail? Surely, it is not as easy as saying he is sexist in one instance but not, or "less so," in another. Could the same or universal critique be applicable across these uses?

One of the earliest charges of sexism and patriarchal arrogance came from no less prominent a figure as Simone De Beauvoir (1989). Succinct as it was, in little more than footnotes, De Beauvoir's critique is as powerful and enduring as any; almost every commentator on Levinas and women feel compelled to reference De Beauvoir. Levinas's portrayal of woman, she says in a summative nutshell, is of oppressive patriarchy, patently stereotypical in its portrayal of women as gentle, frail, weak, tender, a homemaker, and at the same time, an erotic seductress. Levinas's woman is one "defined and differentiated with reference to man and not he with reference to her; she is the incidental, the inessential as opposed to the essential. He is the Subject, he is the Absolute- she is the other" (De Beauvoir, 1989, p. xxii). Levinas perpetuates stereotypical tropes, and for all it wants to do philosophically, it betrays masculine privilege (Sikka, 2001) and denies women full subjectivity (Irigaray, 1991).

De Beauvoir, however, only had access to the early work, which may cast some doubt on such a "straightforward dismissal" inasmuch as it did not benefit from "Levinas's overall philosophical project, which is to elevate the notion of alterity above the notion of totality" (Chanter, 2001a, p. 2). Even so, at the end of the previous paragraph, I provided references (Sikka, 2001; Irigaray, 1991) that *did* benefit from access to the whole oeuvre but which nonetheless seem to support De Beauvoir's charge, if not also its claims. One cannot, therefore, dismiss De Beauvoir

either, acknowledging as we do that her comments are informed by a partial exposure. But one also recognizes a kind of feminist position that emphasizes reciprocality and a fundamental equality of skill, potential, and being. Might we not argue,
now, that a so-called "third-wave feminism" and a nuanced feminist phenomenology would be more attuned to alterity – to the fact that there *is* a difference in the
lived experience of man and woman. To claim the generality of an earlier view of
equality as sameness (that woman is everything man "is" and can "do" everything
man can) is in reality to take the male experience as default and to silence female
alterity. The fact of the matter is that in pregnancy, childbirth, the experience of
sex, her body and her body in the world, and in socially constituted relations, for
example, there is a world of difference – an alterity – that needs to be articulated,
acknowledged, valorized. Yet if this is in fact what Levinas's developing views
gesture toward, how is it that Irigaray's critique remains salient, concerned now
not only "with the need to avoid reducing women to replicas of men, but . . . also
alert to the danger lurking in Levinas's penchant for allowing the feminine to represent alterity" (Chanter, 2001a, p. 3)? It makes good sense, therefore, to remind
ourselves, briefly, of the main developments and themes of the feminine across the
oeuvre and the chapters of this book.

In the early work, the feminine is presented in terms of alterity, as difference
that cannot be subsumed, incorporated, or mastered through labor, knowledge, or
possession. The descriptive terms for such feminine difference that escapes comprehension are of "mystery," "hiding," "modesty," and a slipping "away from the
light" (Levinas, 1987b, pp. 86–87). The caress, we have seen, is the concrete motif
by which the erotic relationship with alterity seeks transcendence – realized in
fecundity and paternity, with the birth of the son. Moving to *Totality and Infinity*,
however, the feminine as alterity, and the erotic as a way to transcendence, falls
away; she is no longer "the other par excellence," and language, rather than the
caress, becomes the prime relationship to the other (Perpich, 2001). Here, the feminine is what makes the world habitable, the hospitable preparation of the dwelling
for the ethical welcome of the other. "The woman is the condition for recollection" (Levinas, 2013, p. 155), the "gentleness" of the home by which it becomes a
refuge for the inner life (of man). She acts as a brake on (man's) "conquering and
virile attitude" (Chalier, 1991, p. 123); in a way, she enables the ethical even as the
welcome she occasions is not, of itself, ethical (Chalier, 1991). Finally, in *Otherwise than Being*, the feminine finds its most striking presentation in maternity –
exemplifying the other-in-me, of being held hostage and being given over to the
other completely, quite literally as the other in the flesh, under one's skin. It is the
very pattern of substitution (Chalier, 1991) and of an assigned, undeclinable, inex-
tricable responsibility, the central statement of that text.

All of these differing moments have been examined and criticized. In a way,
critique of the early work is "easy"; there is no getting away from the stereotypical
associations to women. Additionally, for all its pretensions to illume a philosophical
movement, the fact of the matter is that transcendence is presented in paternity and
the birth of a child, a son, not a daughter. This, rather simply and straightforwardly,

is disturbing; Luce Irigaray (1991) notes that the mother-daughter is neither thematized nor mentioned, which in fact is as striking an exhibit for a more general observation of woman as "invisible and inaudible," silent as of one who is mute (Brody, 2001; Perpich, 2001). Whereas one could argue that *Totality and Infinity* (and *Otherwise than Being*) presents a more complicated and nuanced challenge, charges of sexism or the blind spots of patriarchal privilege remain. Inasmuch as woman is the condition for the welcome of the dwelling, for the masculine to turn away from the self and the struggle with being, she does not venture out to labor, and her presence is for the benefit of man. Her seemingly (more) heroic role is ultimately to tie her to a rather ideal traditional role of the caretaker who surrender themselves in the service and transcendence of men. Even if the role of feminine in habitation has a positive significance in accomplishing the ethical, it is an equivocal significance: the feminine allows the participation of the man in the domain of the ethical but without herself participating in it (Katz, 2001). Of course, self-sacrifice and self-immolation can be considered heroic, even saintly. But in those instances, it is the unique and singular example of the individual whose life and sacrifice might be inspiring, in the sense of us wanting to be like this exemplary individual but also knowing its impossibility, beyond any reasonable possibility or expectation for most all of us; to expect or imply such sacrifice for woman, as such and as group is where saintly martyrdom is but the extension of a patriarchal ideal by which woman is to selflessly give, without a face, without return, without subjectivity. "One simply cannot ignore the fact that throughout history, women have been systematically forced to sacrifice themselves, literally and metaphorically, for men, as if this social context were immaterial or irrelevant to Levinas's claims" (Chanter, 2001a, p. 26).

Such notions of woman cast in traditional, sexist roles and associations extends to *Otherwise than Being*. There is no denying the power of the image and metaphor of maternity for substitution, "the-other-in-the-same" and the "one-for-the-other." At the same time, however, Chanter (2001a, 2001b) argues convincingly that maternity robs woman from eroticism and pleasure; the sexual end is a sanitized maternity, woman as child bearer and mother for whom erotic pleasure is scandalous. In maternity, the beloved woman births the future, a son; she makes the ethical possible, makes subjectivity possible – for the man and at her expense. "She is left without subjectivity, without access to the ethical, and outside any relation to God" (Katz, 2001, p. 155).

By Levinas's explanation, we make a grave error when we equate the conceptual that is the feminine with an empirical and gendered view. That is, the feminine here does not refer to an actual or biological woman (Peperzak, 1993), does not "designate a being" (Chanter, 2001a, p. 16) as much as a tendency, a way, or a metaphor (Guenther, 2006). Fecundity, Levinas writes, "goes beyond the biologically empirical" (Levinas, 2013, p. 277), and "the empirical essence of the human being of the 'feminine sex' in a dwelling in nowise affects the dimension of femininity which remains opens there, as the very welcome of the dwelling" (p. 158). Some authors point to Levinas intentionally mixing the gender of French words to make this point – for example, *aime*, which is masculine (loved), written as *aimee* (beloved). This, however, is not a consistent practice at all, and in several instances, Levinas "drops his guard and resorts to language that invokes the actual empirical women that at other places in his texts he assures us he does not have in mind" (Chanter, 2001a, p. 16). In several interviews, as well, the same dynamic can be noticed: of a back and forth where woman is not an empirical entity but then she is as well, where "feminine is other for a masculine being not only because of a different nature but also inasmuch as alterity is in some way its nature" (Levinas, 1985, p. 65). It seems that the language of maternity is both metaphorical and literal, which Lebeau reads generously as the intent to signal an "overflow of meaning, or an evocation, an excess or surplus of signification" (LeBeau, 2017, p. 339). Yet even as metaphoric indicators, the use of these terms betray masculine patriarchal language privilege, and as literal pointer, Levinas's blindness to mothers who have risked their lives in childbirth "to ensure that through the child time may achieve the element of infinity" (Manning, 1991, p. 140) is revealing.

Finally, we agree with Katz, who has perhaps been the most vocal proponent of the view that Levinas's use of the feminine attains relief against the backdrop of his Judaism and confessional writings. We've mentioned Levinas's own insistence to keep the philosophical and Talmudic streams separate, and it is indeed the case that most commentators do so as well. In this instance, however, we think it particularly illuminating to read intertextually. For example, in Levinas's gloss on creation, it may be possible to argue the creation of the human, a face without sexed characteristics such that "woman and man are created from what is human" (Katz, 2004, p. 156).[5] Such a reading is generous to the argument of sexed language as metaphor and not empirical being. Another reference illustrates this complication: in a rather direct acknowledgment of Biblical inspiration, Levinas's references the book of Numbers to illustrate proximity and the maternal:

> In proximity, the absolutely Other, the stranger whom 'I have neither conceived nor given birth to,' I have already on my arms, already I bear him, according to the Biblical formula, 'in my breast as the wet-nurse bears the nursling' (Numbers XI, 12).
>
> (Levinas, 2004b, p. 91)

In this case, not only is the demand for responsibility towards the stranger as for a nursing child, which I did not bear or have capacity to bear, but as Guenther reminds us (Guenther, 2006), the wet nurse in this case is neither a mother nor even a woman; it is Moses. On the other hand, and in other instances, however, Levinas wholly endorses the Talmudic notion of woman as "a keepsake of the hearth" (Levinas, 1997, p. 32), or as that secret, invisible, silent, marginal presence/absence which permeates the philosophical work. The orthodoxy of the public man in the world against the private and childbearing woman of the home is also a feature of the dwelling, as we have seen. If the Judaic version is clear about reference to concrete women and men, the slippage of its transposition to metaphor in the philosophical work is quite understandable. One could also bring a religiopolitical and religiohistorical inflection to bear on notions such as fecundity, for example: the birth of the (Jewish) child is the futurity of Israel, is to fulfill an immemorial Biblical commandment (a view Levinas articulates in the essay *Judaism and the Feminine* [Levinas, 1997]). Ultimately, the following is not inconceivable:

> Levinas's Hebrew roots give him profound insight into the obligation and responsibility for the other, for those who are most vulnerable. And yet it is his Judaism that precisely allows his inadequate view of women to emerge and take hold.
>
> (Katz, 2001, p. 163)

In the end, the question seems more difficult than a simple dismissal or accusation of willing patriarchy or sexism. One is hard-pressed not to think of the feminine in biological terms, Levinas's statements that we shouldn't notwithstanding, and no less so because he replicates all the stereotypical aspects we have come to associate with femininity – frailty, secrecy, voluptuousness, and so on. "How does one read Levinas as a woman, that is, without reading over what is said of the feminine as if it had nothing to do with being a woman?" Chanter (2001a, pp. 1–2) asks poignantly. It is a question we should all be asking, perhaps even especially those of us who identify as men. The gendered vocabulary retains its connotations of gender even if we are told it does not; the language never escapes its conditioned context nor does it question the association with the socially conditioned to any satisfactory extent. As Karen Horney remarks in her brilliant challenge to penis envy by offering womb envy (and as I challenge my students: if you subscribe to penis envy, there is absolutely no reason why you could not do the same for womb envy), it is impossible to plead innocence if you use gendered theoretical references in a social and cultural context where it is overdetermined. The language is tripped up by ontology inasmuch as the language resurrects its totality. Feminist concerns remain: neither Levinas's assertions, nor ignoring it, nor dismissing it as minor, nor minimizing it in characterizations of metaphor, nor that it does not designate a being as much as a tendency are sufficient. It seems we end at a place where we have to acknowledge some features of Levinas's account as irredeemable for feminism, while an appreciation for an inherent complexity and ambiguity, and for the feminine in relation to the philosophical project as a whole, provides resources to a feminism that can think Levinas differently, that can read Levinas in ways he was not radical enough, or equipped enough, to do himself.

## Race and/or Culture

Critical accusations of androcentrism and sexism have been coupled with those of Eurocentrism and ethnocentrism, even racism. There is hardly any mention of politics, racism, or colonialism, for example, in the work itself; Levinas appears, Drabinski (2011, p. 1) writes, "utterly unaware of and unconcerned with the accusing face of the political." One might argue that such an omission makes perfect sense if we accept that Levinas's philosophical concern is with an infinite, transcendent, and metaphysical ethical responsibility and not with politics or racism which would represent "the ontological betrayal (an 'after') of such (a 'prior') responsibility in a material present and presence" (Laubscher, 2022). Still, one can express some surprise at Levinas's "critical neglect of the political dimension," as Caygill (2000) does, given his (Levinas's) closeness to the "convulsions of twentieth-century political history" and as the philosopher "most directly touched" by such history (Caygill, 2000, p. 6).

Levinas, however, is not entirely silent on issues of race, culture, and/or politics. Firstly, he did comment on international and political events in several interviews. Some of those comments were rather unfortunate, unsavory, and/or downright horrible. It has opened him up to charges of racism directly. We will reference some of these comments but also ask how, or if, these statements are betrayed in the philosophy itself. There is a second way in which we are mistaken to argue that Levinas's philosophy has nothing, or little, to say, imply, or offer politics and/or the political. The truth is that it permeates and percolates in the recurring references to justice, war, tyranny, and morality.[6] Thirdly, some authors (e.g. Alpert, 2015; Anderson, 2017; Eisenstadt, 2003) have argued, rather compellingly, that Levinas's Jewish/Talmudic and/or "confessional writings" (which, we reiterate, he took great pains to keep separate from his philosophical work) contain a rich source for an analysis and understanding of the political and that it – as such – should really be read alongside the philosophical.

We are reminded that, for Levinas, the ethical precedes the encounter with an other as an infinite and transcendent "condition" of possibility for the finite and materialized "actual" encounter of the singular self with a singular other. This ethical responsibility for the other is anarchic, diachronic, imposed, asymmetrical, and an irrefusable obligation; it is not a function of any historical attribute, psychological quality, or sociopolitical context. It is there before, or more precisely, outside (anarchic) history and time and before the appearance of the other as such, before culture, and before one notices the color of her eyes or the hue of their skin. If one does notice the eyes or the shape of the nose, one has entered into the spatial and the ontological, and if the comparison and adequation is of a racist sort, one has betrayed the responsibility of the ethical call in totalizing, systematic violence. Levinas reminds us that "the ethical exigency is not an ontological necessity" (Levinas, 1985, p. 87), that the "malignancy of evil" is a possible response to a face "dominated by perception," even if it "cannot be reduced to that" (p. 87). The ethical is, quite simply put, "first philosophy" from which all else (including politics and "political philosophy") flows. Politics and the political is already a "falling away" from the transcendent and infinite ethical demand into the totalizing and economic rule of law and accounting.

Several scholars and philosophers have taken such Levinasian views on justice and the political to critical task.[7] Bernasconi questions the approach of the other outside of culture, arguing that to do so is to repeat and perpetuate a violent and abstract humanism that "reduces the other to nothing more than a man" (2005, p. 17). A face without characteristics and a non-particular, "abstract," trans-individual universal "humanity" to all real ends is effectively to argue a white, male, European face. The Black who attempts to live thus, "simply as a human being . . . soon discovers that to do so calls for living simply as a white" (Gordon, 2005, p. 4). It may be possible, as a consequence, to levy the argument that "despite every appearance to the contrary, Levinas' philosophy is politics in the purest sense" (Froese, 2019, p. 7). Frantz Fanon (Fanon, 2008) proves a particularly trenchant interlocutor: the conquering and colonial European promise, to "become like me to be a man," is not only a false and impossible one for the Black, inherently and foundationally inassimilable to white Europe, but is also the way in which Europe absolves itself precisely from responsibility, from itself.

Justice requires the visibility of faces and the fact of seeing, notwithstanding Levinas's charge to see without seeing. As a question of justice, what justice is to me, it is a face that poses the question. I am born to justice by someone who "has already presented himself . . . as a face" (Levinas, 2013, p. 177). "Hence, even conceding the question's anarchic and diachronic (non)address, outside of history and place, as the question of the human (my humanity authorized), the addressee is in history and the material present (my humanity authored)" (Laubscher, 2022). The ethical call may precede the self's encounter with the other, but it is only in the encounter with the other that the self can be ethical. Could we not argue, now, that the Levinasian ethical command is (also) political – that "to welcome the widow, orphan, or stranger . . . is already implicated in a political world" (Drabinski, 2011, p. 189). In fact, by Levinas's own formulation of the neighbor, there is no single aspect of existence without the plurality of others, such that the obligation to justice may be no less of a first question than ethics, and "all responsibility has to be borne politically" (Wolff, 2011, p. 25).

The ethical relation presupposes a (human) other, with a (human) face. Is it so, however, that the Black appear as a human? Mbembe argues that the Black is "the very prototype of the animal . . . no more than a 'body-thing' . . . neither the substrate nor the affirmation of any mind or spirit" (Mbembe, 2001, pp. 26–27). A "phobogenic object," the Black has no subjectivity, only materialized objecthood and a canvas for the projections of the white (Fanon, 2008). The Black enters, not as a man "but a new type of man, a new genus. Why, a Negro!" (Fanon, 2008, p. 116). As an object, without a face, the Black is a being which issues no ethical command, cannot order or ordain. This is not, for many (Afropessimists like Wilderson [2010], Sexton [2015], Warren [2018], Marriott [2018] especially), a mere "falling away" from a prior ethical human but a fundamental ontological characteristic of the world itself. Not a matter of perception or representation or of individual prejudice, blackness is ontologically negative, defined as an absence of humanity and possibility.

Levinas's philosophy positions itself as a tension between Athens and Jerusalem, between the Greeks and the Bible. He goes further, though, to also present it as humanity's tension: "I always say – but under my breath – that the Bible and the Greeks present the only serious issues in human life; everything else is dancing . . ." (Levinas, 2001b, p. 149); "Man is Europe and the Bible, and all the rest can be translated from there" (p. 65). The Latin American philosopher, Enrique Dussel, writes:

> Levinas always speaks of the other as 'the absolute other' . . . he has never though that the other could be Indio, African, or Asian . . . Not even Levinas has been able to transcend Europe. We are the ones born outside, we have suffered it.
> (Dussel, 1974)[8]

In an early paper, written shortly after Hitler came to power, Levinas argues that Hitler has awakened an "elemental feeling" within the German populace, based as it was on "primitive powers" (Levinas, 1990). One could connect this early essay to later statements in interviews about "dancing primitives" and "the Asiatic peril"[9] who are too attached "to the elements, to the earth, to the body. They cannot get out of being" (Alpert, 2015, p. 22). Like the pagan, they lack transcendence and are bound to the instinctual and a failure of ethical subjectivity – a failure that presumably also enabled the horror of the Shoah. Hitler's moment, though, can be thought as a temporary failing, a historical aberration given that ethical subjectivity, wrought by the yoke of Athens and Jerusalem, is precisely Europe's gift of humanity, Europe's disjoining of spirit from body, making room as such for transcendence (Levinas argues thus in another early paper, from 1935, *On Escape* [Levinas, 2003]). Thus, while "Europe has many things to be reproached for. . . . a history of blood and war . . . it is also the place where this blood and war have been regretted and constitute a bad conscience" (Levinas, 2001b, p. 63).

Is it really that far-fetched, now, to argue that there are others, other others, whose alterity does not quite evoke an ethical command, their appearance being "radically strange," lacking as they do, a "sacred history," and being too closely beholden to "instinctual passions," rendering them incapable of ethical transcendence and subjectivity? Not quite capable yet of excendence in hypostasis from the elemental, "They cry in another way"[10] (Levinas, 2001b). Drabinski (2011) argues as much; there are those who are near, to whom I am kin and responsible, and then there are those who "appear as radical and alien" and who could be an enemy (Caygill, 2002, p. 1). As such, there opens up an "epistemological distance" between a center and a periphery, the latter of which waits for a responsibility which does not arrive (Froese, 2019). By this reading, the refrain of Bernasconi's question, "Who is my neighbor?" (Bernasconi, 1992), may well render the philosophical answer of (European) kin, kith, and the familiar and proximate same.

Not unlike the responses to charges of sexism, there are those who completely ignore the possibility of a "Eurocentric imperialism" (Caygill, 2002) and/or an anti-Black prejudice – in the work and/or the person. Then there are those who provide all kinds of agile intellectual acrobatics with which to defend him and his philosophy. Some would have nothing to do with his philosophy on the basis of his personal pronouncements. But there are also those who do not find it impossible to acknowledge his statements, even aspects of his philosophy, as sexist, racist, and androcentric (and indefensible) at the same time as there are resources within the philosophy to combat all of those. I tend to find myself in the latter camp.

## Notes

1  A term coined by David Abram (1996), arguably the most inspirational figure for ecopsychology, to refer to earthly nature. The term has been taken up with remarkable alacrity by scholars, therapists, and activists alike.
2  Some examples include Edelglass et al. (2012), Atterton and Wright (2019), and Guenther (2007).
3  Atterton (2011), among a handful of others, has taken Levinas's characterization of Darwin to task as uninformed or a serious misreading. Arguing for the possibility of a biological basis for morality/ethics, "Darwin's idea" in fact does include a moral sense or conscience.
4  Invaluable contributions include Chanter (2001a, 2001b), Sandford (2000), Chalier (1991), and the remarkable essays of Luce Irigaray, *The Fecundity of the Caress* (2001) and *Questions to Emmanuel Levinas* (1991)
5  I quote Katz here to demonstrate this argument, but it is important to note that this is not Katz's view; she disagrees with it.
6  The powerful first lines of *Totality and Infinity* may serve as evidentiary reference par excellence: "Everyone will readily agree that it is of the highest importance to know whether we are not duped by morality. Does not lucidity, the mind's openness upon the true, consist in catching sight of the permanent possibility of war?" (Levinas, 2013, p. 21).
7  These include Eagleton (for whom the Levinasian focus is "self defeating and ineffectual," as it turns politics into "the problem, not the solution" [2009, p. 233]), Zizek (for whom the Levinasian distinction needs to be upended in a choice "*against* the face, for the *third*" [2005, p. 183, emphasis in original]), or Reinhard (who also argues for a reversal, such that the political, in fact, "is the condition of the ethical . . . the *two* can only be created by passing through the *three*" [2005, p. 49, emphasis in original]).
8  There is a simultaneously inspiring and disappointing connection between Dussel and Levinas, who knew each other from their participation in an intensive seminar at Louvain in 1972. "As a South American," Dussel asked Levinas if the "fifteen million Indians slaughtered during the conquest of Latin America, and the thirteen million Africans who were made slaves" were as other to Levinas as the victims of anti-Semitism (Dussel, 1999, p. 125). To which Levinas responded, "That's something for you to think about" (pp. 125–126). Which Dussel did in his "liberation philosophy," which transforms Levinas's absolute alterity to proximate exteriority, to a philosophizing from the position of the damned. It is abundantly clear that Dussel is as inspired and informed by Fanon as he is by Levinas.
9  Caygill (2002) analyzes and lists a range of such statements from various essays and interviews, for example, of "innumerable masses advancing out of Asia" or the "yellow peril" which is "not racial, it is spiritual" and whom eschews a "radical strangeness" where "Abraham, Isaac, and Jacob no longer mean anything" (pp. 182–194).
10  Levinas refers here to televised images of Black South Africans "dancing" at a funeral.

# Chapter 9

# Where Endings Are Beginnings

In a way, the chapter heading says it all. I wanted to introduce Levinas to psychology, in so doing responding to, and participating in, a conversation that already started. I wanted to add to a dismally small gathering of psychologists and helping professionals who have taken Levinas seriously and who wrestle and struggle with ways to think and imagine a psychology inspired, which is to say breathed into, by his insights. But I also hoped to take the conversation in new directions, to raise new questions and possibilities; that, too, is Levinas's idea about what teaching is about, what conversation is about – indeed, what scholarship is about.

The intention was never to deliver a systematic Levinasian psychology. The very idea strikes at the spirit of Levinas's project. At best, it was to wonder what a Levinasian-inspired psychology might look like or have to consider. To that end, we've raised several questions, posed a number of challenges, and offered some suggestions about routes to travel. Still, what is clear is that there are some basic givens. In the same way that one cannot "be" a Christian if you don't believe in the divinity of Jesus, or a psychoanalyst if you don't believe in the primacy of the unconscious, one cannot "be" or practice a Levinasian psychology if you don't proceed from the notion of *ethics as first psychology* and of *responsibility* as the marching order for all one does. We are sometimes too quick to dismiss such "big" framing ideas from what one does, to separate the grime of method and procedure from the supposedly ideal of epistemology, ontology, and metaphysics. Consider, for example, pausing to ask why we do what we do – why, as therapists, we choose to muck about in someone else's pain and suffering, or as researchers to meet with others and ask them to help answer a question we have, or to stand in a classroom to teach about self and others. Consider the answer to that question, not simply as "wanting to help," wanting to "give back," or wanting to "make the world a better place," all of which may laudably be true, but also – primarily and fundamentally – as having been called, elected, singled out to a responsibility that only I can answer for.

Levinas does not provide a normative ethics. He has said so himself – that is not his task. Nor does he provide a psychological how to. And whereas Levinas's project is about the subject and subjectivity, a philosophical subject, to be sure, it is also "one that has flesh, mind and spirit" (Rozmarin, 2007, p. 334), and which, as such, is an eminently psychological subject as well. In the end, we agree with

DOI: 10.4324/9781003315612-9

Bernasconi completely that Levinas's thinking and inspiration "matters not at all unless it impacts on our approach to concrete situations so that we come to them as ethical" (Bernasconi, 2002, p. 250).

Several years ago, I was involved in a large research project which involved collecting stories of apartheid in South Africa. These were ordinary stories, told by "ordinary" people about their earliest memories of apartheid, of experiences that stood out to them and remained with them. On one occasion, I accompanied a young graduate student in his late 20s perhaps to collect precisely such stories for this Apartheid Archive Project. A doctoral student, he was writing his dissertation on trauma, and we saw an opening to simultaneously collect "data" for his dissertation *and* stories for the archive. So we set out early one morning from the leafy university town of Stellenbosch through the exquisitely beautiful winelands of the area, across the mountains to Franschoek (literally "French corner," to honor the French Huguenots, persecuted and exiled from France to settle in South Africa, where they would come to persecute and exile the indigenous peoples whose land they now introduced winemaking to). There, we were to interview a number of farmworkers about their experience of apartheid and for this student, particularly, about the experience of apartheid as trauma. That was the matter of his dissertation, that was what mattered. On the way there, and in the car, this student talked animatedly and enthusiastically about his theoretical background and how he framed and wanted to take up trauma – notably from his readings of Heidegger (2001) and Stolorow (2007) of trauma as the "taking up of being-towards-death in the authentic and anticipatory resoluteness of a struggle." We got to the farm and conducted our first interview in a living room of a farmworker's house, a living room which in a three-room dwelling meant just that, a place where everyone slept, ate, and died, which is to say lived. We spoke to a 75-year-old man who related, with clarion clarity, a clarity clearer than sight, a moment 62 years earlier, from when he was 13 years old. He told us how he was a bright kid, about how smart he was, and how he taught himself to read and how all the teachers at his two-room little farm school told him he was destined for great things. He told us about how he wanted to be a doctor and help people and that he studied his math by the light of a candle, the only candle they had. And how, when he was 13, the owner of the farm came and told his class that he needed them to harvest the bumper crop of fruit – thick, bursting, and juicy export grapes destined for places like America and England; some of your parents may well have eaten grapes from this farm. He told us how the farmer took all the children 13 and older out of school and how, when his father went to plead with the white owner to make an exception and have him stay in school, the farmer said the child was free to go to school but then the family had to vacate their house and move off his farm, as his was not a charity. An impossible choice, our 13-year-old went into the vineyard that mid-January and for 62 more harvest seasons after that. In fact, we interviewed him on the very farm where all of this happened and which he never left.

After the interview, my student walked outside, off into a distance. I walked up to him, and we stood for a while in silence, looking out over the vineyards and the valley below, so beautiful, it hurt. He pulled out a pack of cigarettes, lit one, and as he sucked in the white autumn air, mixed now with the burnt comfort of nicotine and tar, he turned to me and asked, haltingly and pleadingly, "How do I write this?"

My response was "By allowing it to write you."

I would like to believe this was a "Levinasian" moment, an instance where the psychological research enterprise caught sight of ethical responsibility and where the course of that enterprise was challenged and changed in the recognition that what my student saw was not data or a text to be read as much as an *exposure* to an experience, an other, that was to be suffered (that is, a weight to bear: from the Latin *sub* – "from below" + *ferre* – "to bear"). Halling, already in the first extant attempt to bring Levinas to psychology, psychotherapy in particular, caught a glimpse of this insight which "resides not in the wisdom and cleverness of the therapist, but in the fact that we are in the presence of someone who may dispossess us of our understanding, our comprehension, and call us to hear and speak" (Halling, 1975, p. 221).

Ethical responsibility is exorbitant. It includes not only the presence of the other in Halling's therapy room or the interviewee of our example earlier. Several years ago, another student and I set out to research political violence in South Africa. Mindful of the reductionism of natural science psychology, we smugly positioned our study squarely within a qualitative and human science psychology – one of *understanding*. The event that would provide us access to the phenomenon was a particularly horrific instance of "necklacing," a practice of killing that involves putting a gasoline-filled car tire over the neck and shoulders of the victim and setting it alight. Appearing on the South African scene in the mid-1980s, it all but disappeared postapartheid. Usually, this brutal form of execution was perpetrated by a group of people and of someone branded as a traitor to the anti-apartheid cause, a collaborator or a "sell out."[1] We surveyed the literature on political violence, placed "necklacing" squarely in political terms and political context, and designed an elegant qualitative study. We would interview the convicted murderers, the perpetrators found guilty of one such necklacing murder. In addition, we had the transcripts of their trial, as well as the transcripts of the Truth and Reconciliation Commission, which examined the case in question, and heard testimony from the perpetrators and family members of the deceased. Each of these accounts, each of these "data points," provided a different perspective on the same event which we read hermeneutically and intertextually. We looked for similarities and differences, and we were sensitive to how the text was made to mean. We listed all the places where mainstream psychology and social psychology were right and on target around the conceptual of conformity, of obedience, of normativity, of deindividuation, and of dehumanization. And we offered the gifts of our own hermeneutic insights – for example, of betrayal or the importance of context. In short, we produced a rigorous research product, well worth publication in the most prestigious journals, or presentations at the most scholarly research conferences.

But something was "missing." Somehow, we *felt* and knew, knew in our skin and by the sense of our bodies, not by consciousness (How could reason know what it does not know, after all?), that we missed something. In retrospect, one might argue that niggling unease in terms of Levinasian proximity and substitution, but in the moment, then, it was also a vague consciousness (a reason) of the fact that our research product was simply another widget on the scholarly production line. We could now say it was simply another said. And so, good researchers that we wanted to be, we went looking for what was missing in the said of the data, but this time, we rummaged in the scraps of footnotes or story snippets that never made it into our thematic telling and in "data" that ended up on the cutting floor. There was one such moment: in the court transcripts, we read of something rather puzzling. In the heat of the murdering moment, it appears that Nombulelo Dilato's killers do something curious: they throw sand on her face so that it does not burn. The judge, employing the linear logic of the rational, also finds this act strange. He notes:

> Number 3 accused . . . ordered him [State Witness] to throw sand over the head of the deceased to prevent that portion of her body from burning. This he did, though is not clear what the purpose of this operation was.
>
> (Supreme Court of South Africa, 1986)

And then the judge moves on, and it is never mentioned again. Sixteen years later, at the TRC hearings, one of the commissioners mention that "They threw sand on her face as she was burning. Why?" He poses this question to Nombulelo's sister, who says she does not know. To which the commissioner responds, "I wouldn't know why either," and continues to other matters.

Thus, it was that – our research to all intents and purposes "done," a dissertation written, an article prepared – we had to go back to the perpetrators themselves to ask them about this business with the sand. What would they say? Why throw sand on their victim's face as the rest of her body burns? One responded that he didn't know. "It was just, you know, *izikizi*." The interview was in isiXhosa, and whereas the word can be translated as "scary," or "gruesome," that is not really the full of it. It is an abomination and a kind of dread, a kind of expectation of something about to happen, not to you directly or materially, but nonetheless that something is about to happen that will haunt you forever. It is like looking out your window and seeing your child in the front yard playing with a ball, the ball bouncing into the street, and a truck which the child does not see coming down the hill; this is the moment of *izikizi*, the dread of something that might happen, that hasn't happened yet, and that does not happen to you, even as it does and even as it always and forever will. It comes from elsewhere; it is an unspeakable and untranslatable word for what is unspeakable, for what cannot be worded. It is always from elsewhere, for the other, and from the other, an abomination, as in ab homine – "away from man" – an omen from an other or otherworldly realm. The second perpetrator, in response to our question, uttered the following: "*into engathethekiyo*" which, if you plug it into Google Translate, will come back as "something unspeakable" or "something extraordinary" – something that you cannot bear to talk about, as well as what language cannot bear.

It is here, then, that the order of our research changed. It is here now that we realized:

> for all our interest in her death, Nombulelo Dilato was nowhere present, really, or to the extent that she was, she was a mere catalyst, variable, or tool for others to explain themselves with, or for us to understand 'political violence' by.
>
> (Laubscher & Mbuqe, 2020, pp. 74–75)

Facing up to the face of a ghost, we stood accused. The marching orders for our research was no longer a question that we posed as much as our being questioned, being deposed. We were being addressed, we were in an apostraphizing relationship with the one person who could tell us most about political violence and whose proximity mandated our response. Claimed it, truth be told, so that it was no longer for our study to grasp in understanding than to *be* grasped in responsibility. There are many more touchpoints to Levinas than I mention here and many more ways we wrestled with what it might mean for the scholar to give countenance to the dead,[2] the scholar who is to "say the loneliness of those who thought themselves dying at the same time as Justice" (Levinas, 1996b, p. 120).

There are many ways to "get to" a Levinasian-inspired psychology. In the example earlier, we certainly did not go to the data with Levinas in hand; one might say the primordial responsibility and the expiation of subjectivity was there before Levinas, who provided the words for our recognition. We did not know that our latching onto that scrap of discarded data could be thought as the trace of a saying or for our research to attempt an unraveling, unfurling unsaying. In a sense, we do not need Levinas to hear the call of the other, but we can hear the call so much clearer by heeding Levinas. The thing is, whether one is a humanistic or psychoanalytic psychologist, existential, Gestalt, or any number of others, it is wholly possible "to make ethics, conceived as responsibility for the other" (Marcus, 2008, p. 221) the basis for psychological theory and/or practice. From this recognition, one almost wants to say from this "simple recognition," we start from where we are. Therapy, teaching, research – these are all ethical events; in all instances, it is ethical because a claim is made on me (Dueck & Parsons, 2007). There is no need to build a whole new psychology, a systematic Levinasian psychological edifice. Where we are is good enough for Levinas to breathe into the embers of our theory and practice. Indeed, this image is one Donna Orange (2011) borrows from Levinas to characterize her own invitation to Levinas, between a relational psychoanalysis and hermeneutics. The hospitality of Levinas's dwelling becomes a model for her therapy, a nonjudgmental and nonviolent welcome which remains "experience-near" and honors asymmetry over mutuality (Orange, 2011). Or to rethink affect, as Marcus (2007, 2008) does, not as derivative "expressions of libidinal and/or aggressive drives" (2008, p. 227) but as an experience of the other and the other in me, myself returned to me, as obligation. One does not even need Marcus's psychoanalytic inflection for Levinas to help us think affectivity as sensibility. It is the strangest thing this, that psychology has long not quite known what to do with emotion, that very thing of psychology, of what it is to be human. Behavioral, cognitive, and cognitive behavioral theories have sidelined it completely, at worst, or saw it as derivative of some reciprocally determined triad of behavior, cognition, and affect. Natural science looks for solace and certainty in neurochemicals and neurotransmitters as its "cause" (sometimes I wonder whether they know, quietly and secretly, that such reasoning is nonsense, as I believe conspiracy theorists must know their beliefs are crazy). But if we think affect as sensibility, as a different kind of knowing, a knowing of the body and the prereflective, as its source in the other and the other in the same, then we can also "know," like Job's friends did, when it is appropriate just to sit in silence. We recall that when they hear of Job's terrible suffering, his friends travel some distance and put up with expense and discomfort to be with him – Eliphaz from Ideumea, Bildad from Shuah, and Zophar from Na'amah, we are told. They do so because they care for him, he is their friend, and they love him and want to "be there for him," as it were. Not unlike many of us who become psychologists because we care about human suffering, or activists who want to shine a light on injustice, or researchers who want to make the world a better place – by a certain discernment, the movement, the motivation, we say, is often born from a sense of care, borne by a charity, which is to say a certain benevolence of love. But when the friends finally come upon Job, they are stunned, they are silenced by the enormity of his suffering. Job, once familiar to his friends, has now been made strange, frightfully uncanny, both recognizable and not. They cannot understand, they cannot get what is happening in their grips. So they just sit with him, silently, for seven days and nights we are told. Without words. In silence. Eventually, they will speak, and what they will say will not be helpful. But before they do, the silence of their compassion (*com* – together + *pati* – to suffer) and companionship (*com* – with + *panis* – bread, literally to "break bread together") speaks to a knowing of sensibility, of an exposure before which knowledge and the reasoned word is impotent. As we've indicated at greater length elsewhere in the book, Levinas can teach psychology to listen to and take seriously the wisdom of the sensible, of the body.[3]

But yet again, the importance of embodiment and sensibility is not reserved for the encounter in the present or the face-to-face. I've made mention in an earlier chapter of an undergraduate course I teach on the Holocaust and psychology, which has a mandatory travel component associated with it. For this course, I ask students, at the beginning of the semester, why they take the course and what their expectations are for it; it is a favorite of university professors everywhere, and my money is safe on a bet that most of you have asked or been asked a similar question yourself. Some of the most prominent responses from students are that they want to learn about the Holocaust and they want to understand why and how it happened; others say they want to learn about theories of genocide in order to know what can be done to prevent it. Some say they were always "interested" in the Holocaust and thought it would be "cool" to see where it all happened. I teach at a private Catholic university and have yet to have a student in this class who identifies as Jewish or whose interest comes from a closer family member's suffering of the Shoah. Their reasons are all rather distant, intellectualized, egoic, and selfish (in the etymological sense of the for-itself). We keep a journaling record throughout; and sometimes on the bus ride from Krakow to Auschwitz-Birkenau, several students scribble away (or type away on their phones) in such journals. We spend the better part of a full day at the camps, and somewhere in the day, they all fall silent – at some point, at one of the many points of address by the dead. For some, it is in Block 4, where they are confronted with 2 tons of human hair, shorn from inmates before they were marched into the gas chamber, hair that was to be recycled into carpets and clothing. Sometimes it is in Block 11 and the death wall or in the gas chamber itself as they look up to see the holes in the roof through which the canisters of zyklon B were dropped. Sometimes it is the eerie, uncanny, *unheimliche* silence and presence of Birkenau itself which settles in the glands just behind their eyes, surprises them there without them knowing why, and not unlike Antigone, whose tears, Derrida tells us, "reminds us that the eyes are not for seeing, but for crying" (Derrida, 2000, p. 115). There, and thereafter, these students realize, in the seizure of their witness, that is, in the surprise of proximity, that there is nothing to understand there. They come to glimpse what escapes understanding, what precedes their ability to bring into language the possession and obsession, in the skin, of the other's assignation.

But they cannot remain speechless. Deposing reason cannot leave us without response. Quite literally, my students have to write term papers, the student of my example in South Africa has to write his dissertation, and Sipho and I had to submit a manuscript for publication. Job's friends also had to speak, eventually. When they did, they reasoned, "There must be a reason, a why, to your suffering, Job. You must have done something wrong. Surely, God would not punish the righteous like this. Search your memory and confess the secret sins hidden from view." Job's friends seek to understand the disaster. They want to grasp it and seize it and use the power of reason and cognition to tame it; and they want to do so in the service of a remedy. If they know why it happened, if they know what went wrong, they can fix it, or at the very least, try to prevent it; they will know not to do it themselves or tell others not to do it, not unlike the motivations of my students at the beginning of class. And so Job's friends offer to him the remedy to confess, to them and to God, and to pray and pray. While they came for his sake, came to a call of his, their response and remedies, their therapy room as confessional for absolution, closure, and cure betrays *their* interest, the interest of being for whom essence is interest (Levinas, 2004b). Small wonder that Job screams his no to them and the heavens. "What," he asks, "could I have done, could I have possibly done, to deserve this, to have this happen to me?" It is a cry that echoes through the ages, from Job's land of Uz to the classrooms of Sandyhook elementary and the cities of Ukraine. From the Rwandan hills to a wine farm in Franschoek. It is a cry we are beholden to in response, responsibility, and justice. It is a response that demands us rethinking reason and the ego – not as a tool for possession and mastery but as the means to justice.

The knowledge of encounter does not discard "objective" or "dynamic" or "procedural" or "professional" knowledge but puts it in question, questions it, and subjects it to the demands of the ethical and of justice. Elsewhere (Laubscher, 2010a,

2010b), I have argued for a particular way of responsible and ethical scholarship by the figures of witness and testimony. One does not renounce knowledge and understanding as if that were even a possibility. Mindful of the limits of representation, we do not abandon representation; we use it to reveal its failures: "There is something unrepresentable that we nevertheless seek to represent, and that paradox must be retained in the representation we give" (Butler, 2020, p. 144). The figures of the witness and testimony are arguably most available to us by the example of the law and the juridical. There, the witness is assumed to provide firsthand knowledge of the event and is called upon to provide the truth of the event in testimony, to settle questions about the event before the call of truth, having been there, having seen. The witness is summoned under penalty (*sub poena*) to provide a measured account, evidence, of what was obvious to sight and/or mind. Clearly, already, this is not quite the model of witness and testimony I have in mind, but it already concedes the aporetic scandal that inheres to it, lurks within it, and haunts it. Remember, firstly, the threat of the sub poena, the under penalty, should one refuse the testifying injunction or violate the summons to truth in perjury. It is premised on a rather public sanction of the commons, of an accounting of the one for the neighbor by the institutions of the commons, under the inspiration of the for-the-other, corruptible as it may end up in totalizing practice. But moreover, and in addition, the summons concedes, I venture, precisely the inspiration of the other-in-me. After all, we are asked to swear an oath, to answer the summons on pain of an oath. And an oath is always to an other, always to promise before an other, a divine witness to my witnessing. The "so help me God" always concedes that whereas there may be no consequences to my perjurious and lying testimony, if I lie in secret, if no one knows, *that* no one knows is only true in the world of the living and the empirical. The divine witness to whom one promises nonetheless sees and commands, nonetheless "orders and ordains" from a no-place wholly elsewhere and exterior, which is also to say wholly interior by the substitution of the other-in-the-same. The guilt and shame one feels for lying is not (only or necessarily) because God sees but because the other-in-the-same sees. To witness, now, as to testify, is consequently a summons to a wholly different order of truth than fact or proof and is – in ironic fact – nothing less than a summons to justice, to the self that is myself by the other in me.

To bear witness is to carry a singular and irreplaceable responsibility, "to bear the solitude of a responsibility, and to bear the responsibility, precisely, of that solitude" (Felman & Laub, 1992, p. 3). To bear witness is to be marked and to bear the mark of the other as a haunted subject. It may be no accident that we couple so easily, as if it cannot be uncoupled, the notions of witnessing and bearing, which is to say, suffering it; to bear something is etymologically to suffer it. And by the same fluid way we bear witness, in the couplet of the term, so, too, do we "offer testimony." We learn that suffer and offer depart from the same etymological port (suffer – sub + ferre; offer: ob + ferre . . . "to bring" "to carry" "to someone"). To offer testimony is not to bring back a representational copy, in clear opposition to the expectation of the court of law. Rather, inasmuch as testimony allows for a recuperation, a reiteration, a bringing back, it is to see again, for the first time, which is to say a seeing differently, which is to say an unseeing, which is to say a response, not from knowledge but from a command to responsibility, from an address. It is to offer a singular said, from a singular encounter with the other in responsibility and from the force of an ethical subjectivity that has been lying in wait for the singular signature and proper name that is me, the oneself, to the response in the wager of an otherwise than being in a being otherwise. This signatory emplacement is nothing but the concern for justice. Derrida writes:

> No justice – let us not say no law . . . we are not speaking here of laws – seems possible or thinkable without the principle of some *responsibility*, beyond all living present, within that which disjoins the living present, before the ghosts of those who are not yet born or who are already dead, be they victims of wars, political or other kinds of violence, nationalist, racist, colonialist, sexist, or other kinds of exterminations, victims of the oppressions of capitalist imperialism or any of the forms of totalitarianism.
>
> (Derrida, 1994, p. xix, emphasis in original)

Of course, we have to make sense. We operate in the arena of acts and things to do. We have to make meaning – we are in the world, we are in a room with another, we are in the field conducting research. But there is a difference between meaning as totalization and meaning as arising from ethical encounter and responsibility (Downs et al., 2012) – meaning which operates precisely to question and challenge totalizing meaning, meaning which is of the unsaying sort and relies on sensibility as much as reason, indeed, where the very distinction is a banality. Levinas's dizzying philosophical reflection proposes to start with human being in its concrete and material existence. Even so, this concrete and material existence reads and feels quite differently to the concrete of an other, in therapy, before us, or the research subject I speak to, directly, or the ethnographic space I inhabit and live in. Psychology is where Levinas's rubber meets the road.

## Notes

1 But it was also used by the South African apartheid police, we would learn later, as a dirty trick maneuver to execute antiapartheid activists but to make it look like they were "killed by their own."
2 The interested reader is referred to Laubscher and Mbuqe (2020).
3 Psychology's neglect of the body and the sensible is all the more strange because we rely on it so much in practice. Of the most sage advice I received as a beginning therapist, for example (and although it runs counter to some of what I've argued here), was from a valued and experienced mentor who told me, "If, at the end of the first session, something feels 'off,' you feel disoriented, but you did everything 'right' and you cannot put your finger on 'it' and seem to ask yourself, 'What just happened?' start thinking in the direction of personality disorder."

# References

Abram, D. (1996). *The spell of the sensuous*. Vintage Books.

Adams, W. W. (2023). *A wild and sacred call: Nature-psyche-spirit*. SUNY Press.

Alford, C. F. (2000). Levinas and Winnicott: Motherhood and responsibility. *American Imago, 57*(3), 235–259.

Alford, C. F. (2002). *Levinas, the Frankfurt school and psychoanalysis*. Continuum.

Alpert, A. (2015). Not to be European would not be "to be European still": Undoing Eurocentrism in Levinas and others. *Journal of French and Francophone Philosophy, 23*(1), 21–41.

American Psychological Association (APA). (2010). Psychology as a core science, technology, engineering, and mathematics (STEM) discipline (Report of the APA 2009 Presidential Task Force on the future of psychology as a STEM discipline). *American Psychological Association*. https://www.apa.org/pubs/reports/stem-report.pdf.

Anderson, P. D. (2017). Levinas and the anticolonial. *French and Francophone Philosophy, 25*(1), 150–181.

Arendt, H. (1978). Politics and philosophy of history: Martin Heidegger at eighty. In M. Murray (Ed.), *Heidegger and modern philosophy: Critical essays*. Yale University Press.

Atterton, P. (2010). Editor's introduction: The early Levinas (1930–49) and the escape from being. *Levinas Studies, 5*, vii–xiv.

Atterton, P. (2011). Nourishing the hunger of the other: A rapprochement between Levinas and Darwin. *Symploke, 19*(1–2), 17–33.

Atterton, P., & Wright, T. (Eds.). (2019). *Face to face with animals: Levinas and the animal question*. State University of New York Press.

Azari, N. P., Nickel, J., Wunderlich, G., Niedeggen, M., Hefter, H., Tellmann, L., Herzog, H., Stoerig, P., Birnbacher, D., & Seitz, R. J. (2001). Neural correlates of religious experience. *The European Journal of Neuroscience, 13*, 1649–1652.

Bahler, B. (2015). Levinas and the parent-child relation: A Merleau-Pontyian critique of applying Levinas's thought to developmental psychology. *The Humanistic Psychologist, 43*, 128–147.

Bakewell, S. (2016). *At the existentialist cafe: Freedom, being, and apricot cocktails*. Other Press.

Barrett, L. F. (2017). *How emotions are made: The secret life of the brain*. Houghton Mifflin Harcourt.

Barsalou, L. (2020). Challenges and opportunities for grounding cognition. *Journal of Cognition, 3*(1), 1–24.

Baumgartner, H. L. (2005). *Visualizing Levinas: Existence and existents through Mulholland drive, memento, and vanilla sky.* Bowling Green State University.

Bergson, H. (1960). *Time and free will: An essay on the immediate data of consciousness* (F. L. Pogson, Trans.). Harper.

Bernard-Donals, M. F. (2005). Difficult freedom: Levinas, laguage, and politics. *Diacritics, 35*(3), 62–77.

Bernasconi, R. (1991). Skepticism in the face of philosophy. In R. Bernasconi & S. Critchley (Eds.), *Re-reading Levinas* (pp. 149–162). Indiana University Press.

Bernasconi, R. (1992). *Who is my neighbor? Who is the other? Questioning "the generosity of Western thought"* [Symposium presentation]. Simon Silverman Phenomenology Center, Duquesne University.

Bernasconi, R. (1998). Different styles of eschatology. *Research in Phenomenology, 28*(1), 3–19.

Bernasconi, R. (2001). Foreword. In *Existence and existents.* Duquesne University Press.

Bernasconi, R. (2002). What is the question to which 'substitution' is the answer. In S. Critchley & R. Bernasconi (Eds.), *The Cambridge companion to Levinas* (pp. 234–251). Cambridge University Press.

Bernasconi, R. (2005). No exit: Levinas' aporetic account of transcendence. *Research in Phenomenology, 35*, 101–117.

Beyers, M. S., & Reber, J. S. (1998). The illusion of intimacy: A Levinasian critique of evolutionary psychology. *Journal of Theoretical and Philosophical Psychology, 18*(2), 176–192.

Bible, K. J. (Producer). (2021). *The Bible – American Standard Version.* https://www.rasv.org.

Binswanger, L. (1958). The case of Ellen West. In R. May, E. Angel, & H. F. Ellenberger (Eds.), *Existence* (pp. 237–364). Basic Books.

Bion, W. (1989). *Experiences in groups.* Routledge. (Original work published 1961)

Blanchot, M. (1973). *Thomas the obscure.* Station Hill Press.

Blanchot, M., & Derrida, J. (2000). *The instant of my death* (E. Rottenberg, Trans.). Stanford University Press.

Blanke, O., & Arzy, S. (2005). The out-of-body experience: Disturbed self-processing at the temporo-parietal junction. *The Neuroscientist, 11*, 16–24.

Boothroyd, D. (2019). Levinas on ecology and nature. In M. L. Morgan (Ed.), *The Oxford handbook of Levinas* (pp. 769–788). Oxford University Press.

Borg, J., Andree, B., Soderstrom, H., & Farde, L. (2003). The serotonin system and spiritual experiences. *The American Journal of Psychiatry, 160*(11), 1965–1969.

Boss, M. (1963). *Psychoanalysis and daseinsanalysis* (L. B. Lefebre, Trans.). Basic Books.

Brody, D. (2001). Levinas's maternal method from "time and the other" through "otherwise than being". In T. Chanter (Ed.), *Feminist interpretations of Emmanuel Levinas* (pp. 53–77). Pennsylvania State University Press.

Brody, D. H. (1995, January 1). Emmanuel Levinas: The logic of ethical ambiguity in otherwise than being or beyond essence. *Research in Phenomenology, 25*(1), 177–203. https://doi.org/10.1163/156916495X00103.

Burgat, F. (2015). Facing the animal in Sartre and Levinas. *Yale French Studies, 127*, 172–189.

Burns, L. (2017). What does the patient say? Levinas and medical ethics. *Journal of Medicine and Philosophy, 42*, 214–235.

Burston, D., & Frie, R. (2006). *Psychotherapy as a human science.* Duquesne University Press.

Butler, J. (2020). *Precarious life: The powers of mourning and violence*. Verso.

Capili, A. D. (2011). The created ego in Levinas' totality and infinity. *Sophia, 50*, 677–692.

Casasanto, D. (2013). Different bodies, different minds: The body-specificity of language and thought. In R. Caballero & J. E. Diaz-Vera (Eds.), *Sensous cognition: Explorations into human sentience, imagination, (e)motion and perception* (pp. 9–17). De Gruyter.

Caygill, H. (2000). Levinas's political judgement: The esprit articles 1934–1983. *Radical Philosophy*, (104), 6–15.

Caygill, H. (2002). *Levinas and the political*. Routledge.

Chalier, C. (1991). Ethics and the feminine. In R. Bernasconi & S. Critchley (Eds.), *Re-reading Levinas* (pp. 119–129). Indiana University Press.

Chanter, T. (1999). The betrayal of philosophy: Emmanuel Levinas's otherwise than being. *Budhi, 3*(1).

Chanter, T. (Ed.). (2001a). *Feminist interpretations of Emmanuel Levinas*. Pennsylvania State University Press.

Chanter, T. (2001b). *Time, death, and the feminine: Levinas with Heidegger*. Stanford University Press.

Chung, M. C., & Hyland, M. E. (2011). *History and philosophy of psychology*. Wiley-Blackwell.

Churchill, S., & Wertz, F. J. (2001). An introduction to phenomenological research in psychology: Historical, conceptual, and methodological foundations. In K. Schneider, J. F. T. Bugental, & J. F. Pierson (Eds.), *The handbook of humanistic psychology* (pp. 231–245). SAGE.

Churchill, S. D., Aanstoos, C. M., & Morley, J. (2021). The emergence of phenomenological psychology in the United States. *Journal of Phenomenological Psychology, 52*, 218–274.

Ciocan, C. (2009). The problem of embodiment in the early writings of Emmanuel Levinas. *Levinas Studies, 4*, 1–19.

Clegg, J. W., & Slife, B. D. (2005). Epistemology and the hither side: A Levinasian account of relational knowing. *European Journal of Psychotherapy, Counselling and Health, 7*(1–2), 65–76.

Clifton-Soderstrom, M. (2003). Levinas and the patient as other: The ethical foundation of medicine. *The Journal of Medicine and Philosophy, 28*, 447–460.

Cohen, B. (2008). The trace of the face of god: Emmanuel Levinas and depth psychology. *Jung Journal: Culture & Psyche, 2*(2), 30–45.

Cohen, R. (1986). *Face to face with Levinas*. State University of New York Press.

Cohen, R. (2001). *Ethics, exegesis, and philosophy: Interpretation after Levinas*. Cambridge University Press.

Cohen, R. (2005). Book review: Emmanuel Levinas, on escape. *European Journal of Psychotherapy, Counselling and Health, 7*(1–2), 109–115.

Cohen, R. (2007). Emmanuel Levinas: Judaism and the primacy of the ethical. In M. L. Morgan & P. E. Gordon (Eds.), *The Cambridge companion to modern Jewish philosophy*. Cambridge University Press.

Cohen, R. (2015). Preface. In K. C. Krycka, G. Kunz, & G. G. Sayre (Eds.), *Psychotherapy for the other: Levinas and the face-to-face relationship* (pp. vii–xiv). Duquesne University Press.

Cole, M. (1996). *Cultural psychology: A once and future discipline*. Harvard University Press.

Comings, D. E., Gonzales, N., Saucier, G., Johnson, J. P., & MacMurray, J. P. (2000). The DRD4 gene and the spiritual transcendence scale of the temperament and character index. *Psychiatric Genetics, 10*, 185–189.

Conn, W. E. (1998). Self-transcendence, the tue self, and self-love. *Pastoral Psychology*, *46*(5), 323–332.

Cools, A. (2005). Revisiting the il y a: Maurice Blanchot and Emmanuel Levinas on the question of subjectivity. *Paragraph*, *28*(3), 54–71.

Coon, D., & Mitterer, J. O. (2014). *Introduction to psychology* (14th ed.). Cengage.

Correia, C. J. (2018). Levinas and the question of time. In J. M. Justo, P. A. Lima, & F. M. F. Silva (Eds.), *From Heidegger to Badiou* (pp. 91–100). Centre for Philosophy at the University of Lisbon.

Critchley, S. (2002). Introduction. In S. Critchley & R. Bernasconi (Eds.), *The Cambridge companion to Levinas* (pp. 1–32). Cambridge University Press.

Critchley, S. (2015). *The problem with Levinas* (A. Dianda, Ed.). Oxford University Press.

Csikszentmihalyi, M. (1991). *Flow: The psychology of optimal experience*. Harper Perennial.

Davis, C. (1996). *Levinas: An introduction*. University of Notre Dame Press.

Davis, T. (1995). Deconstructing prejudice: A Levinasian alternative. *Journal of Theoretical and Philosophical Psychology*, *15*(1), 72–83.

Davy, B. J. (2007). An other face of ethics in Levinas. *Ethics and the Environment*, *12*, 39–65.

De Beauvoir, S. (1989). *The second sex* [Le deuxieme sexe] (H. M. Parshley, Trans.). Vintage Books. (Original work published 1949)

Derrida, J. (1973). *Speech and phenomena* (D. B. Allison, Trans.). Northwestern University Press.

Derrida, J. (1978). *Writing and difference* (A. Bass, Trans.). University of Chicago Press. (Original work published 1967)

Derrida, J. (1992). Force of law: The 'mystical foundation of authority'. In D. Cornell, M. Rosenfeld, & D. G. Carlson (Eds.), *Deconstruction and the possibility of justice* (pp. 68–94). Routledge.

Derrida, J. (1994). *Specters of Marx: The state of the debt, the work of mourning, and the new international* (P. Kamuf, Trans.). Routledge.

Derrida, J. (1999). *Adieu to Emmanuel Levinas*. Stanford University Press.

Derrida, J. (2000). *Of hospitality* (R. Bowlby, Trans.). Stanford University Press.

Derrida, J. (2003a). And say the animal responded? In C. Wolfe (Ed.), *Zoontologies: The question of the animal*. University of Minnesota Press.

Derrida, J. (2003b). Derrida avec Levinas, Interview with Alain David. *Le Magazine Litteraire*, *419*, 30–31.

Diamond, S. (2001). Wundt before Leipzig. In R. W. Rieber & R. K. Robinson (Eds.), *Wilhelm Wundt in history: The making of a scientific psychology* (pp. 3–70). Plenum.

Diehm, C. (2000). Facing nature: Levinas beyond the human. *Philosophy Today*, *44*, 51–59.

Diehm, C. (2003). Natural disasters. In C. S. Brown & T. Toadvine (Eds.), *Eco-phenomenology: Back to the earth itself* (pp. 171–185). State University of New York Press.

Dilthey, W. (1977). *Descriptive psychology and historical understanding* (R. M. Zaner & K. L. Heiges, Trans.). Martinus Nijhoff. (Original work published 1894)

Dostoevsky, F. (2002). *The brothers Karamazov* (R. Pevear & L. Volokhonsky, Trans.). Farrar, Straus and Giroux.

Downs, S. D., Gantt, E. E., & Faulconer, J. E. (2012). Levinas, meaning, and an ethical science of psychology: Scientific inquiry as rupture. *Journal of Theoretical and Philosophical Psychology*, *32*(2), 69–85.

Drabinski, J. E. (2011). *Levinas and the postcolonial: Race, nation, other*. Edinburgh University Press.

Dueck, A., & Goodman, D. (2007). Expiation, substitution and surrender: Levinasian implications for psychotherapy. *Pastoral Psychology*, *55*, 601–617.

Dueck, A., & Parsons, T. D. (2007). Ethics, alterity, and psychotherapy: A Levinasian perspective. *Pastoral Psychology*, *55*, 271–282.

Dussel, E. (1974). *Method for a philosophy of liberation* [Método para una filosofía de la
liberación]. Ediciones Sigueme.

Dussel, E. (1999). Sensibility and otherness in Emmanuel Levinas. *Philosophy Today*,
(Summer), 125–133.

Eagleton, T. (2009). *Trouble with strangers: A study of ethics*. Wiley-Blackwell.

Ebbinghaus, H. (1973). *Psychology: An elementary text-book*. Arno Press. (Original work
published 1908)

Edelglass, W., Hatley, J., & Diehm, C. (Eds.). (2012). *Facing nature: Levinas and environmental thought*. Duquesne University Press.

Eisenstadt, O. (2003). The problem of the promise: Derrida on Levinas on the cities of refuge. *Cross Currents*, *52*(4), 474–482.

Eisenstadt, O. (2012). Eurocentrism and colorblindness. *Levinas Studies*, *7*, 43–62.

Eisenstadt, O. (2019). Levinas's Jewish writings. In M. L. Morgan (Ed.), *The Oxford handbook of Levinas*. Oxford University Press.

Emery, E. (2000). Facing "O": Wilfred Bion, Emmanuel Levinas, and the face of the other.
*Psychoanalytic Review*, *87*(6), 799–840.

Erikson, E. (1993a). *Gandhi's truth: On the originis of militant nonviolence*. W. W. Norton & Company.

Erikson, E. (1993b). *Young man Luther: A study in psychoanalysis and history*. W. W. Norton & Company.

Fanon, F. (2008). *Black skin, white masks* (R. Philcox, Trans.). Grove Press. (Original work
published 1952)

Faulconer, J. E. (2005). Knowledge of the other. *European Journal of Psychotherapy, Counselling and Health*, *7*(1–2), 49–63.

Felman, S., & Laub, D. (1992). *Testimony: Crises of witnessing in literature, psychoanalysis, and history*. Routledge.

Fetters, A. (2015). Must out of sight mean out of mind? Levinas, language, and the schizophrenic other. *Journal of Humanistic Psychology*, *55*(4), 412–428.

Fisher, L., & Embree, L. (Eds.). (2000). *Feminist phenomenology*. Kluwer.

Frankl, V. (1963). *Man's search for meaning*. Washington Square Press. (Original work published 1959)

Frankl, V. E. (1964). The philosophical foundations of logotherapy. In E. W. Straus (Ed.),
*Phenomenology: Pure and applied*. Duquesne University Press.

Frankl, V. E. (1965). *The doctor and the soul: From psychotherapy to logotherapy* (2nd ed.).
Knopf.

Frankl, V. E. (1969). *The will to meaning: Foundations and applications of logotherapy*. The
New American Library.

Freeman, M. (2012). Thinking and being otherwise: Aesthetics, ethics, erotics. *Journal of
Theoretical and Philosophical Psychology*, *32*(4), 196–208.

Freeman, M. (2013). *The priority of the other: Thinking and living beyond the self*. Oxford
University Press.

Freeman, M. (2014). Listening to the claims of experience: Psychology and the question of
transcendence. *Pastoral Psychology*, *63*, 323–337.

Freud, S. (1964). *Leonardo Da Vinci and a memory of his Childhood* (A. Tyson, Trans., J. Strachey, Ed.). W. W. Norton & Company.

Freud, S. (1989). *Group psychology and the analysis of the ego.* W. W. Norton & Company. (Original work published 1921)

Friedlander, J. (1990). *Vilna on the Seine: Jewish intellectuals in France Seine 1968.* Yale University Press.

Froese, R. (2019). Levinas and the question of politics. *Contemporary Political Thought, 19*(1), 1–19.

Fromm, E. (1994). *Escape from freedom.* Henry Hold and Company. (Original work published 1941)

Fryer, D. (2004). *The intervention of the other: Ethical subjectivity in Levinas and Lacan.* Other Press.

Fryer, D. (2007). What Levinas and psychoanalysis can teach each other, or how to be a Mensch without going Meshugah. *Psychoanalytic Review, 94*(4).

Gallagher, S. (2010). Phenomenology and non-reductionist cognitive science. In S. Gallagher & D. Schmicking (Eds.), *Handbook of phenomenology and cognitive science.* Springer.

Gantt, E. E. (2000). Levinas, psychotherapy, and the ethics of suffering. *Journal of Humanistic Psychology, 40*(3), 9–28.

Gantt, E. E., & Williams, R. N. (Eds.). (2002). *Psychology for the other: Levinas, ethics and the practice of psychology.* Duquesne University Press.

Garcia-Romeu, A. (2010). Self-transcendence as a measurable transpersonal construct. *The Journal of Transpersonal Psychology, 53*(1), 26–47.

Garza, G., & Landrum, B. (2010). Ethics and the primacy of the other: A Levinasian foundation for phenomenological research. *The Indo-Pacific Journal of Phenomenology, 10*(2), 1–12.

Gendlin, E. T. (1982). *Focusing.* Bantam Books. (Original work published 1978)

Giannopoulos, P. J. (2019). *Levinas's philosophy of transcendence* (M. L. Morgan, Ed.). Oxford University Press.

Giorgi, A. (1970). *Psychology as a human science: A phenomenologically based approach.* Harper & Row.

Giorgi, A. (2000). Psychology as a human science revisited. *Journal of Humanistic Psychology, 40*(3), 56–73.

Giorgi, A. (2012). The descriptive phenomenological psychological method. *Journal of Phenomenological Psychology, 43*, 3–12.

Giorgi, A. (2014). Phenomenological philosophy as the basis for a human scientific psychology. *The Humanistic Psychologist, 42*, 233–248.

Goodman, D., & Freeman, M. (Eds.). (2015). *Psychology and the other.* Oxford University Press.

Goodman, D. M. (2012). *The demanded self: Levinasian ethics and identity in psychology.* Duquesne University Press.

Goodman, D. M., & Collins, A. (2019). The streaming self: Liberal subjectivity, technology, and unlinking. *Theoretical and Philosophical Psychology, 39*(3), 147–156.

Goodman, D. M., Dueck, A., & Langdal, J. P. (2010). The "heroic I": A Levinasian critique of western narcissism. *Theory & Psychology, 29*(5), 667–685.

Goodman, D. M., Walling, S., & Ghali, A. A. (2010). Psychology in pursuit of justice: The lives and works of Emmanuel Levinas and Ignacio Martin-Baro. *Pastoral Psychology, 59*, 585–602.

Gordon, L. (2005). Through the zone of nonbeing: A reading of *Black Skin, White Masks* in celebration of Fanon's eightieth birthday. *The CLR James Journal, 11*(1), 1–43.

Gorelik, G. (2016). The evolution of transcendence. *Evolutionary Psychological Science, 2,* 287–307.

Griffiths, R. R., Richards, W. A., McCann, U., & Jesse, R. (2006). Psilocybin can occasion mystical-type experiences having substantial and sustained personal meaning and spiritual significance. *Psychopharmacology, 187,* 268–283.

Group for the Advancement of Psychiatry. (1976). *Mysticism: Spiritual quest or psychic disorder.* Brunner-Routledge.

Guenther, L. (2006). "Like a maternal body": Emmanuel Levinas and the motherhood of moses. *Hypatia, 21*(1), 119–136.

Guenther, L. (2007). Le Flair animal: Levinas and the possibility of animal friendship. *PhaenEx, 2,* 216–238.

Guenther, L. (2021). Six senses of critique for critical phenomenology. *PUNCTA: Journal of Critical Phenomenology, 4*(2), 5–23.

Gutting, G. (2001). *French philosophy in the twentieth century.* Cambridge University Press.

Hall, T. (2015). *Trauma at the limit: Bearing witness to the impossible of survivor testimony.* Duquesne University.

Halling, S. (1971). The implications of Emmanuel Levinas' totality and infinity for therapy. In A. Giorgi, C. T. Fischer, & E. L. Murray (Eds.), *Duquene studies in phenomenological psychology* (Vol. 2, pp. 206–223). Duquesne University Press.

Halling, S. (1975). The implications of Emmanuel Levinas' totality and infinity for therapy. In A. Giorgi, C. T. Fischer, & E. L. Murray (Eds.), *Duquesne studies in phenomenological psychology* (Vol. 2, pp. 206–223). Duquesne University Press.

Ham, B. J., Kim, Y. H., Choi, M. J., Cha, J. H., Choi, Y. K., & Lee, M. S. (2004). Serotonergic genes and personality traits in the Korean population. *Neuroscience Letters, 354,* 2–5.

Hamer, D. (2004). *The God gene: How faith is hardwired into our genes.* Doubleday.

Hand, S. (2009). *Emmanuel Levinas.* Routledge.

Harrington, D. R. (1993). *Person, system, and subjectivity: Psychology and the philosophy of Emmanuel Levinas* [Doctoral dissertation, Pennsylvania State University].

Harrington, D. R. (2002). A Levinasian psychology? Perhaps . . . In E. E. Gantt & R. N. Williams (Eds.), *Psychology for the other* (pp. 209–224). Duquesne University Press.

Hatzfeld, J., Coverdale, L., & Sontag, S. (2006). *Machete season: The killers in Rwanda speak.* Farrar, Straus and Giroux.

Hecker, J. C. (2010). *Levinasian ethical turn in psychology.* Regent University.

Hegel, G. W. F. (2018). *The phenomenology of spirit* (M. Inwood, Trans.). Oxford University Press.

Heidegger, M. (2001). *Being and time* (J. R. Macquarrie, Edward, Trans.). Blackwell Publishers. (Original work published 1927)

Heidegger, M. (2002). The origin of the work of art. In J. Young & K. Haynes (Ed. & Trans), *Off the beaten track.* Cambridge University Press. (Original work published 1950)

Heinrichs, M., Von Dawans, B., & Domes, G. (2009). Oxytocin, vasopressin, and human social behavior. *Frontiers in Neuroendocrinology,* (30), 548–557.

Herzog, A. (2013). Dogs and fire: The ethics and politics of nature in Levinas. *Political Theory, 41*(3), 359–379.

Hofmann, W., & Nordgren, L. F. (2015a). Introduction. In W. Hofmann & L. F. Nordgren (Eds.), *The psychology of desire* (pp. 1–13). The Guilford Press.

Hofmann, W., & Nordgren, L. F. (Eds.). (2015b). *The psychology of desire*. The Guilford Press.

Hofmeyr, B. (2012). On escaping the seemingly inescapable: Reflections on being in Levinas. *Filozofia, 67*(6), 460–471.

Holt, R. (1999). *Heidegger: An introduction*. Cornell University Press.

Huett, S. D., & Goodman, D. M. (2012). Levinas on managed care: The (A)proximal, faceless third-party and the psychotherapeutic dyad. *Journal of Theoretical and Philosophical Psychology, 32*(2), 86–102.

Hunt, M. M. (1993). *The story of psychology*. Doubleday.

Husserl, E. (1960). *Cartesian meditations* (D. Cairns, Trans.). Martinus Nijhoff.

Husserl, E. (2001). *Logical investigations (Volume 2)* [Logische Untersuchungen] (J. N. Findlay, Trans., D. Moran, Ed.). Routledge. (Original work published 1900/1901)

Hutchens, B. C. (2004). *Levinas: A guide for the perplexed*. Continuum.

Irigaray, L. (1991). Questions to Emmanuel Levinas: On the divinity of love. In R. Bernasconi & S. Critchley (Eds.), *Re-reading Levinas* (pp. 109–118). Indiana University Press.

Irigaray, L. (2001). The fecundity of the caress: A reading of Levinas, totality and infinity, 'phenomenology of eros'. In T. Chanter (Ed.), *Feminist interpretations of Emmanuel Levinas* (pp. 119–144). Pennsylvania State University Press.

Jackson, S. A., & Marsh, H. W. (1996). Development and validation of a scale to measure optimal experience: The flow state scale. *Journal of Sport and Exercise Psychology, 18*, 17–35.

Jacques, J. (2017). Where nothing happened: The experience of war captivity and Levinas's concept of the "there is". *Social and Legal Studies, 26*(2), 230–248.

James, W. (1982). *The varieties of religious experience*. Penguin. (Original work published 1902)

James, W. (2001). *Psychology: The briefer course*. Dover. (Original work published 1892)

Janicaud, D. (2000). The theological turn in French phenomenology (B. G. Prusak & J. L. Klosky, Trans.). In D. Janicaud, J.-F. Courtine, J.-L. Chrétien, M. Henry, J.-L. Marion, & P. Ricoeur (Eds.), *Phenomenology and the "theological turn"*. Fordham University Press.

Kant, I. (2007a). *Critique of judgment* (J. C. Meredith, Trans., N. Walker, Ed.). Oxford University Press. (Original work published 1790)

Kant, I. (2007b). *The critique of pure reason* (D. Burnham & H. Young, Eds.). Indiana University Press. (Original work published 1781)

Katz, C. E. (2001). Reinhabiting the house of ruth: Exceeding the limits of the feminine in Levinas. In T. Chanter (Ed.), *Feminist interpretations of Emmanuel Levinas* (pp. 145–170). Pennsylvania State University Press.

Katz, C. E. (2004). From eros to maternity: Love, death, and "the feminine" in the philosophy of Emmanuel Levinas. In H. Tirosh-Samuelson (Ed.), *Women and gender in Jewish philosophy*. Indiana University Press.

Kitson, A., Chirico, A., Gaggioli, A., & Riecke, B. E. (2020). A review on research and evaluation methods for investigating self-transcendence. *Frontiers in Psychology, 11*(547687), 1–27.

Kleinberg, E. (2019). Levinas as a reader of Jewish texts: The Talmudic commentaries. In M. L. Morgan (Ed.), *The Oxford handbook of Levinas* (pp. 443–458). Oxford University Press.

Kockelmans, J. J. (Ed.). (1987). *Phenomenological psychology: The Dutch school*. Martinus Nijhoff Publishers.

Kok, B. E., Coffey, K. A., Cohn, M. A., Catalino, L. I., Vacharkulksemsuk, T., Algoe, S. B., & Fredrickson, B. L. (2013). How positive emotions build physical health: Perceived positive social connections account for the upward spiral between positive emotions and vagal tone. *Psychological Science*, (24), 1123–1132.

Kong, B.-H. (2008). Levinas' ethics of caring: Implications and limits in nursing. *Asian Nursing Research, 2*, 208–213.

Krycka, K. C., Kunz, G., & Sayre, G. G. (Eds.). (2015). *Psychotherapy for the other: Levinas and the face-to-face relationship*. Duquesne University Press.

Kunz, G. (1998). *The paradox of power and weakness: Levinas and an alternative paradigm for psychology*. State University of New York Press.

Kunz, G. (2006). Interruptions: Levinas. *Journal of Phenomenological Psychology, 37*(2), 241–266.

Kunz, G. (2007). An analysis of the psyche inspired by Emmanuel Levinas. *Psychoanalytic Review, 94*(4), 617–638.

Kunz, G. (2012). Conscience of a conservative psychologist: Return of the mysteriously illusive psyche. *The Indo-Pacific Journal of Phenomenology, 12*, 1–13.

Lajoie, D. H., & Shapiro, S. I. (1992). Definitions of transpersonal psychology: The first twenty-three years. *Journal of Transpersonal Psychology, 24*(1), 79–98.

Larios, J. (2019). Levinas and the primacy of the human. *Ethics and the Environment, 24*(2), 1–22.

Laubscher, L. (2010a). Facing the apartheid archive, or, of archons and researchers. *South African Journal of Psychology, 40*, 370–381.

Laubscher, L. (2010b). Working with the apartheid archive: Or, of witness and testimony. *Psychology in Society*, 49–63.

Laubscher, L. (2022). When "there is" a Black: Levinas and Fanon on ethics, politics, and responsibility. *Middle Voices, 2*(1), 1–18.

Laubscher, L., & Mbuqe, S. (2020). A case study of 'necklacing': When the case has a face. *Psychology in Society (PINS), 59*, 66–85.

Lavoie, M., De Koninck, T., & Blondeau, D. (2006). The nature of care in light of Emmanuel Levinas. *Nursing Philosophy, 7*(4), 225–234.

LeBeau, C. S. (2017). Ontological and ethical guilt: Phenomenological perspectives on becoming a mother. *The Humanistic Psychologist, 45*(4), 333–347.

Lescourret, M.-A. (1994). *Emmanuel Levinas*. Flammarion.

Levi, P. (1989). *The drowned and the saved*. Vintage.

Levin, J., & Steele, L. (2005). The transcendent experience: Conceptual, theoretical, and epidemiologic perspectives. *Explore, 1*(2), 89–101.

Levinas, E. (1978). Signature. *Research in Phenomenology, 8*, 175–189.

Levinas, E. (1982). *On escape*. Stanford University Press. (De l'evasion, Original work published 1935)

Levinas, E. (1985). *Ethics and infinity* (R. Cohen, Trans.). Duquesne University Press.

Levinas, E. (1987a). *Collected philosophical papers* (A. Lingis, Trans.). Martinus Nijhoff.

Levinas, E. (1987b). *Time and the other* (R. Cohen, Trans.). Duquesne University Press.

Levinas, E. (1988). The paradox of morality: An interview with Emmanuel Levinas. In R. Bernasconi & D. Wood (Eds.), *The provocation of Levinas: Rethinking the other* (pp. 168–180). Routledge.

Levinas, E. (1989). Is ontology fundamental. *Philosophy Today, 32*(2), 121–129 (L'Ontologie est-elle fondamentale? *Revue de Metaphysique et de Morale, 56* (1951), 88–98).

Levinas, E. (1990). Reflections on the philosophy of hitlerism. *Critical Inquiry*, *17*(1), 62–71. (Original work published 1934)

Levinas, E. (1995). *The theory of intuition in Husserl's phenomenology* (A. Orianne, Trans., 2nd ed.). Northwestern University Press.

Levinas, E. (1996a). *Emmanuel Levinas: Basic philosophical writings* (A. T. Peperzak, S. Critchley, & R. Bernasconi, Eds.). Indiana University Press.

Levinas, E. (1996b). *Proper names*. Stanford University Press.

Levinas, E. (1997). *Difficult freedom: Essays on judaism* (S. Hand, Trans.). Johns Hopkings University Press. (Original work published 1963)

Levinas, E. (1998a). *Entre Nous – thinking-of-the-other* (M. B. Smith & B. Harshav, Trans.). Columbia University Press.

Levinas, E. (1998b). The understanding of spirituality in French and German culture. *Continental Philosophy Review*, *31*.

Levinas, E. (1999). *New Talmudic readings* (R. Cohen, Trans.). Duquesne University Press.

Levinas, E. (2001a). *Existence and existents*. Duquesne University Press. (Original work published 1947)

Levinas, E. (2001b). *Is it righteous to be? Interviews with Emmanuel Levinas* (J. Robbins, Ed.). Stanford University Press.

Levinas, E. (2003). *On escape (De l'evasion)* (B. Bergo, Trans.). Stanford University Press. (Original work published 1935)

Levinas, E. (2004a). Ethics of the infinite. In R. Kearney (Ed.), *Debates in continental philosophy* (pp. 65–84). Fordham University Press.

Levinas, E. (2004b). *Otherwise than being, or beyond essence* (A. Lingis, Trans.). Duquesne University Press. (Original work published 1974)

Levinas, E. (2007). *Beyond the verse: Talmudic readings and lectures* (G. D. Mole, Trans.). Continuum. (Original work published 1982)

Levinas, E. (2009). *Carnets de captivité: suivi de Écrits sur la captivité et Notes philosophiques diverses*. Bernard Grasset/IMEC.

Levinas, E. (2013). *Totality and infinity: An essay on exteriority* (A. Lingis, Trans.). Duquesne University Press. (Original work published 1961)

Levinas, E. (2019). *Nine Talmudic readings* (A. Aronowicz, Trans.). Indiana University Press. (Original work published 1968)

Lingis, A. (1987). Translator's introduction. In *Collected philosophical papers*. Martinus Nijhoff.

Lingis, A. (2004). Translator's introduction. In *Otherwise than being or beyond essence* (pp. xvii–xlviii). Duquesne University Press.

Lingis, A. (2010). The environment: A critical appreciation of Levinas's analysis in existence and existents. *Levinas Studies*, *5*, 65–81.

Livshetz, M., & Goodman, D. M. (2015). Honoring the sensate bond between disparate subjectivities in psychotherapy. *The Humanistic Psychologist*, *43*, 177–193.

Llewelyn, J. (1991). Am I obsessed with bobby (humanism of the other animal). In R. Bernasconi & S. Critchley (Eds.), *Re-reading Levinas* (pp. 234–246). Indiana University Press.

Llewelyn, J. (1995). *Emmanuel Levinas: The genealogy of ethics*. Taylor & Francis Group.

Loewenthal, D., & Kunz, G. (2005). Editorial: Levinas and the other in psychotherapy and counselling. *European Journal of Psychotherapy, Counselling and Health*, *7*(1–2), 1–5.

Lorenzi, C., Serretti, A., Mandelli, L., Tubazio, V., Ploia, C., & Smeraldi, E. (2005). 5-HT1A polymorphism and self-transcendence in mood disorders. *American Journal of Medical Genetics, Part B*, *137*, 33–35.

Maldonado-Torres, N. (2002). *Thinking from the limits of being: Levinas, Fanon, Dussel and the cry of ethical revolt*. Brown University.

Malka, S. (2006). *Emmanuel Levinas: His life and legacy* (M. Kigel & S. M. Embree, Trans.). Duquesne University Press.

Mandell, A. J. (1980). Toward a psychobiology of transcendence: God in the brain. In J. M. Davidson & R. J. Davidson (Eds.), *The psychobiology of consciousness* (pp. 379–464). Plenum Press.

Manning, R. J. S. (1991). Thinking the other without violence? An analysis of the relation between the philosophy of Emmanuel Levinas and feminism. *Journal of Speculative Philosophy*, *5*(2), 132–143.

Marais, E. (2017). *The soul of the white ant* [Die Siel van die Wit Mier] (W. De Kok, Trans.). A Distant Mirror. (Original work published 1937)

Marcus, P. (2006). Religion without promises: The philosophy of Emmanuel Levinas and Psychoanalysis. *Psychoanalytic Review*, *93*(6), 923–951.

Marcus, P. (2007). You are, therefore I am: Emmanuel Levinas and psychoanalysis. *Psychoanalytic Review*, *94*(4), 515–527.

Marcus, P. (2008). *Being for the other: Emmanuel Levinas, ethical living and psychoanalysis*. Marquette University Press.

Marion, J.-L. (2018). The phenomenon of beauty. *Journal of Aesthetics and Phenomenology*, *5*(2), 85–97.

Marriott, D. (2018). *Whither Fanon? Studies in the blackness of being*. Stanford University Press.

Maslow, A. (1968). *Toward a psychology of being*. Van Nostrand.

Maslow, A. (1977). A conversation with Abraham Maslow. In R. E. Schell (Ed.), *Readings in developmental psychology today*. CRM Books. (Original work published 1968)

Mbembe, A. (2001). *On the postcolony*. University of California Press.

McDonald, H. (2011). Levinas in the hood: Portable social justice. *The Humanistic Psychologist*, *39*, 305–311.

Mensch, J. R. (2015). *Levinas's existential analytic: A commentary on totality and infinity*. Northwestern University Press.

Merleau-Ponty, M. (1983). *The structure of behavior* (A. L. Fisher, Trans.). Duquesne University Press.

Merleau-Ponty, M. (2012). *Phenomenology of perception* (D. A. Landes, Trans.). Routledge. (Original work published 1945)

Meskin, J. (2000). Toward a new understanding of the work of Emmanuel Levinas. *Modern Judaism*, *20*(1), 78–102.

Misiak, H., & Sexton, V. S. (1973). *Phenomenological, existential, and humanistic psychologies: A historical survey*. Grune & Stratton.

Moore, I. A., & Schrift, A. D. (2017). Existence, experience, and transcendence: An introduction to Jean Wahl. In A. D. Schrift & I. A. Moore (Eds.), *Jean Wahl: Transcendence and the concrete*. Fordham University Press.

Moran, D. (2000). *Introduction to phenomenology*. Routledge.

Moran, D. (2005). *Edmund Husserl: Founder of phenomenology*. Polity Press.

Morgan, M. L. (Ed.). (2011). *The Cambridge introduction to Emmanuel Levinas*. Cambridge University Press.

Morgan, M. L. (Ed.). (2019). *The Oxford handbook of Levinas*. Oxford University Press.

Moyaert, P. (2000). The phenomenology of eros: A reading of totality and infinity, IV. B. In J. Bloechl (Ed.), *The face of the other and the trace of god* (pp. 30–42). Fordham University Press.

Moyn, S. (2003). Emmanuel Levinas's Talmudic readings: Between tradition and invention. *Prooftexts: A Journal of Jewish Literary History*, *23*(3), 338–364.

Moyn, S. (2005). *Origins of the other: Emmanuel Levinas between revelation and ethics.* Cornell University Press.

Nietzsche, F. (2003). *Beyond good and evil: Prelude to a philosophy of the future* (R. J. Hollingsdale, Trans.). Penguin.

Nortvedt, P. (2003). Levinas, justice and healthcare. *Medicine, Healthcare and Philosophy*, *6*(1), 25–34.

Noyes, A. (2016). *The magic casement: An anthology of fairy poetry.* Westphalia Press. (Original work published 1909)

Ohayon, A. (2006). *Psychology and psychoanalysis in France: The impossible encounter (1919–1969).* La Découverte.

Orange, D. (2011). *The suffering stranger: Hermeneutics for everyday clinical practice.* Routledge.

Orange, D. (2018). Traumatized by transcendence: My other's keeper. In E. Boynton & P. Capretto (Eds.), *Suffering and the limits of theory* (pp. 70–82). Fordham University Press.

Peperzak, A. T. (1993). *To the other: An introduction to the philosophy of Emmanuel Levinas.* Purdue University Press.

Peperzak, A. T. (1997). *Beyond: The philosophy of Emmanuel Levinas.* Northwestern University Press.

Perpich, D. (2001). From the caress to the word: Transcendence and the feminine in the philosophy of Emmanuel Levinas. In T. Chanter (Ed.), *Feminist interpretations of Emmanuel Levinas* (pp. 28–52). Pennsylvania University Press.

Perpich, D. (2005). Figurative language and the 'face' in Levinas's philosophy. *Philosophy and Rhetoric*, *38*(2), 103–121.

Perpich, D. (2008). *The ethics of Emmanuel Levinas.* Stanford University Press.

Plato. (2002). *Phaedrus* (R. Waterfield, Trans.). Oxford University Press.

Pollan, M. (2019). *How to change your mind: What the new science of psychedelics teaches us about consciousness, dying, addiction, depression, and transcendence.* Penguin Books.

Porges, S. W. (2007). The polyvagal perspective. *Biological Psychology*, *74*, 116–143.

Purcell, M. (2006). On hesitation before the other. *International Journal for Philosophy of Religion*, *60*(1/3), 9–19.

Reinhard, K. (2005). Towards a political theology of the neighbor. In S. Zizek, E. L. Santner, & K. Reinhard (Eds.), *The neighbor: Three inquiries in political theology* (pp. 11–75). University of Chicago Press.

Rhodes, C., & Carlsen, A. (2018). The teaching of the other: Ethical vulnerability and generous reciprocity in the research process. *Human Relations*, *71*(10), 1295–1318.

Richardson, F. C. (2014). Investigating psychology and transcendence. *Pastoral Psychology*, (63), 355–365.

Ricoeur, P. (1987). *À l'école de la phenomenologie.* Vrin.

Robinson, D. N. (1995). *An intellectual history of psychology.* University of Wisconsin Press.

Ron, Y. (Director). (2014). *Absent god – Emmanuel Levinas and the humanism of the other* [Film]. Arnavaz Productions.

Rozmarin, E. (2007). An other in psychoanalysis: Levinas's critique of knowledge and analytic sense. *Contemporary Psychoanalysis*, *43*(3), 327–360.

Salanskis, J.-M. (2010). The early Levinas and Heidegger. *Levinas Studies*, *5*, 43–64.

Sallis, J. (1998). Levinas and the elemental. *Research in Phenomenology*, *28*, 152–159.

Sandford, S. (2000). *The metaphysics of love*. The Athlone Press.

Sartre, J.-P. (1991). *The psychology of imagination*. Citadel. (Original work published 1940)

Sartre, J.-P. (2000). *The emotions: Outline for a theory* (B. Frechtman, Trans.). Philosophical Library. (Original work published 1939)

Sayre, G. G. (2005). Toward a therapy for the other. *European Journal of Psychotherapy, Counselling and Health, 7*(1–2), 37–47.

Sayre, G. G., & Kunz, G. (2005). Enduring intimate relationships as ethical and more than ethical: Inspired by Emmanuel Levinas and Martin Buber. *Journal of Theoretical and Philosophical Psychology, 25*(2), 224–237.

Schrift, A. D., & Moore, I. A. (Eds.). (2017). *Transcendence and the concrete: Selectted writings*. Fordham University Press.

Sealey, K. (2010). Levinas's early account of transcendence: Locating alterity in the il y a. *Levinas Studies, 5*, 99–116.

Sealey, K. (2013). The 'face' of the il y a: Levinas and Blanchot on impersonal existence. *Continental Philosophy Review, 46*, 431–448.

Seligman, M. E. P., & Csikszentmihalyi, M. (2000). Positive psychology: An introduction. *American Psychologist, 55*(1), 5–14.

Seligman, M. E. P., Steen, T. A., Park, N., & Peterson, C. (2005). Positive psychology progress: Empirical validation of interventions. *American Psychologist, 60*(5), 410–421.

Severson, E. R. (2012). Beyond hermeneutics: Levinas, language and psychology. *Journal of Theoretical and Philosophical Psychology, 32*(4), 251–260.

Sexton, J. (2015). Unbearable blackness. *Cultural Critique, 90*, 159–178.

Shabot, S. C., & Landry, C. (Eds.). (2018). *Rethinking feminist phenomenology: Theoretical and applied perspectives*. Rowman & Littlefield.

Sikka, S. (2001). The delightful other: Portraits of the feminine in Kierkegaard, Nietzsche, and Levinas. In T. Chanter (Ed.), *Feminist interpretations of Levinas* (pp. 96–118). Pennsylvania State University Press.

Simms, E. M. (2008). *The child in the world: Embodiment, time, and language in early childhood*. Wayne State University Press.

Skalski, J. (2017). The historical evolution of tolerance, the experience of tolerating, and the face of the other. *The Humanistic Psychologist, 45*(1), 62–70.

Smith, R. (1997). *The Norton history of the human sciences*. W. W. Norton & Company.

Sollod, R., Wilson, J. P., & Monte, C. F. (2009). *Beneath the mask: An introduction to theories of personality*. John Wiley.

Stolorow, R. D. (2007). *Trauma and human existence: Autobiographical, psychoanalytic, and philosophical reflections*. Routledge.

Strhan, A. (2012). *Levinas, subjectivity, education: Towards an ethics of radical responsibility*. Blackwell Publishing.

Supreme Court of South Africa. (1986). *Case number cc755.86*. South African Government Press.

Tallon, A. (2007). Can Levinas's ethical metaphysics contribute to psychoanalysis? *Psychoanalytic Review, 94*(4), 657–680.

Talmud (n.d.). *Sanhedrin Tractate, 37a*. https://halakhah.com/sanhedrin/index.html.

Taylor, E. (2001). Positive psychology and humanistic psychology: A reply to seligman. *Journal of Humanistic Psychology, 41*(1), 13–29.

Thorne, B. M., & Henley, T. B. (2001). *Connections in the history and systems of psychology*. Houghton Mifflin.

Urgesi, C., Aglioti, S. M., Skrap, M., & Fabbro, F. (2010). The spiritual brain: Selective cortical lesions modulate human self-transcendence. *Neuron, 65*, 309–319.

Vandenberg, B. (1999). Levinas and the ethical context of human development. *Human Development, 42*(1), 31–44.

Van Kaam, A. (1966). *Existential foundations of psychology*. Duquesne University Press.

Van Manen, M. (2016). *Researching lived experience: Human science for an action sensitive pedagogy* (2nd ed.). Routledge. (Original work published 1997)

Varakukalayil, J. J. (2015). Body as subjectivity to ethical signification of the body: Revisiting Levinas's early conception of the subject. *Sophia,* (54), 281–295.

Varela, F. (1996). Neurophenomenology: A methodological remedy for the hard problem. *Journal of Consciousness Studies, 3*(4), 330–349.

Wade, C., Tavris, C., & Gary, M. (2015). *Invitation to psychology* (6th ed.). Pearson.

Walsh, R. (2005). Beyond therapy: Levinas an ethical therapeutics. *Journal of Psychotherapy, Counselling and Health, 7*(1–2), 29–35.

Walsh, R., & Vaughan, F. (1980). Beyond the ego: Toward transpersonal models of the person and psychotherapy. *Journal of Humanistic Psychology, 20*(1), 5–31.

Warren, C. L. (2018). *Ontological terror: Blackness, nihilism, and emancipation*. Duke University Press.

Watson, J. (2003). Love and caring: Ethics of face and hand – an invitation to return to the heart and soul of nursing and our deep humanity. *Nurse Administration Quarterly, 27*, 197–202.

Weiss, G., Murphy, A. V., & Salamon, G. (Eds.). (2020). *50 concepts for a critical\* phenomenology*. Northwestern University Press.

Wertz, F. J. (2011). The qualitative revolution and psychology: Science, politics, and ethics. *The Humanistic Psychologist, 39*, 77–104.

Wertz, F. J. (2015). Phenomenology: Methods, historical development, and applications in psychology. In J. Martin, J. Sugarman, & K. L. Slaney (Eds.), *The Wiley handbook of theoretical and philosophical psychology: Methods, approaches, and new directions for social sciences* (pp. 85–1010). Wiley-Blackwell.

Westermann, R., Spies, K., Stahl, G., & Hesse, F. (1996). Relative effectiveness and validity of mood induction procedures: Analysis. *European Journal of Social Psychology, 26*, 557–580.

Whitman, W. (2019). *Leaves of grass* (B. Bennett, Ed.). Macmillan. (Original work published 1855)

Wiesel, E. (2011). *One generation after*. Schocken Books.

Wilber, K., Engler, J., & Brown, D. P. (1986). *Transformations of consciousness: Conventional and contemplative perspectives on development* (1st ed.). New Science Library.

Wilber, K., & Wilber, K. (2000). *Integral psychology: Consciousness, spirit, psychology, therapy* (1st pbk. ed.). Shambhala.

Wilderson, F. B. (2010). *Red, white & black: Cinema and the structure of U.S. antagonisms*. Duke University Press.

Williams, R. N. (1992). The human context of agency. *American Psychologist, 47*(6), 752–760.

Williams, R. N. (2005). Self-betraying emotions and the psychology of heteronomy. *European Journal of Psychotherapy, Counselling and Health, 7*(1–2), 7–16.

Williams, R. N. (2007). Levinas and psychoanalysis: The radical turn outward and upward. *Psychoanalytic Review, 94*(4), 681–701.

Williams, R. N., & Gantt, E. E. (1998). Intimacy and heteronomy: On grounding psychology in the ethical. *Theory & Psychology, 8*(2), 253–267.

Williams, R. N., & Gantt, E. E. (2002). Pursuing psychology as science of the ethical: Contributions of the work of Emmanuel Levinas. In E. E. Gantt & R. N. Williams (Eds.), *Psychology for the other: Levinas, ethics and the practice of psychology* (pp. 1–31). Duquesne University Press.

Wolff, E. (2011). *Political responsibility for a globalised world: After Levinas' humanism.* Transaction Publishers.

Wyschogrod, E. (1974). *Emmanuel Levinas: The problem of ethical metaphysics.* Martinus Nijhoff.

Yaden, D. B., Iwry, J., & Newberg, A. (2016). Neuroscience and religion: Surveyiong the field. In N. K. Clements (Ed.), *Religion: Mental religion: Part of the Macmillan interdisciplinary handbooks: Religion series.* Macmillan.

Yaden, D. B., Vago, D. R., Haidt, J., & Newberg, A. (2017). The varieties of self-transcendent experience. *Review of General Psychology, 21*(2), 143–160.

Yalom, I. (1980). *Existential psychotherapy.* Basic Books.

Yee, R. (2001). *An approach to psychotherapy: Self-in-ethical-relationship; the contributions of Emmanual Levinas.* Fielding Institute.

Young, I. (1980). Throwing like a girl: A phenomenology of feminine body comportment, motility, and spatiality. *Human Studies, 3*, 137–156.

Zimmer, C. (2004, October). Faith boosting genes: A search for the genetic basis of spirituality. *Scientific American,* 291 (4), 110–111.

Zizek, S. (2005). Neighbors and other monsters: A plea for ethical violence. In *The neighbor: Three inquiries in political theology.* University of Chicago Press.

# Index

For Product Safety Concerns and Information please contact our EU
representative  GPSR@taylorandfrancis.com
Taylor & Francis Verlag GmbH, Kaufingerstraße 24, 80331 München, Germany